KU-125-514

Spectacular Allegories
Postmodern American Writing and the Politics of Seeing

Josh Cohen

Pluto  Press

LONDON • STERLING, VIRGINIA

First published 1998 by Pluto Press
345 Archway Road, London N6 5AA
and 22883 Quicksilver Drive,
Sterling, VA 21066-2012, USA

Copyright © Josh Cohen 1998

The right of Josh Cohen to be identified as the author of this work has
been asserted by him in accordance with the Copyright, Designs and
Patents Act 1988.

British Library Cataloguing in Publication Data
A catalogue record for this book is available from the British Library

ISBN 0 7453 1212 8 hbk

Library of Congress Cataloging in Publication Data
A catalog record for this book is available from
the Library of Congress

Designed and produced for Pluto Press by
Chase Production Services, Chadlington, OX7 3LN
Typeset by Stanford DTP Services, Northampton
Printed in the EC by TJ International, Padstow

KING ALFRED'S COLLEGE
WINCHESTER

813.5
COH   KA0273 6837

For Abigail

How things withstand the gaze.
Walter Benjamin,
'Hashish in Marseilles'

Fading somewhere – don't take my eyes.
James Ellroy, *White Jazz*

Contents

Acknowledgements

Portions of this book have been published in different forms as 'The look of the sight machine: Robert Coover and the question of cinematic vision' in *diatribe* no. 4; 'The melancholic gaze: Joan Didion and the opacity of urban spectacle' in *Over Here: A European Journal of American Culture* vol. 16, no. 1 (summer 1996); 'James Ellroy and the spectacular crisis of masculinity' in *Women: A Cultural Review* vol. 7, no. 1 (spring 1996), reprinted in Peter Messent (ed.) *Criminal Proceedings: The Contemporary American Crime Novel* (Pluto Press, 1997)

I would like to thank Peter Nicholls for his acute, imaginative and dilligent supervision of the thesis that formed the basis for this book. Thanks also to Pete Messent, James Annesley, Maria Balshaw, Caroline Blinder, Ben Cohen, Rick Crownshaw, Helen Carr, Richard Godden, David Herd, Julian Levinson and Linus Cohen, all of whom have provided valuable insight and intellectual stimulus during the course of this project. My parents, Raquel Goldstein and Edward Cohen, have each provided limitless practical and personal support over the years. Sadly, my late grandfather, Haham Dr Solomon Gaon, never got to see this book completed; I look back on our conversations about it, like all my time with him, with untold love and affection.

Finally, Abigail Cohen, to whom this book is dedicated, is due much more than thanks. Her love, support and sense of humour, along with her own adventures in the field of vision, have lighted the way.

Introduction

The pervasive presence of visual forms is one of the defining features of our postmodern condition. In the 'society of the spectacle', sight has become the most privileged and the most relentlessly stimulated of the senses.[1] This book will explore the many ways in which this spectacular culture has impacted upon the processes of writing and, in particular, contemporary American writing.[2]

For cultural theorists of a wide range of philosophical and political persuasions, contemporary America is almost synonymous with the spectacle. In the highly influential work of Jean Baudrillard, this conflation has the radical consequence of severing American culture from its historical determinants.[3] For Baudrillard, 'America' is the ultimate name for the process by which lived history is absorbed into its 'hyperreal' simulation. Thus his notorious contention that 'the Gulf War did not take place' is intended to describe the way in which real events in the postmodern West have become interchangeable with their media-generated representations.[4]

I want to argue here that Baudrillard's central error, repeated by much subsequent postmodern cultural theory, is to conceive of the spectacle as somehow *opposed* to, rather than implicated in, historical experience. In this, he reproduces a historical tendency of philosophy to think of sight as abstracted from, rather than a part of, bodily experience.[5] At the heart of this book, in contrast, is the argument that vision belongs to lived private and public experience. Its readings of recent American writing will attempt to show that to understand the experience of *seeing* as dramatised by such writing, is also and necessarily to inquire into some of postmodern America's most pivotal social, economic and cultural struggles.

Implied in this project is a particular conception of the relation between theory and fiction. My intention is not simply to read texts 'through' a particular theoretical framework, but to demonstrate how representations of seeing, and of spectacular culture, overlap the boundaries of theory and fiction. Both forms of writing, I suggest, seek to address the conditions and crises of the postmodern culture of the image. This is not to argue that theory and fiction are 'the same' but, on the contrary, to suggest that the intrinsic generic differences built into their specific ways of negotiating these questions are precisely what makes them mutually illuminating.

1

Thus, if theory can help identify the dilemmas being articulated in fiction, fiction, in turn, enables us to see how these dilemmas are actually *lived* in determinate private and public contexts.

In positing literature as a means of dramatising the lived experience of specific cultural and historical conditions, I have been informed in particular by the work of Richard Godden.[6] In his readings of modern American fiction, Godden painstakingly excavates the historical meanings underlying the preoccupation with consumerist spectacle in, especially, Fitzgerald and Mailer. My own attempts to explore the same preoccupations in postmodern American writing will involve both extending and critiquing Godden's historical materialist model of narrative. I shall develop a model of postmodern narrativity which refuses the depth hermeneutics of base and superstructure, in which narrative merely reflects the shifting history of the economic.

This model will be constructed by way of a four-fold argument that will take shape during the course of the first chapter. First, with the aid of both theory and cultural history, I will identify the new primacy of spectacle as a constitutive force of both state and economic power which has penetrated everyday life in postmodern America. I will further argue that recent fiction has both reproduced and intervened in this 'spectacularisation' of American culture. Second, I will suggest that the representation of visual experience in both modern and postmodern cultural practice is thoroughly inscribed by the question of gender. More explicitly, I will identify a tendency in both fiction and theory to figure the spectacular lifeworld of modernity and postmodernity as a struggle between a 'masculine' visual consciousness and 'feminised', and feminising, mass culture.[7] The third stage of my theoretical argument, then, will be to explore the disruption of masculine perception, both visual and narrative, by the feminine image-sphere it seeks to control and repress, a disruption enacted in what Craig Owens calls the 'allegorical impulse' of postmodernism.[8] Finally, I will address the question as to how visual agency, or the critical empowerment of the eye, might be possible in the face of this crisis of 'subject-centred' (masculine) vision and, implicitly, of narrative authority. I will argue for a conception of seeing that is premised not on the eye's domination of its object, but on a mutually constitutive relation between the two. This dialogic conception of vision owes much to Walter Benjamin's conception of the 'porosity' of the gaze, a concept which counters the tendency to conflate vision with domination.[9] As Martin Jay has recently shown, this conflation is present throughout the modern Western (and especially French) philosophical tradition.[10]

Each of the writers under discussion can be situated in relation to this model of vision, insofar as they are each concerned with the plight of the seeing subject in a culture of spectacle. Chapter 2 will attempt to trace in the trajectory of Norman Mailer's career a mounting crisis of visual authority, produced by American society's spectacular postwar transformation. It will examine the shifting means by which Mailer confronts this crisis, focusing particularly on the increasing untenability of the 'metaphysics of vision' developed in his early career, in the face of the body's inexorable penetration by an expanding corporate capitalism. Chapter 3 will identify, in what I have termed 'cinematographic writing' (specifically the writing of Jerzy Kosinski, Robert Coover and Stephen Dixon), different ways of responding to the privileged place of the filmic image in postmodern culture. It will argue that the filmic exemplifies the 'allegorical' model of narrative set out in Chapter 1. Chapter 4 will posit Los Angeles as postmodern American writing's paradigmatic allegorical space. Its readings of two Los Angeles writers (Joan Didion and James Ellroy) will foreground the 'catastrophic' implications of an urban experience defined by the spectacle.

Throughout the book, a diverse range of theories will be in play, which should, however, coalesce to form an interrelated matrix of critical concepts, rather than an unwieldy accumulation of related ideas. It is to the task of fleshing out that matrix, and of expounding its relevance to the context of postmodern American fiction, that I now turn.

1

Visuality, allegory and postmodern American writing

Visuality and postmodernism: the problem of abstraction

I have pointed, in my introduction, to a tendency within postmodern theory, exemplified by Jean Baudrillard, to view the spectacular culture of postmodernity as floating above, and oblivious to, material reality. Nevertheless, rather than dismiss wholesale the likes of Baudrillard and his contemporary, Paul Virilio, it may be more productive to recuperate their insights into the primacy of the image in the postmodern for historical inquiry.[1]

Baudrillard's key terms – the 'hyperreal', 'simulation', 'the code' – describe the processes by which lived experience comes to be preceded by its own representation, and cultural forms are 'conceived from the point of view of their reproducibility'.[2] Simulationary events such as Watergate, and, more recently, the Gulf War, are produced not by determinate historical struggles, but by the 'mediascape'- TV, radio, cinema, the print media – and as such are consumed rather than experienced.

This diagnosis consciously short-circuits the possibility of political resistance. For Baudrillard, any critical gesture is unwittingly complicit with the simulationary logic it purports to contest. Underlying any opposition to the mediascape's 'deceit' in the name of 'truth' or 'justice' is the assumption of the reality of such distinctions as subject and object, appearance and reality; distinctions based in a metaphysical conceit liquidated by the logic of the hyperreal.

Baudrillard, then, claims to have dissolved the subject–object opposition which any concept of resistance assumes. Douglas Kellner's trenchant critique of Baudrillard, however, persuasively argues that the latter less dissolves than inverts this distinction: in postmodernity's 'nexus of information and communication networks ... the subject becomes transformed into an object'.[3] At the same time, simulationary culture comes to usurp the position of the subject. Baudrillard, that is, posits the 'triumph of objects over subjects within the obscene proliferation of an object world so completely out of control that it surpasses all attempts to understand, conceptualize and control it' (Kellner, p. 155). The mediascape, then, in its sublime omnipresence, renders the subject politically impotent.

Moreover, Baudrillard codes this displacement of the subject's authority in explicitly gendered terms. The simulationary universe does not so much dominate the human subject as *seduce* him – him, because the triumph of seduction is also the triumph of the feminine, of 'a universe where the feminine is not that which opposes itself to the masculine, but that which *seduces* the masculine'.[4] In projecting this 'object-world' of hyperreality as feminine, then, Baudrillard again deploys the binary logic whose demise he claims to be announcing, inserting himself into a French cultural and philosophical tradition that repeatedly figures mass culture as a 'feminine' assault on masculine integrity.[5]

In what follows, I will take up Baudrillard's identification of simulationary culture as a primary site of postmodern cultural experience, as a point of departure for a critical engagement with the postmodern. At the same time, I will refuse his claim that the dissolution of the modern 'master-subject' necessarily entails the eclipse of any form of political agency.

Postmodernity, narrative and historical materialism

What the dissolution of the 'master-subject' by postmodernity's culture of the image does eclipse, however, is a certain form of historical materialism which conceives of history in terms of a dialectic of progress. Any model of postmodern narrative must acknowledge the insufficiency of 'the logic of capital' as an explanatory principle. Postmodern literary forms, that is, are not, as the economistic view might suggest, narrative enactments of shifts in the history of capital, so much as of their own failure to make sense of that history. Spectacular culture, this book will argue, is characterised by an opacity and an indeterminacy which manifests itself in what I call an allegorical impulse.

Allegorical narrative, in the sense intended here, is rooted in a discontinuous, non-linear experience of time famously theorised by Walter Benjamin in 'Theses on the philosophy of history' and elsewhere.[6] This conception of time has been influential on a number of contemporary theorists, including Christine Buci-Glucksmann and Craig Owens.[7]

As I have suggested, this allegorical model is different in a number of respects from Richard Godden's more orthodoxly Marxist hermeneutics.[8] For Godden, modern American fictional narratives are a means of metaphorically representing social experience. Taking up Paul Ricoeur's definition of metaphor as the communicative meanings opened up by conflicting social intentions, he argues that such meanings, 'in Fordist USA are largely engineered by capital' (p. 8). Shifts in narrative options, then, are both generated by, and expressive of, 'the changing economy of consumption' (p. 9). This is not to suggest, however, that Godden's model of narrative is unproblematically deterministic; the work of each writer is read as a complex response to, and negotiation of, key moments in the American growth economy, rather than a simple reflection of it. That said, it remains the case for Godden that 'a prevalent form of capital ... promotes preferred narratives' (p. 251), so that the economy remains the primary determining force of literary production.

Godden's materialist interpretative strategies are nicely exemplified by his reading of Fitzgerald's *Tender is the Night*, a reading which tellingly foregrounds the related forces of visuality and gender. Fitzgerald, he argues, dramatises the erosion of the binary division of gender power represented in James' figuration of the wealthy female, passively displaying the accumulated riches of her class. With the new dominance of everyday life by the culture of the spectacle, the female is no longer a mere decorative object for an accumulative masculine subject. In *Tender is the Night*, the female 'object' of Fordist consumerism, represented by Rosemary, the rising screen star, embodies a new paradigm of selfhood, generated by consumerism's 'programmatic multiplication of selves' (Godden, p. 119). Rosemary, that is, signifies the shift from the hegemony of the regime of accumulative to that of reproductive capitalism, dominated by the consumerist economy of spectacle.

The point which I am most concerned to contest in Godden's critical method is his designation of narratives as metaphorical condensations of primarily economic meanings. One consequence of such a method is that the visualities of American modernism are reduced to little more than an *effect* of capital, a metaphorical superstructure to an emphatically economic base. This framework posits culture as constituted by the logic of capitalism, a position that leads to a certain elision of the subject's capacity to think and act critically. For if Fordism 'cinematises' subjects, producing disintegrative, synthetic and reproducible selves in the service of mass consumption, there remains little room for these subjects to resist their own 'cinematisation'.

It is not merely, however, a series of philosophical differences that distinguish my own 'allegorical' model of narrative from Godden's 'metaphorical' one. Godden's critical focus is on modernism, which produces different kinds of visual relations to those of the postmodern. More specifically, writers such as Hemingway and Fitzgerald cannot have the same awareness of the spectacle's *autonomy*, its status as a central site of cultural contestation, as their postmodern counterparts. Indeed, a significant strain of modernism, as Peter Nicholls has shown, is premised on resistance to precisely this growing autonomy of consumer culture, and as such is characterised by a kind of will to objectification, whereby 'a fear of "possession" by the other' results in 'the need for clear boundaries to be drawn around the self'.[9] Nicholls further draws attention to the hostility of both Eliot and Pound to a 'feminine' writing, marked by diffuseness and opacity, qualities which attest to its 'failures of objectification'.

The condition of postmodernity, however, arguably renders impossible this project of perceptual mastery. Indeed, Godden himself begins to suggest this impossibility in his reading of *Tender is the Night* as a narrative of the new sovereignty of the cinematised subject, and especially in his reading of Mailer's *Armies of the Night*. In that text, the erosion of masculine visual authority reaches an apotheosis, as the author relates the displacement of his own phallic command by the 'deoedipalized' force of corporate, TV-dominated USA, ironically embodied in Beverly, his actress wife.

There is an important sense, then, in which Godden's readings in American modernism convey precisely the sense of an encroaching hegemony of spectacle, and, correspondingly, the increasingly *reversible* relations between masculine subject and feminine object in the field of vision which, I am arguing, most distinguishes the postmodern from the modern. Postmodern narrative's allegorical impulse, that is, fully releases the discontinuous temporality and subjectivity which in modernism, as Craig Owens argues, '*remains in potentia*' (p. 74).

For Godden, consumer spectacle produces a condition in which the narrating subject's eroded authority reproduces the political impotence of the collective. This equation of narrative and political crisis, however, can be traced to his understanding of spectacle as an epiphenomenon of the logic of capital. Such an understanding needs to be countered by an awareness of spectacle as an autonomous site of contestation, rather than as a mere effect of capital. This in turn would demand a different reading of the feminine within postmodern culture. Whilst Godden acutely identifies the feminine as the bearer of a new, 'spectacular' self, his insight risks reifying Woman as a mere manifestation of the new logic of capital. An attentiveness to the autonomy of spectacle, in contrast, would restore to the female 'object' her status as agent; for if the culture of modernity has persistently encoded the feminine as its irrational Other, then, as Buci-Glucksmann astutely posits, 'its irratio has to be deciphered and made dialectical' as an 'eminently political task' (p. 48).

It is my contention, then, that the condition of postmodernity, governed as it is by the fragmentary logic of the image, demands of historical materialism a move beyond the unproblematic equation between the culture of mass spectacle and a monolithic form of domination. If an internally critical relation to contemporary culture is to remain viable, Guy Debord's dictum that 'the unification [spectacle] achieves is nothing but an official language of separation' needs to be superseded by an argument for the postmodern subject's 'porous' relation to the lifeworld of spectacle.[10]

Spectacular history: postmodern America's visualised culture

Dale Carter's ambitious cultural history of the postwar American state helps demonstrate the constitutive force of visual forms in this period of history.[11] Carter borrows Hannah Arendt's formulation of a transition from imperialism to 'incipient totalitarianism', defined by a sustained project of cultural propogandism whose most prominent product is the space programme.

Carter reads Thomas Pynchon's *Gravity's Rainbow* as a potent narrativisation of these strategic shifts in ideological practices, in particular via the representation of its protagonist's increasingly fractured subjectivity. Tyrone Slothrop, Carter argues, in his successful attempt to outwit the security guards at the Potsdam Conference, enacts each stage in his guise as the cartoon character Rocketman, whose identity consists in 'visual images independent of any natural or historical basis' (p. 17). In Pynchon can be glimpsed a shift into an era in which 'conflict is reconstituted towards a civilian struggle over the "universe of images"' on whose 'communication and manipulation ... the structures of power are increasingly predicated' (p. 36).

David Harvey similarly identifies the centrality of the image to the logic of postmodernity in his seminal study of the period.[12] For Harvey, as for Godden, the economic remains the primary explanatory ground of the visualised culture of late capitalism. Harvey's historical field of inquiry, however, directly supersedes Godden's, and the contrast is registered by way of the former's marked emphasis on postmodernity's disjunctive visuality, its fragmentation of modernity's key narratives. His account of the emergent regime of 'flexible accumulation' provides the context for his description of the postmodern aesthetic. In an economy characterised by perpetual flux and elasticity in labour processes and markets, in patterns of production and consumption and by ceaseless technological and organisational innovation, he notes,

> the relatively stable aesthetic of Fordist modernism has given way to all the ferment, instability and fleeting qualities of a postmodern aesthetic that celebrates difference, ephemerality, spectacle, fashion, and the commodification of cultural forms. (p. 156)

This is not, in other words, an aesthetic given to the linear narration of the history of capital. Indeed, as if to underline the point, Harvey's summary diagnosis of 'Postmodernity as a historical condition', points to a culture in which 'images dominate narratives' (p. 328).

Hal Foster's writings on the relationship between late twentieth-century art and commodity spectacle provide a third account of the centrality of the image to the constitution of the postmodern social and political terrain, as well as an intervention in that terrain.[13] Foster attempts to appropriate critically Baudrillard's notorious contention that the economic and semiotic (the realm of signs) have fused into a single, totalising 'code' that structurally paralyses any form of cultural resistance. Foster's strategy here dovetails with the intention of the present study to absorb Baudrillard's diagnostic insights into a renewed cultural politics, whilst refusing his corresponding disavowal of resistance as 'collusive with the very action of capital' (p. 147). What is most immediately useful for Foster in Baudrillard's identification of 'a commutation of the cultural and the economic' is that it provides the condition for a critical theory in which 'the cultural is not strictly an effect of economic determination of ideological reflection ... it is a site of contestation' (p. 146).

Revealed through the thrice-filtered lens of state (Carter), economy (Harvey) and culture (Foster), is the extent to which the realm of images functions as both a constitutive force of, and contestatory terrain within, the postmodern. To these accounts can be added Anthony Woodiwiss's illuminating analysis of the fate of the narrative of social modernism in postmodern America.[14] For Woodiwiss, 'the United States is literally a postmodern society in which there is an incredulity towards the modernist metanarrative that for the past thirty years or so has explained and legitimated what occurs within it' (p. 145). The Lyotardian terms invoked here underpin a sociological argument that the American state's economic and political logic has undergone a crucial shift premised in 'an involuntary forgetting of social modernism' (p. 145).

'Social modernism' designates the agglomeration of those key narratives of the American state from Roosevelt to Johnson, through which macropolitical and economic life were organised. Where, between the former's New Deal and the latter's Great Society, political discourse 'metanarrativises' government as a self-evident source of beneficence and foregrounds the redistributive role of the state, the social postmodernism inaugurated by Reaganism eschews that role. As the consensual principle underlying large-scale administrative projects is gradually eroded by crises within capitalism, so the dominant discourse of politics mutates to account for this erosion, generating a kind of pervasive amnesia in the US political mainstream. The motifs of the minimalist state and the imperative to individual assumption of responsibility supersede those of the managerial state and its role in maintaining socioeconomic equilibrium. The new fragmentation of labour markets and consumption is thus accompanied by the break-up of a previously consensual ideology.

An important consequence of this forgetting is that it divests social life of a unifying narrative through which collective experience might be represented. This divestment, I will argue, is evinced by the allegorical turn in the narrative strategies of postmodern American writing. These texts actualise the condition of narrative recognised by Benjamin in 1936.[15] In 'The storyteller', Benjamin attributes the demise of storytelling to the fact that 'the communicability of experience is decreasing' (p. 86). Narrative can no longer be rooted in the eternal verities of tradition; the modern novel conveys rather the unmooring of experience from any stable guarantors of truth, and so 'gives evidence of the profound perplexity of the living' (p. 87). This perplexity has been brought into being by 'the secular productive forces of history', forces subtended by the removal of narrative from 'the realm of living speech' (p. 87). This removal, insofar as it frustrates the fundamentally illustrative impulse of storytelling, serves to sever the narrative sign from any determinate meaning, and to introduce into it a new opacity and (Benjamin's term) 'incommensurability'. It is this opacity which distinguishes also the visually charged narrativity of much postmodern fiction.

The question insistently arises, however, as to whether this foregrounding of opacity merely affirms the paralysis of political agency that Debord, and later Baudrillard, attribute to the society of the spectacle. It is worth returning to Foster's work to obtain at least a provisional response to this question. Foster projects a range of cultural–political practices that might be forged in the face of the cultural commodification of everyday life. These would be characterised foremost by an attentiveness to 'the need to *connect* the buried (the nonsynchronous), the disqualified (the minor), and the yet-to-come (the utopian, or, better, the desired)' (p. 179).

These posited conditions for cultural resistance suggest in usefully condensed form some of the central themes I wish to develop during the remainder of this chapter. Foster's notion of non-synchronicity dovetails directly with the idea of an anti-progressive temporality, through which I intend to construct a discontinuous model of narrative. Such a model is intimately bound up with a utopian historical sensibility which privileges a projective engagement with the past, in which the ephemeral image of redemption, persistently invoked by Benjamin, contests the stable narrative of progress. Moreover, Foster's use of the category of the 'minor', informed by Deleuze and Guattari's essay of that title, is convergent with my own deployment of the feminine, insofar as it 'stands for a critical activity that reactivates the conflictual history of sign-systems so as to break through the (ahistorical) logic of the code' (p. 179). If the containment of the feminine object within the culture of modernity can be seen as thoroughly complicit with that '(ahistorical) logic of the code', then Buci-Glucksmann's previously cited injunction to the 'eminently political task' of 'making dialectical the feminine *irratio*' seems particularly commensurate with this kind of critical activity. Indeed, Foster speaks directly to this task when he observes that, within a proliferating (postmodern) economy of the sign, 'it may be "woman as artifice" rather than "woman as nature" that feminism must now contest' (p. 10).

The remainder of this chapter will thus elaborate these forms of critical activity within the context of a model of postmodern narrative.

Merleau-Ponty, Benjamin and the time of seeing

Informing this model is a particular conception of time and its relation to vision. Two philosophical traditions inform this conception: first, a Benjaminian tradition, elaborated below; and second, an existential tradition whose most important representative for our purposes is Maurice Merleau-Ponty.

I want now to show how Merleau-Ponty's account of subject–object relations can help ground Benjamin's critique of the dialectic of progress. This account contests the 'subject-centred' conception of vision common to both idealist and empiricist philosophical traditions.[16] Merleau-Ponty's critique of subject-centre optics is not, of course, without precedent. Perhaps its most significant prefiguration is to be found in Nietzsche's figuration of the relation between time and the image.

Nietzsche repeatedly attributes the greatest significance to the changeable, deceptive realm of appearances. Thus, in *Thus Spoke Zarathustra*, if gold has the highest value, 'it is because it is uncommon and useless and shining and mellow in lustre'.[17] Virtue, Zarathustra contends, 'has its origin and beginning in images' (p. 101) and 'the best images speak of time and becoming ...' (p. 111). The virtue of the image, then, is precisely its temporality, its representation of experience as process, reinvention, 'becoming', defying the atemporal fixity of the Platonic Form. Images are the basis for a disruptive visual ontology, which refuses, in Zarathustra's memorable phrase, 'immaculate perception' (p. 145), in favour of what Gary Shapiro terms Nietzsche's 'vision at risk'.[18]

Perhaps the most conscious of Nietzsche's progeny in the critique of 'immaculate perception' is Heidegger, whose project is also historically and philosophically close to Merleau-Ponty's. Heidegger strongly implicates vision as the primary means through which the dominating subject of Western metaphysics (whose ultimate manifestation is Nietzsche's Will to Power) perpetuates itself, most explicitly in his essay 'The age of the world picture'.[19] Heidegger here argues that 'the fundamental event of the modern age is the conquest of the world as picture' (p. 134), an event that might be glossed as the triumph of a subject-centred vision over an objectified lifeworld. This mode of visual being reduces the diversity of the phenomena it encounters to quantifiable units of meaning; thus historiography objectifies the past, whilst science instrumentalises the natural world. Heiddeger thus reveals the objectification of time to be the very ground of subject-centred vision, throwing into relief the crucial relation between temporality and visuality.

Whilst situated in the same post-Husserlian tradition as Heidegger, Merleau-Ponty's ontology of sight avoids the latter's tendency to equate modern forms of seeing with domination. Where Heidegger locates the condition for a new form of seeing outside of everyday modernity, in the transhistorical realm of Being, Merleau-Ponty looks to the perceptual experience of an embodied, historically situated subject as a way into the same. This insistence on the historicity of the seeing subject, I suggest, enables the forging of a critical visual agency, resistant yet aware of its limitations, and active whilst refusing the privileged perspective of the master-subject.

In *Phenomenology of Perception*, Merleau-Ponty describes visual perception as a 'subject–object dialogue', a 'drawing together, by the subject, of the meaning diffused through the object, and by the object, of the subject's intentions'.[20] Seeing, in other words, is a dialogic activity, in which the relations of the seer and the seen are defined not by domination but by mobility and reversibility. The *Phenomenology*'s chapter on temporality elaborates explicitly how this theory of visuality might inform a critique of abstract time.

Merleau-Ponty here refutes the notion of abstract time, demonstrating that time arises rather out of the subject's phenomenological experience of the world. Time works, that is, 'not ... as a system of objective positions, through which we pass, but as a mobile setting which moves away from us, like the landscape seen through a railway carriage window' (p. 240). This figuration of time in terms of visual perception throws into relief Merleau-Ponty's critique of an abstracting gaze that would reduce time to a series of objectified coordinates. A mobile temporality is shot through with the 'thickness' of lived experience, its present moments charged by both the memory of the past and the horizon of the future.

This critique of the philosophical abstraction of time is fleshed out less technically in his essays on Marxism. Marxism, he contends, envisions history as 'both logical and contingent', so that 'nothing is absolutely fortuitous but ... also ... nothing is absolutely necessary'.[21] This interplay of the logical and the contingent enables a dialectical analysis of history, without reducing it to an abstract narrative of capital's 'progress'. This is a 'Marxism without illusions, completely experimental and voluntary' (p. 124), which would recognise that political actions are always shot through with a plurality of meanings and motivations, and so cannot be made transparent by a putative 'science' of politics. This is the necessary consequence of positing 'concrete human intersubjectivity', rather than abstract laws of motion, as 'the vehicle of history and the motivating force of the dialectic' (p. 129).

Written five years before the *Phenomenology*, Benjamin's 'Theses on the philosophy of history' can be read as an intervention within just such a 'non-objective' Marxism, in spite of the apparent gap between its apocalyptic messianism and Merleau-Ponty's more conventional humanism.[22] What these thinkers share, I suggest, is a conception of history that refuses the perspective of the master-subject, or, to use Benjamin's own revealing term, 'the victors'. The essay's famous opening paragraph is a critique of the linear narrative of history, in the form of a parable. It tells of a chess-playing automaton programmed to beat all conceivable opponents. Sat amongst 'a system of mirrors' that creates the illusion of the table's transparency, the puppet is in fact powered by a 'little hunchback who was an expert chess player' sitting inside it and guiding its hands 'by means of strings':

> One can easily imagine a philosophical counterpart to this device. The puppet called 'historical materialism' is to win all the time. It can easily be a match for anyone if it enlists the service of theology, which today, as we know, is wizened and has to keep out of sight. (p. 245)

This, in other words, is the deliberate *reductio ad absurdam* of Marxist-Leninism's 'inevitability thesis', which would project history as the inevitable march of progress to socialism. This thesis is premised on the objectified time of the automaton.

Written in the face of the bleak forces so ominously on the rise by 1940, Benjamin's essay struggles to conceive of a historical materialism that recognises the untenability of the inevitability thesis. The historian, he consequently asserts, must refuse the distinction between 'major' and 'minor' events, for 'nothing that has ever happened should be regarded as lost to history' (p. 246). Where history seen from the lofty vantage-point of the logic of capital may organise itself around a hierarchy of events, Benjamin's 'projective' past works to salvage those fleeting, redemptive moments elided by that very narrative.

Significantly, this new relation between past and present is registered in the form of *images*: 'The past can be seized only as an image which flashes up at the instant when it can be recognised and is never seen again' (p. 247). No longer a narrative of teleological progress, history, the way in which the present lives the past, takes the new form of fragmentary flashes, or image traces. Any such image 'not recognised by the present as one of its own concerns threatens to disappear irretrievably' (p. 247). Blasted out of the continuum of time, the image is that which resists narrative resolution and which interrupts its explanatory logic. Images figure the possibility of messianic redemption precisely because they cannot be coopted into a narrative of historical progress grounded in 'homogeneous, empty time' (p. 253). The past as envisaged by Paul Klee's 'Angelus Novus', a single, catastrophic wreckage of fragments blowing the Angel of History 'into the future to which its back is turned' (p. 248), is a past which refuses to be made transparent. Against the linear time of the narrative of progress, Benjamin posits a 'time of the now', 'which is shot through with chips of Messianic time' (p. 255). The redemptive future can be glimpsed fleetingly, then, in our present, or 'now-time', rather than as a mere teleological projection of strictly progressive time.

Buci-Glucksmann insists on the critical place of this disruptive temporality in the aesthetics of modernity, and finds in Klee's Angel of History its most concentrated representation. Buci-Glucksmann's 'Angelic Space' 'shatters the temporal continuum (social-democratic faith in progress), replacing it with a catastrophic, messianic instance that will release the future buried in the past and build it with the present' (p. 44). The modern aesthetics of Baudelaire and Proust enact 'the *untimely* experience of modernity' (p. 110), rather than the progressive one.

Discontinuous time and visual agency

This model of time, however, inevitably invites the objection that it disables political action, in divesting the subject of stable positions in time and space from which it can think and act. Drawing on a number of theorists within the broad materialist tradition, I want to engage this objection directly, by arguing that a form of agency can in fact be forged out of such a temporality, one acutely informed, moreover, by the specific conditions of the society of the spectacle.

Benjamin's essay 'Surrealism' elaborates how the visual experience of modern commodity (and especially urban) culture doubles, in its imaginative reinvention by the likes of Andre Breton, as a repository of subversive political energies, with the potential to transform the degraded experience of mass consumption into a source of explosive 'revolutionary nihilism':[23]

> Noone before these visionaries and augurs perceived how destitution – not only social but architectonic, the poverty of interiors, enslaved and enslaving objects – can be suddenly transformed into ... revolutionary experience, if not action. (p. 229)

Here, then, is Benjamin's notion of 'profane illumination' at work, revealing the repressed messianic force buried in the routinised visual experience of consumer capitalism. Surrealism's valorisation of image over concept, as Martin Jay has argued, refuses the definition of the image as the representation of an external object, perceiving it instead as 'the revelation of an inner state'.[24] This redefinition has crucial political implications: as the expression of the internal rather than a reflection of the external, the realm of images can no longer be seen as a mere 'superstructure'; it is a sphere of contestation over, rather than reflection of, the meanings of capitalism. Furthermore, in drawing out the hidden currents of the uncanny generated by the commodity and the machine, surrealism yields traces of a 'projective' past, of those moments of messianic illumination which refuse to be absorbed into an abstract narrative of progress.

Benjaminian temporality is thus allied to a theory of agency which locates the possibility of resistance in the buried internal energies of capitalism itself. As Michael Taussig argues, this is an agency figured very much in terms of visual perception.[25] Drawing on Benjamin's essay on film and photography, Taussig suggests that the 'optical unconscious' opened up by modernity's great 'mimetic machines' can produce not only a new sensory experience, but a new relation between subject and object. Filmic experience, in throwing the minutest interactions of everyday life into intense relief, confers an unprecedented perceptual acuity on the spectator, dissolving the spatial distance between subject and object, 'merging the object of perception with the body of the spectator and not just the mind's eye' (Taussig, p. 208). Taussig provides here a suggestive means for establishing a point of convergence between Benjamin and Merleau-Ponty. In each thinker, visual perception opens up a new subject–object relation, in which domination yields to dialogue, spatial distance to the interplay between the eye and its object.

Benjamin's conception of temporality, foregrounding those marginal images put out of political play by a hegemonic narrative of progress, along with Merleau-Ponty's theory of perception as an ongoing dialogue between subject and object, offers the basis for a critical mode of seeing which can engage the specific historical demands of the postmodern consumer society.

One of the most interesting attempts to rethink historical materialism in the light of the conditions of postmodernity has been made by Stanley Aronowitz.[26] Aronowitz insists that Marxism can remain visible only by recognising difference as 'an ineluctable feature of reality' (p. 26). The intellectual history of Marxism, he claims, has been dogged by the imperative to uncover history's concealed 'laws of motion'. Relations of production, within this tendency, override gender, race, sexuality and culture as the determining force of social life. Consequently, the project of politics becomes defined by the domination of nature in the service of human needs. Time and history, in this context, take on the logic of Benjamin's automaton, that is, of the narrative of the neccessary development of capitalism, a narrative which dissolves all indeterminacies in (to use Adorno's term) a 'dialectic of identity'.

For Aronowitz, however, the persistence of difference, its resistance to assimilation by a single master-narrative, to which the struggles of women, ethnic and sexual minorities, and environmentalists all bear testament, is the most potent discovery of this century. The foremost lesson provided by 'the crisis of historical materialism', is that 'there is no question of representation of even a master discourse that is fated to assume the logical centre of historical change' (p. 126). The terms have a real resonance in the context of an argument about postmodern literature, in that it is just the kind of narrative 'representation' premised on revealing history's progressive laws of motion, that the writing under discussion continuously frustrates.

Aronowitz locates in the category of time a source of opposition to the dominant tradition of historical materialism. Drawing on Ernst Bloch's concept of 'non-synchrony', he posits a temporality in which past, present and future are multilayered rather than uniform. There is, he argues, an objective 'non-synchrony' in history, expressed in the temporalities of, for example, feminism and ecology, both of which contest the dominant, quantified time of modernity.

Taking the historical experience of non-synchronicity and marginality as its point of departure, Homi Bhabha argues that the disruptive temporality produced by this experience can enable, rather than constrain, politics.[27] Bhabha marshalls the terminology of postcolonial theory – migrancy, dispersal, borderlines, diaspora – for a sustained critique of what he terms 'the Occidental stereotomy' of subject and object at the heart of Western philosophy. The same critique opens up the possibility of an alternative political project: the transnational displacements, for example, of Salvadorean and Filipino workers, 'part of the massive economic and political diaspora of the modern world ... embody the Benjaminian "present": that moment blasted out of the continuum of history' (p. 8). Bhabha's injunction is to grasp this moment born out of enforced exile and social discrimination in order to forge a 'revisionary time' and 'in-between space' interruptive of hegemonic space and time.

Bhabha's postcolonial temporality, then, is the basis for a new politics of cultural difference, 'a process by which objectified others may be turned into subjects of their own history and experience' (p. 178). It is just this attempt to endow the object with political agency, to interrupt the objectifying (masculine) gaze of the master-subject with a new, dialogic conception of visual relations, which informs the model of postmodern narrative I want now to develop.

Postmodernity, narrativity, allegory

This model of narrative is to be conceptualised via Benjamin's theory of allegory, and some of its postmodern derivations. Allegory will thus emerge as a terminological counterpart to Godden's metaphoricity; where the latter designates the forms in which latent, primarily economic meanings are condensed into metaphorical distortions (for example, Fitzgerald's and Mailer's incest plots enact the previously 'taboo' penetrations of the body wrought by shifts in the American regime of accumulation), allegory is that which *resists* being rendered readable in terms of any privileged interpretative code such as the economic.

Susan Buck-Morss's account of Benjamin's seminal study of the German baroque *Trauerspiel* usefully identifies the central features of the allegorical aesthetic.[28] Allegory comes into being once the written sign fails to find meaning fulfilled in itself:

> The result is that nature, far from an organic whole, appears in arbitrary arrangements, as a lifeless, fragmentary, untidy clutter of emblems. The coherence of language is similarly shattered ... Allegorists, like alchemists, hold dominion over an infinite transformation of meanings, in contrast to the one, true word of God. (p. 173)

It is well worth noting the 'emblematic' character of these fragmentary signs. The shattering of linguistic coherence emerges out of the unprecedented proliferation of visual signs found in baroque culture. Language's newly lost transparency of meaning is thus registered first of all in the image. The weakened ontological and epistemological grounding that defines the subject's interpretative relation to the baroque is expressed in a new privileging of the visual sign, as an examination of the Benjamin text itself further affirms.[29]

Benjamin's baroque allegorical universe is marked by a new and profound awareness of nature's mortality, an awareness made visible in its projection of an 'object-world of emblems' (p. 230). Baroque drama exerts an unprecedented fascination on the transience of nature and history. No longer perceived in terms of the eternal verities of myth, the signs of nature are seen anew, as subject to the processes of decay and dissolution. This vision of nature gives rise to the baroque cult of the 'ruin'. This cult, insofar as its central preoccupation is with the lost transparency of the sign, can be termed allegorical, for in allegorical narrative, 'Any person, any object, any relationship can mean absolutely anything else' (p. 175). Thus, 'In the field of allegorical intuition, the image is a fragment, a rune' (p. 176). This 'field' is profoundly melancholic, for it is only 'under the gaze of melancholy' that 'the object becomes allegorical' (p. 183); that is, only under such a gaze will the object reveal its intrinsic transience, its vulnerability to historical processes.

Thus, where recent deconstructive treatments of allegory have located the indeterminacy of the form in the rhetorical structures of language itself, Benjamin's *Trauerspiel* study situates this indeterminacy in the traumatic historical transition to modernity.[30]

The imagistic 'runes' of baroque culture, with their fixation on the signs of mortality (the death's head, the ruin, the fractured torso), are the most prominent emblems of this trauma. Benjamin conveys a world in which things are suddenly endowed with a life of their own:

> ... lifeless objects, forests, trees, stones, may speak and act, while ... words, syllables and letters appear in personified forms ... It is perfectly clear that fragmentation in its graphic aspects is a principle of the allegorical approach. (p. 186)

This 'graphic fragmentation' has significant implications for the development of narrative subjectivity. Specifically, it generates a crisis of the transcendent perspective which would enable the narrator to apprehend and control his or her object. This crisis is palpably augured by the object's new autonomy, the uncanny sentience of the inanimate that Benjamin describes above; where subject–object relations were once perceived as fixed, they are now revealed as shifting and reversible. As 'ideas evaporate in images' (p. 199), so does the stable ontology that grounds those 'ideas' yield to the disruptive ontology of 'images'.

Postmodern narrative, I suggest, is governed by just this visual ontology. Its images, shot through with a surfeit of meanings, produce an unstable relation between reader and text, whereby straightforward communication gives way to perpetual interpretation: hence 'allegory', a story which generates an infinite number of interpretations. This relation is indicated in Craig Owens' claim that

'The allegorical impulse that characterizes postmodernism is a direct consequence of its preoccupation with reading' (p. 74). This preoccupation, commonly designated in recent literary criticism as postmodernism's 'self-reflexive' tendency, reproduces in the relation between reader and artwork the destabilising of subject–object relations described above.[31]

Owens further draws attention to the melancholy sensibility produced by the ephemerality of the allegorical aesthetic. Photography, he argues, is an expression of this sensibility, responding to the lost transparency of the sign by playing out 'our desire to fix the transitory, the ephemeral, in a stable and stabilizing image' (p. 56). In so doing, however, it reveals the object's refusal of this stabilising impulse, 'and thus affirms its own arbitrariness and contingency' (p. 56), exacerbating the very melancholy it wishes to overcome.

The last of the general features of allegory identified by Owens is its discontinuous, anti-dialectical temporality. He describes allegorical artworks as 'not dynamic, but static, ritualistic, repetitive', and thus, 'the epitome of counternarrative, for it arrests narrative in one place, substituting a principle of syntagmatic disjunction for one of diegetic combination' (p. 57). Allegorical narrative is not linear diegesis, so much as the process by which diegesis is frustrated, unable to proceed. I want to show this 'counternarrative' impulse at work by way of a brief reading of a representative piece of postmodern American fiction, Robert Coover's much-anthologised short story 'The babysitter'.[32]

The story comprises a series of narrative fragments which recount the experiences of a young girl as she babysits the Tucker children in a standard American suburban home. These fragments, however, produce narratives which are mutually contradictory, none of which distinguishes itself as the privileged 'authentic' account of the evening. The reader's perspective is shifted discomfitingly amongst narrative options, in one of which the babysitter is sexually assaulted by her boyfriend and his friend, in another of which she humiliates the two latter with her own voracious appetite; other scenarios see her forcibly seduced by Mr. Tucker, Mr. Tucker caught *in flagrante* by his wife, and the babysitter set upon by the unruly children in her care. Shadowing these foregrounded narratives, meanwhile, are a range of diegetic background 'noises' from the television, ranging from Western to crime thriller to weepie. These TV plots are surreptitiously bled into the babysitter narrative, rendering indistinguishable 'real' life and consumer culture's representation of it.

The story, then, enacts precisely the 'ritualistic, repetitive' counternarrative temporality that characterises, for Craig Owens, postmodern allegory. Eschewing the linear thrust of conventional

narrative, it repeats various motifs, exclamations and images across
its contradictory narrative contexts. For example, two fragments
– one in which the Tuckers come home to find the three teenagers
huddled 'half-naked under the blanket, caught utterly unawares',
the other in which Mr. Tucker bursts drunkenly into the house where
the babysitter sits alone – each open with an exclamation of 'Hey!
What's going on here?' One of the boys, Jack, repeats the refrain,
'This baby's cold! She needs your touch!', to his friend Mark,
speaking first of a pinball machine, and later of the babysitter
herself, when she resists their forcible advances.

These repetitions both 'ritualise' the narrative patterns of the
story and draw attention to a disjunctive temporality in which
progress gives way to contradictory simultaneity. The past of
Coover's story is projective rather than linear, directed by
potentialities in mutual tension, rather than by a univocal and
authoritative perspective. The insistent shadow of television's
flattened, repetitive and fragmentary images provides a cultural
context for this narrative logic.

Coover's story thus emerges as an exemplary postmodern allegory,
conferring on the apparently singular event an irreducible multiplicity
of meanings. Each character, each incident and each relation in
the story stands perpetually – in accordance with Benjamin's
definition of allegory – for something else, transforming its meanings
as it traverses the diverse scenarios.

The fragmentation of narrative temporality is attended by a
corresponding fragmentation of visual perception. The story's
contradictory narratives each imply a specific visual perspective vying
for an authority which must be denied it. Moreover, the story's visual
perspectives are defined by their reversibility; the babysitter is both
represented as victimised object of Mr. Tucker's, Mark's and
Jack's predatory gazes, and, elsewhere, is herself endowed with a
gaze that controls and objectifies even her boyfriend and the little
boy in her charge.

It is significant, of course, that the babysitter, as feminine subject
and object of desire, serves as the embodiment of this allegorical
ambiguity and reversibility. She enacts Buci-Glucksmann's
conception of the feminine as modernism's paradigm allegory,
emerging as an interruptive force, blocking the forward thrust of
narrative time, and the unified perspective of subjective vision.
Narration is divested of its integrity, frustrated by the feminine object
it cannot render readable. The babysitter, in short, is opacity itself,
an illegible agglomeration of contradictory motives and desires,
repelling the authoritative gaze and opening up the instability of
the relation between seeing subject and visible object.

Two of the most cogent treatments of narrative in terms of the
relation between a fractured visual perspective and shifts in gender

relations are to be found in the work of Buci-Glucksmann and Peter Nicholls.[33] As I have indicated, Buci-Glucksmann's work is an ambitious attempt to excavate the feminine as the defining principle of allegory: 'allegory discovers all its depths of forgetting and being forgotten, its true destructive principle, its most precious booty [in] woman' (p. 78). It is in Baudelaire that these depths are most visibly realised, that allegory's destruction of the semantic fullness of language, and the consequent shattering of the object into a multiplicity of meanings, is most explicitly conflated with Woman. Baudelaire's prostitute, embodied in his poem 'Allegorie', displays all of the feminine's discomfiting ambiguity, as 'dispenser alternately of perfume and poison, seraphic and hell-black by turns' (Buci-Glucksmann, p. 78).

Baudelaire's tortured ambivalence towards the feminine object, however, is only a concentrated expression of a more widespread crisis of masculinity. This crisis is engendered by the newly pervasive force of urban mass culture, a force which gathers increasing intensity within the chronology of modernity.[34] The emergence of consumer culture brings about 'the symbolic redistribution of relations between the feminine and the masculine' (Buci-Glucksmann, p. 97), as the poetic aura invested in woman's 'natural' qualities by premodern culture is displaced by the commodification of women in the spheres of production and consumption. For Baudelaire, the prostitute is the exemplary embodiment of the penetration of organic femininity by the deceptive logic of the market, and as such produces a crisis of definition at the heart of his masculine identity: 'The integrity of Baudelaire's poetic Ego is exploded by the allegorical impulse to destroy the appearances of nature and the social order' (p. 97).

Whilst conceiving of woman as the allegory of modernity, however, Buci-Glucksmann strives to avoid reifying the feminine as a mere object, albeit a disruptive one, in the masculine field of vision. The indeterminacy of the feminine sign, that is, is not only a projection of the beleaguered masculine imagination, but a potential condition for the activation of women's agency. The figures of the lesbian and the androgyne, whose presence continuously if fleetingly surfaces throughout Benjamin's writings, constitute two historical manifestations of such an agency. In these two figures, 'woman is not only *allegory of modernity* ... she is also a *heroic protest against this modernity*' (p. 104). Thus, the 'proliferation of forms generating non-identity logics' (p. 132) that defines allegory becomes, when activated in the field of sexual politics, a point of entry into a form of resistance outside the assimilative mechanism of the dialectic of identity, one which dovetails productively with Aronowitz's and Bhabha's non-synchronous politics of time.

Moreover, it may be just this account of non-identity logics that can provide the ground for a theory of postmodern writing. Peter Nicholls' theorisation, informed by Lyotard, of how 'figural' discontinuity operates as postmodernism's dominant principle, is predicated on just such logics.[35] Lyotard's conception of the postmodern, Nicholls argues, can be read as a counterargument to Fredric Jameson's developmental view, which famously ascribes to the contemporary a set of cultural shifts, including the waning of modernist 'affect' and hermeneutic depth, along with a new privileging of space and a schizophrenic subjectivity.[36] Lyotard, in contrast, enables us to trace the continuities, as well as the ruptures, which mark the transition from modernity to postmodernity. In particular, the postmodern can be understood as that moment at which the modernist subject can no longer name itself as the 'narrator of history'. The definition serves also as a useful counterpoint to Godden's modernist metaphoricity, which locates the narrator of history in capital itself. In postmodernism, in contrast, capital can no longer serve as the ground of history's narrative explanation, but only, as I have tried to suggest, as the enactment of that explanation's necessary failure.

This failure of narrative explanation, Nicholls claims, can be illuminated by Lyotard's notion of the 'figure'. The figural is that which interrupts the systems of modern knowledge by introducing into them that which exceeds perspectival representation, that is, by revealing the 'openness' that those systems seek to forget. Significantly, in the present context, Nicholls points to 'the visual and spatial nature of a text' (p. 6) as a key guise in which the figural appears. Moreover, the figural is shown to be 'strongly marked by the historical ambiguities of the "feminine"' (p. 7), once again affirming the interplay of the visual, the feminine, and postmodern narrativity.

Perhaps the most productive element in Nicholls' deployment of the figural in relation to postmodern American fiction, however, is his insistence on its temporal nature. The temporal figure, or 'event' is that 'which can't be incorporated into a dialectic or reduced to a "meaning" within a historical narrative or equivalent other meanings' (p. 14). What this argument achieves is a recuperation of postmodern writing's *historicity* in the face of a pervasive tendency within postmodern cultural theory, exemplified above all by Baudrillard, to project history as having been absorbed into the proliferating circuit of 'simulationary' signs. Nicholls' critique of the figuring of postmodernity as a 'closed circuit' of spectacular signs enables a reading of postmodern fiction as less the affirmation of history's disappearance than of its grounding in a discontinuous temporality that defies mimetic representation. This reassertion of postmodern fiction's inextricable relation to a disjunctive history makes available an understanding of the 'divergences' within this fiction. As Nicholls puts it, 'these very different forms of writing all seek to disrupt from within the discourse of the modern' (p. 15). In the readings that follow, I hope to establish this impulse to destabilise modern ways of seeing as a point of continuity between otherwise very different writers. Whether this impulse is released, as in the likes of Coover and Stephen Dixon, or repressed, as in Jerzy Kosinski and Joan Didion, or ambivalently negotiated, as in Norman Mailer and James Ellroy, it remains an insistent presence.

Cold War visions: the development of Norman Mailer's allegorical impulse

The previous chapter identified a crisis of seeing in postmodern American fiction, generated by the newly dominant cultural logic of the image. In the present chapter, I intend to trace a literary history of the American crisis of visuality since World War II, as enacted by the development of Norman Mailer's long career. In so doing, I hope to demonstrate the origins of postmodern allegory in the historically specific conditions of the Cold War.

Mailer's own designation of his work as an attempt to appropriate and critique European existentialism in order to reinvent a spiritually and sensually impoverished collective American identity, provides a way into clarifying his conception of modernity. His literary project, that is, is broadly continuous with what Thomas Flynn describes, in reference to European existentialism, as a concern 'to humanize, indeed to "personalize" a world disenchanted by the rise of modern science and rendered impersonal by technology and the mass culture it fosters'.[1] Mailer's corpus can be read as a kind of protracted engagement with the disenchanted lifeworld of technological modernity, the experience of which is repeatedly registered on the plane of the visual, as evinced, for example, by his hypertrophied polemics against modern architecture and the mass media. In this respect, as Joseph Wenke has argued, Mailer's less than systematic engagement with existentialism should be seen less as a new moment in that movement's intellectual history, than as a heuristic means of finding a language for a critique whose concerns are very much in the broad tradition of American letters.[2] Nevertheless, it may be productive to examine critically Mailer's model of existential selfhood in relation to his European counterparts, in order to account for the increasing vulnerability of that model in the face of the penetration of lived experience by corporate capitalism and its various cultural apparatuses.

I intend to focus, then, on Mailer's diagnosis of the modern American 'plague' of technological standardisation and mass cultural 'banalisation', and on his attempt, from the 1950s, to frame a response to these phenomena in the form of an elaborate metaphysics of the body. I will go on to locate, at the crucial juncture of the late 1960s, the onset of the postmodern turn, a crucial shift in his conception of existential subjectivity, in which the 'authentic' body, living in proximity to its own primitive drives, is inexorably penetrated by the logic of an expanding corporate capitalism. As Richard Godden persuasively argues, *Why Are We in Vietnam?* most explicitly dramatises these penetrations of the lived body, and the consequent eclipse of Mailer's earlier prescriptions for resistance.[3] Extending my critical dialogue with Godden from the previous chapter, however, I shall take issue with his reading of the fractured narratorial subjectivity of the novel as primarily a metaphorical displacement of economic crisis, in order to restore to it what I would term its allegorical indeterminacy. In the last part of this chapter, I shall read Mailer's *Harlot's Ghost*[4] as an attempt to negotiate this indeterminacy as an irreducible fact of the lifeworld of American (post)modernity.

Throughout, I shall draw attention to the ways in which Mailer's shifting relation to American culture and society is articulated in terms of visual experience.

Cold War and the politics of opacity: early novels

From the beginning of his career, Mailer evinces a fascination with the loss of clearly delineated, 'readable' ideological distinctions wrought by Cold War culture. The context for this pervasive blurring of political meaning is valuably provided by Dale Carter.[5] The seismic geopolitical shifts wrought by the Allies after World War II, Carter argues, are managed by way of 'the control of communication and manipulation of images', producing a map of global power in which 'the illusionist replaces the soldier' (p. 36) as the arbiter of ideological meaning. What emerges from these new conditions of struggle is 'a state where what were once discrete combat zones dissolve into one continuous no man's land, boundless in domain but besieged at all times, ostensibly unrestricted and demobbed but potentially hostile at all points' (p. 69). Appropriately, Mailer's postwar writings provide an important point of reference for Carter, in establishing an emergent consciousness of this state of 'boundlessness' and dissolution. Indeed, the above-cited description constitutes an apposite definition of Mailer's metaphor for the impending American crisis, namely 'cancer' or the 'plague'. Cancer, or the 'incipient totalitarianism' of the Cold War American state, like Carter's no man's land, encroaches into every dimension of lived experience, indifferent to the hitherto unpenetrated boundaries of body, soul and nation. In couching his description in spatial terms, moreover, Carter highlights the ways in which this condition is experienced through the modality of vision in the form of a proliferating image-sphere of propagandistic spectacle. The dissolution of political boundaries renders the landscape of America opaque, resistant to the critical gaze. It is this opacity, which I have designated as a mark of the allegorical, that Mailer perpetually identifies in his ongoing critique of modern American architecture and mass culture. His self-proclaimed war against the totalitarian impulses of technological modernity can be recoded as a challenge to the abstraction, by the pervasive spectacles of consumer capitalism, of the visual from its origins in the primitive, lived body. The sensual drives of the authentic masculine body constitute the locus of resistance to the flattening logic of mass culture, whose fetish of the surface does a kind of violence to the American eye. As I hope to demonstrate, however, the status of this imagined body as a site unsullied by modernity is rendered increasingly tenuous by the shifts in American culture that Mailer is forced to absorb during the course of his career. Mailer's opening salvo, in a protracted and combative diagnosis of the American plague, is to be located in his first novel. *The Naked and the Dead*, a war epic in the politically engaged tradition of Dos Passos and Farrell, famously catapulted Mailer into overnight celebrity.[6] Some distance from the breathlessly intricate stylistic mannerisms that would later become the hallmark of his prose, the consciously derivative realism of the novel conveys little sense of the esoteric version of existentialism he would come to develop. The distinction is useful in that it points to the grounded perceptual clarity with which Mailer attempts to negotiate the emergent conditions of Cold War culture and society. The eye of the realist, that is, sees the world through a relatively transparent lens, one which clouds in correspondence with Mailer's development as a writer.

The Naked and the Dead projects the shifting coordinates of American culture and society as they will emerge in the aftermath of the war. Its trio of central protagonists function as barely veiled embodiments of the dominant forms of power coming into being at this historical moment: General Cummings' meditations on the meaning of the war provide an augury of the forces of technological massification that will become power's latest mutation in the new global order; Sergeant Croft's raw brutality and sadism represents the latent force by which this apparently seamless power mechanism is impelled, and on which it is unacknowledgedly parasitic; whilst Lieutenant Hearn's half-hearted attachment to a stable ethic in the conduct of politics, with which he challenges Cummings' aristocratic contempt for democracy, suggests the waning of the traditional liberal paradigm of American politics. The redundancy of this paradigm is symbolically affirmed when Croft's machinations during the climactic mission on Mount Anaka lead to Hearn's death.

If the emergent postwar global order is moving relentlessly towards a pervasive bureaucratic systematisation, which flattens cultural distinctions and produces a new opacity in social life, Mailer's response at this point is nevertheless to write a clear figurative map of these conditions. Mailer, that is, is not yet conceiving his protagonists allegorically, insofar as the likes of Cummings and Croft are mimetically stable, representatives of recognisable social forces. Where later characters and events will be charged by an indeterminacy that frustrates the interpreting eye, Mailer's early writing struggles to maintain a distance between narrating subject and represented object which can guarantee perceptual clarity.

Cummings' journal entries in the latter part of the novel exemplify this striving for distance and clarity. In his reflections on the broad historical trends being instituted by the war, Cummings attempts to take up the perspective of the seer, subjecting past and future to his transcendent gaze. This perspective produces such portentously apocalyptic observations as:

> Battle is an organization of thousands of man-machines who dart with governing habits across a field, sweat like a radiator in the sun, shiver and become stiff like a piece of metal in the rain ... We are not so discrete from the machine any longer ... A machine is worth so many men ... The nations whose leaders strive for the Godhead apotheosize the machine. (p. 567)

Cummings' identification of technology as the master category of modernity presages, of course, the thematics that will dominate Mailer's future writings. Mailer's most enduring preoccupation will be with the proliferation of an abstracted, 'second-order' lifeworld generated by the penetration of technology into every realm of experience. Cummings' vision of this lifeworld, filtered through a lens evocative of a Junger or a Marinetti (that is, in its aestheticisation of technological warfare), transforms the body of individual soldiers into a unified mechanism as coldly efficient as it is visually spectacular. The reign of the machine is here simultaneously the sovereignty of the aesthetic, severing the objective surfaces of military combat from its subjective experience.

The novel, however, tellingly enacts the waning of Cummings' charismatic authority in the emergent power structures of the postwar world. The conclusion sees Cummings reluctantly acknowledge that 'patience and sandpaper' may have been more instrumental in the conduct of his victorious campaign on Anopopei than his own strategic acumen. More significantly, the unexpected role of Major Dalleson, prime embodiment of the 'totalitarian' reign of banality that Mailer will come to identify as the American cancer, in securing the victory, leads to the former's promotion within the batallion to head of training for the immediate postwar period. The climactic pages of the novel show Dalleson newly established in the operations shack, contemplating new training strategies:

> At this moment he got his idea. He could jazz up the map-reading class by having a full-size colour photograph of Betty Grable in a bathing suit, with the coordinate–ordinate grid system laid over it. The instructor could point to different parts of her and say, 'Give me the coordinates.' (p. 716)

Cummings' ominous pronouncements of impending decline are effectively realised. Dalleson's proposals are for a literal merger of military and mass cultural forces, which inserts the soldier at one stroke into what Carter terms the realm of the illusionist. Tellingly, in the context of my own argument, the increasing proximity of man to machine presaged by Cummings is here enacted on the plane of spectacle. Betty Grable, semi-official icon of American femininity during wartime, becomes a device through which the new structures of global power can be consolidated. That this is the novel's climax further underlines the sense of a fundamental shift being wrought in the dominant cultural and political logic of the West. The conflation of geopolitics with mass cultural spectacle produces a new ideological map rendered illegible by the deceptive effect of entertainment. Moreover, the approaching triumph of mass culture is here crucially embodied by the feminine (in this case the Hollywood pin-up), Christine Buci-Glucksmann's foremost 'allegory of modernity'.[7] This perhaps constitutes the primary condition of the transfer in power from Cummings to Dalleson. Where the former, as we have seen, has striven to maintain a 'masculine' perceptual distance from the objectified 'man-machines' he commands, Dalleson's consciousness, in contrast, has been thoroughly penetrated by the standardising forces at work in the new global order. Cummings' authoritarian perspective, rigidly separate from the phenomena he witnesses, gives way to a subject position much more internal to the new hegemony of mass culture, a perspective that Mailer himself will later polemicise against as the motor of America's 'womanisation' in the late twentieth century.[8]

The protagonists of Mailer's next two novels are situated in just this context of a disorientingly opaque political and cultural lifeworld. *Barbary Shore*, claimed by Mailer himself to be the most autobiographical of his novels, was written at a crucial juncture in his political development.[9] Under the influence of Jean Malaquais, a novelist and intellectual whom Mailer had met in Paris in 1948, after the completion of *The Naked and the Dead*, Mailer found himself taking up a Trotskyist critique of Soviet communism and its Western affiliates as locked into an artificial conflict with American capitalism, both of which in fact functioned collusively in a homogeneous system of global power. Characteristically, Mailer publicly proclaimed his 'third way' at the 1949 Conference for World Peace, whose aim was to bolster mutual tolerance between the superpowers. The protagonists in the Cold War, he claimed, each partook of the same internal contradictions, of monopoly capitalism in the case of the United States, and of 'state' capitalism in the Soviet Union, producing an inherently self-implosive system that must result in war. The experience of this system, then, frustrates any attempt to render its meanings legible. *Barbary Shore* is centred on just this frustration as experienced by Lovett, its narrator and central protagonist. Symbolically dramatising Mailer's own education in the dilemmas of Cold War politics, the novel repeatedly encodes the illegibility of postwar America in an explicitly visual register. Thus, in the opening paragraph of the novel, Lovett informs the reader that his memory of the past has been largely obliterated, probably by a traumatising war injury. He goes on to describe the surgically reconstructed face he sees in his mirror:

> It does not matter how often I decide the brown hair and the gray eyes must have always been my own; there is nothing I can recognize, not even my age. I am certain I cannot be less than twenty-five and it is possible I am a little older, but thanks to whoever tended me, a young man without a wrinkle in his skin stands for a portrait in the mirror. (p. 3)

This failure of recognition, I want to argue, can be read as Mailer's first attempt to convey postwar consciousness allegorically, in the sense I have explicated above. Benjamin's *The Origins of German Tragic Drama* designates as allegorical that object of nature which has been subjected to the play of history, severing it from the eternal verities of myth and so making it available to a limitless multiplicity of interpretations ('Any person, any object, any relationship, can mean absolutely anything else').[10] In this respect, Lovett's self-portrait surely exemplifies the allegorical impulse. The face, primary locus of the self's sense of identity, is here penetrated by the traumas of recent history, divesting Lovett's eye of visual authority, of the capacity to 'recognise' history and his own place in it.

The novel narrates Lovett's struggle to overcome this condition, that is, to forge a literal and figurative vision that would penetrate the opacity of his personal and political horizons. The final paragraphs of the opening chapter provide an allegorical enactment of this struggle in the form of a dream. In this dream, Lovett sees a traveller, emphatically not himself, arriving in the city he understands to be his home. After hailing a taxi, he finds himself travelling across the peaceful landscape of the city. Wearily unfolding a newspaper, he finds that 'the print blurs and he lays the sheet down' (pp. 5–6), whereupon he realises that the driver has taken the wrong route:

> The man lives in this city, but he has never seen these streets. The architecture is strange, and the people are dressed in unfamiliar clothing. He looks at a sign, but it is printed in an alphabet he cannot read. (p. 6)

Once again, Lovett's dream is allegorical precisely in Benjamin's sense, working markedly against the grain of traditional definitions of the term. The dream works not to transform the chaotic texture of lived experience into readable narrative but, on the contrary, to affirm that experience's resistance to reading. The multiple significations of the city become fragmentary images, lacking their previous transparency, producing a correlative shift in narrative subjectivity. Lovett's traveller finds himself suddenly and unexpectedly divested of visual authority, confronted by a lifeworld of signs that, like his own face, withstands the inquisitive gaze. Furthermore, even when the cab driver goes on to interpret the experience for the traveller symbolically, the symbols invoked work to confirm, more than correct, the decentred epistemological perspective from which the traveller is suddenly forced to view the world. The driver informs him that his taxi is the motion of history itself, and the city the material city of lived experience.

Where traditional concepts of allegory place emphasis on the availability of certain narratives for metaphorical appropriation and doctrinal instruction, Mailer's deployment of the dream allegory here, in contrast, frustrates just this didactic motive. If the traveller is confronted by a new crisis of seeing, the driver's gloss merely designates that crisis as a condition of history itself, specifically postwar history. Similarly, if the unreadable city represents material experience, the driver has less illuminated that experience than affirmed its unreadability as its constitutive meaning. Benjamin's contention that the graphic fragmentation of baroque allegory is a product foremost of its historicity is thus demonstrated here on the very different terrain of Cold War America.

That the opacity of the postwar landscape is bound up inextricably with the power structures that control it, is further illustrated by Mailer's portrayal of Hollingsworth, representative of the Cold War American state. Hollingsworth is one of a quartet of players in a microcosmic political and sexual drama enacted in the Brooklyn boarding house in which Lovett is struggling to write a novel. Each of these characters is marked by a set of specific personal and ideological contradictions which combine to form a map of the political dilemmas that Lovett is forced to negotiate during the course of the novel. In this context, Hollingsworth is the official agent of American anti-communism, relentlessly pursuing and, eventually, interrogating the former Communist high official (and coordinator of Trotsky's assassination) McLeod, in order to extract from him an unnamed 'object' and so, apparently, ensure his political neutralisation. Revealingly, Hollingsworth's most remarkable physical characteristics, according to Lovett, are his 'opaque and lifeless' blue eyes (p. 40). Hollingsworth's eyes, that is, can be seen as exemplary allegorical objects of American modernity, depthless, unreadable and exuding artifice. They express foremost the inscrutability of his personal and political motives, his uncanny ability to confound the expectations of others (he appears to be both Christian moralist and womanising hedonist, Southern gentleman and calculating sociopath), and as such, attest to the fundamentally political meaning of opacity, its status as an effective instrument of control in the Cold War structures of the American state.

Indeed, opacity is repeatedly figured as the primary obstacle on Lovett's unsteady journey towards political enlightenment. The personal histories of the other four men and women in his boarding house seem perpetually closed off to him, miming his fragmentary consciousness of his own past. Both Guinevere and Lannie embody Buci-Glucksmann's allegorical feminine; the former, landlady and object of desire for each of the men in the building, is a model of wily artifice, whose vacillating sexual and political commitments articulate a relation between the feminine and the 'inauthentic' that Mailer would come to make increasingly explicit. Lannie, in contrast, embodies a more crisis-ridden political consciousness, one traumatised by the assassination of Trotsky into political defection to Hollingsworth, as well as into the construction of a private and illegible language, through which she reveals a growing madness borne out of the breakdown of a stable system of political reference. Both women serve as destabilising forces for Lovett's already precariously balanced subjectivity, figuring sexually the opacity of his political environment.

In contrast, it is the figure who seems most to frustrate Lovett's interpretative capacity, McLeod, who appears finally to provide a way out of this apparently impenetrable political lifeworld. McLeod's own biography reads as a painful narrative of recognition, during which Soviet communism is gradually but inexorably revealed to be complicit with the very structures of domination at work in American capitalism. During his interrogations by Hollingsworth, to which Lovett compulsively bears witness, McLeod apotheosises the assassination of Trotsky, in which he himself was instrumental, as the moment of implosion in his political consciousness, and the point of departure for a new theorisation of global power and resistance. It is to Lovett that McLeod bequeathes this ideological legacy at the conclusion of the novel, in the symbolic form of the still unnamed 'object'. As Robert J. Begiebing points out, however,

Lovett's political apprenticeship is dramatised allegorically earlier in the novel.[11] A key incident sees Lovett and McLeod venture out on to the streets of Brooklyn, talking as they walk through the night towards the bridge. This setting, Begiebing observes, is marked by 'sea fog, murkiness and dull lights' (p. 33), that is, by a physical obscurity that seems to reproduce metaphorically the ideological opacity of Cold War politics. It is at this moment, however, that McLeod recognises Lovett's aptitude for theoretical political engagement, and consequently undertakes to recruit him to his Trotskyist revolutionary project, a project that resembles, of course, Mailer's own position at this historical juncture. Thus, the restoration of Lovett's physiological vision, as night and fog lift, at just this watershed in his political education, constitutes a symbolic figuration of the potential reactivation of political vision, of the critical re-empowerment of the eye in Cold War America.

However, rather than interpret this visual empowerment, as Begiebing does, via a Jungian definition of allegory as the narrative enactment of mythic truths, Lovett's ongoing negotiation of ideological opacity should be read in Benjaminian terms, as the loss of just this mythic transparency. Lovett's experience, that is, should by understood as produced by the historical (and geographical) contingencies of the Cold War, rather than as a mythic trope. Thus, where Begiebing identifies an unproblematic shift from obscurity to transparency in Lovett's vision, I would suggest that the latter's eye can no more transcend the unreadable world he inhabits, by the end of the novel, than it can elude the play of history itself. Lovett, that is, has learned not to 'see clearly', so much as to acknowledge the necessary containment of his sight within the 'boundless', perpetually hostile 'no man's land' of Cold War America. Extending Merleau-Ponty's argument that the subject's visual perception is always temporally and spatially situated, I suggest that Lovett's glimpse of a redemptive socialist future from the dystopian horizon of 'Barbary Shore' (where the apocalyptic forces of the Cold War will inexorably converge) is not a teleological projection, as Begiebing would have it.[12] Rather, it provides a vantage-point from which to negotiate and critique the political 'blindness' (the concluding sentence prophesies that as 'the boat drifts ever closer to shore ... the blind will lead the blind' (p. 312)), by which he is necessarily contained. The novel's deployment of allegory, then, works not to reenact a transhistorical quest narrative, but to figure the map of the new global order as perpetually unreadable. 'Revolutionary socialism' does not alchemically transform this map, rendering it transparent, so much as it signals the possibility of reactivating political resistance within its opaque confines. As McLeod himself remarks, during his protracted climactic political challenge to Hollingsworth, 'I do not assume that we leap at a bound from hell to Arcady. At least there will be, however, a soil in which man may play out his drama' (p. 285). Far from positing a telos of political transparency, then, McLeod is arguing rather for the challenge of confronting and engaging the opacity of human history from within, and embracing such a project's necessary dangers. Here, then, can be located the embryonic traces of the concept of existential freedom that Mailer would come to develop through a long trajectory of non-fictional writings. If *Barbary Shore* seems to be weighted by a pessimism fixated on the impenetrability of existing political structures, this pessimism can perhaps be attributed to the incomplete development of Mailer's own conception of resistance.

Mailer's next novel, *The Deer Park*, completes a kind of triptych of diagnosis and critique of Cold War American conditions, which, taken together, both precede and prefigure the creation of a specifically American existentialist project.[13] The novel extends Mailer's figuration of postwar America as a stubbornly opaque political landscape to the terrain of mass culture, and in particular of Hollywood. Mailer's portrayal of Desert D'Or, a fashionable Southern Californian resort for the film industry's elite, is very much in the tradition of the Hollywood novel, the most prominent antecedents of which are Fitzgerald's *The Last Tycoon* and West's *The Day of the Locust*. Both setting and narrative, in this sub-genre, draw attention to artifice, inauthenticity and mass manipulation as the thoroughly entrenched principles by which Hollywood lives.

Mailer's specific inflection of this tradition is to be found in the McCarthyist context in which the novel's drama is played out, which serves to reveal the political content of Hollywood's impenetrable artifice. Desert D'Or serves as a symbolic repository of American mass culture's fetish of surfaces, as the novel's narrator and protagonist, Sergius O'Shaughnessy, makes clear in his initial descriptions of the town:

> ... the bars, cocktail lounges, and night clubs were made to look like a jungle, an underwater grotto, or the lounge of a modern movie theatre. The Cerulean Room ... had an irregular space of rose-orange walls and booths of yellow leatherene under the influence of a dark blue ceiling ... a smoky yellow false ceiling reflected into the mirror behind the bar and coloured the etching of a half-nude girl which had been cut into the glass. (p. 13)

Here, synthetic colour serves as the primary marker of 'an object-world of emblems' (Benjamin, *Tragic Drama*, p. 230), whose visual fragmentation conveys the object's 'allegorical' loss of transparency. 'Nature' – a jungle, an underwater grotto – becomes an arbitrary visual signifier, unmoored from its organic origins and inserted into the simulationary history of consumer capitalism. Colour, in this context, becomes enclosed within a Baudrillardian, self-referring circuit of signs, severed from any external reality. Moreover, at the heart of this simulationary microcosm of Hollywood itself is 'the etching of a half-nude girl', evoking the conflation, identified in the previous chapter, of mass culture and the feminine, Woman and artifice.

Mailer's diagnosis of this proliferating lifeworld of images, however, at this stage diverges in important ways from Baudrillard's, most particularly in the way he posits its relation to the political. For Baudrillard, as we have seen, the hyperreal logic of postmodernity severs the image from material human relations, and so from the operation of individual or collective agency, with the consequence that culture becomes nothing more than a closed circuit of signs, oblivious to reality. Mailer, writing over the course of the Korean War, is less ready to identify his Desert D'Or as a mere effect of the diffusion of power into the hyperreal. On the contrary, *The Deer Park*, with its focus on McCarthyism's purge of Hollywood, neatly enacts Carter's thesis that the proliferation of spectacle in the Cold War period is the latest means through which power articulates itself.

The deployment of the Hollywood novel's established narrative tropes, in which aesthetic and moral integrity are gradually corroded by the commercial imperative, takes on a crucially political inflection. This process of corruption is centred on the figure of Charles Eitel, a middle-aged and previously celebrated director whose career has been cut short by his refusal to cooperate with a Congressional investigating committee on communism in Hollywood. As the novel develops, however, Eitel's collaboration on a script with a studio executive, Collie Munshin, comes to challenge his apparently steadfast commitment to political principle.

The significance of this rather familiar narrative resides in the explicit equation it posits between cultural and political surrender. As Eitel reflects on 'how clever was the new script, how effective, how brilliant of its own professional sort' (p. 284), he begins to make overtures to Congressman Richard Crane in order to negotiate the terms of his cooperation with the Congressional committee. Eitel's capitulation to the banal commercial imperatives of Hollywood, in the form of his effortlessly slick script, is simultaneously an absorption into the 'cancerous' logic of Cold War American politics. The novel thus articulates Mailer's growing sense of mass culture's function as the guarantor of American capital's ideological hegemony. Eitel's political and cultural defeatism is intimately bound up with Desert D'Or's proliferating landscape of consumerist imagery. Moreover, the gradual collapse of Eitel's emotionally charged affair with Elena further develops Mailer's sense of a direct relation between political and sexual cowardice in Cold War America.

Like Mike Lovett of *Barbary Shore* however, Sergius O'Shaughnessy's own narrative is intended to provide a counterpoint to the apparent spread of totalitarian logic across the terrain of American culture. Once again, Begiebing points to vision as the modality through which Mailer's notion of resistance is expressed; Sergius's rejection of Hollywood's ambition to appropriate his lifestory for the screen, and his consequent embrace of the marginalised life of the writer, articulates 'a vision that penetrates false surfaces and sees the real connections between things' (Begiebing, p. 42). Begiebing is once more deploying an ahistorical distinction between 'false', fetishistic vision (Munshin, Herman Teppis), and its 'true', transcendent alternative (Sergius). Carrying forward my previous argument, I would suggest that Sergius has less rendered transparent the opaque, synthetic object-world of Desert D'Or, than taken up a critical vantage-point internal to it, from which he might reactivate a historically situated visual agency. The marginal writer, that is, can never hope to elude the play of history; he can seek only to engage it dialogically, to resist absorption into the totalitarian logic of the forces that drive it.

Having asserted the necessary historicity of Sergius's narrative perspective, it is nonetheless worth noting that Mailer's conclusion might in some senses invite Begiebing's unhistorical reading. In particular, the figure of Sergius O'Shaughnessy was to be the prototype for the protagonist of a projected 'heroic cycle' of novels that has remained unwritten.[14] Mailer is looking to forge an archetypal 'existential' subjectivity through which late capitalism might be fictionally negotiated. In this respect, the novel's concluding paragraphs constitute an effective prelude to the protracted series of non-fictional writings that would follow it. In an imagined dialogue with God, Sergius asks whether sex might be seen as the beginning of philosophy, to which his interlocutor replies, "'Rather think of Sex as Time, and Time as the creation of new circuits'" (p. 356). Like Benjamin, Mailer looks to an alternative conception of temporality as the means by which the privileged linear narratives of technological modernity might be exploded. Where he diverges from the likes of Benjamin, however, is in his location of such a temporality in the realm of Sex, or, less obtusely, of bodily experience. Mailer, I suggest, will progressively and consciously open himself up, during the years following publication of *The Deer Park*, to charges of an ahistorical fetishism of the body as a site of resistance to capitalism's technological fix. Indeed, if Sergius's narrative persona is marked by a curious flatness, it is precisely because he has not fully made the 'heroic' leap out of history and into the 'new circuits' of sexual time.

The active dialectical consciousness which Mailer opposes to the deadened and undifferentiated lifeworld of modernity is thus

defined sexually rather than historically. The resulting paradox of
an ahistorical dialectic is surely peculiarly American; posited as the
suspension in time of opposing primal forces, and most particularly
of masculine and feminine, Mailer's dialectic grounds the 'ethic
of risk-taking' (Wenke, p. 4) by which the heroic existentialist
lives, an ethic which, reproducing the manly frontier consciousness
of America itself, privileges ongoing struggle over narrative resolution.
For all his palpable historical consciousness, then, Mailer finally
stages his resistance to technological progress on the terrain of a
curiously Lawrentian sexual dynamic.

Thus, where Mailer's figurations of resistance in his first two novels
are premised on a historicised critique of an emergent permanent
arms economy, his writings from *The Deer Park* onwards would
suggest an increasingly privatised and transhistorical critical project,
articulated via his peculiarly Americanised reinvention of
existentialism. Mailer's steady retreat into his elaborate metaphysics
of the body is attended by an increasingly monolithic conception
of American mass culture. In this context, bodily experience can
be read as a locus of freedom from the insurmountable opacity of
culture and society, an authentic counterpoint to the logic of
technological capitalism.

For Samuel Coale, the mounting 'Manicheanism' of Mailer's
vision, its reading of the world through a bipolar lens that renders
every object shadowy and unreadable, should be seen as a chapter
in a broader trajectory of American letters inaugurated by
Hawthorne.[15] Hawthorne's Manichean sensibility, Coale claims,
perpetually sees 'irreconcilable conflict ... insoluble contradiction
and polarization at the center of things' (p. 5). This mode of
perception charges each object (Coale's example is the 'A' of *The
Scarlet Letter*) with conflicting meanings, rendering the world
impenetrable, resistant to the interpretative gaze. This perceptual
construction of the object would account, moreover, for the
prevalence of allegorical form in this literary tradition, insofar as
every figure and event is made available for a superabundance of
contradictory readings. I have attempted to demonstrate above how,
for Mailer, this impenetrability is increasingly conferred upon the
lifeworld of technological modernity itself and its increasingly spec-
tacularised cultural landscape, suggesting, as Coale has it, 'the
ultimate indecipherability and inscrutability of the world around
him' (p. 28). Nevertheless, I would continue to assert the historicity
of Mailer's Manicheanism, that is, to read his rather conspiratorial
vision of postwar American culture as an autonomous and self-
perpetuating object-world, as itself produced by specific historical
conditions.

I have indicated, via the work of Dale Carter, what these conditions
are; namely, 'the restructuring of the social, psychological, and visual

forms of power which reveal the passing of one control system ... and the inauguration of another', or, more specifically, the junction 'between World War II and the Cold War which emerges from its ashes; in a deeper sense between ... imperialism and totalitarianism' (p. 19). Totalitarianism generates, for Mailer, the need for a new rhetoric of resistance, attentive to the shifting logic of capital and the State, and in particular to the new and debilitating function of mass culture in shaping American collective consciousness. The boundless 'no man's land' of American culture has dissolved not only 'discrete combat zones', but equally discrete zones of political engagement into a flattened continuity. What this new landscape consequently renders redundant is any mode of political agency premised on a dialectic of progress, and any subject that understands itself as the 'narrator of history'.[16] The subject's relation to its history in the emergent condition of postmodernity, as the preceding chapter has argued, is necessarily reversible and dialogic, and as such disallows the subsumption of all the indeterminacies of lived experience under the sign of a single, legible narrative. We should understand in this context Mailer's emphatic rejection of 'the notion of an autonomous self that can understand the universe completely, foresee enlightened progress in all things' (Coale, p. 25). For Mailer, any such conception of the self is collusive with the reifying logic of technological capitalism, and its violent effacement of 'primitive' sensory experience. If a master-subject of modernity can exist for Mailer, then, he is nevertheless not the narrating subject of historical 'progress', but the 'heroic' 'counternarrator' of a new, discontinuous temporality made available through an immersion in the body's many 'mysteries'. Thus, if Mailer's existentialism challenges modernity's abstraction of the eye from embodied experience, along with the regime of visual domination that this engenders in such forms as architecture and television, it does so in the service of constructing an alternative master-subject, a kind of counterhegemonic hero that seeks to explode the dominant time of modern rationality via recourse to the primal.

The American plague: mass culture, 'womanisation' and perceptual distortion

The ten years following publication of *The Deer Park* see Mailer produce a network of non-fictional writings, which combine to form a coherent, if unsystematic exposition of his existentialism. Recurring throughout this corpus of writings are both polemical diagnoses of the American 'plague', and a series of prescriptions for resisting it. It is in *Advertisements for Myself*, his pivotal collection of 1959, that

Mailer chronicles the emergence of this new consciousness, and in particular his movement towards an existential mode of oppositional practice rooted in visceral and unmediated sensual experience.[17] Throughout the collection, Mailer directly identifies the historical conditions that have brought this peculiar fusion of bodily and cultural politics into being.

The most explicit attempt to address these conditions is to be found in Mailer's intriguing foray into Marxist theory, 'From surplus value to the mass media'.[18] Here, as the title suggests, he seeks to trace a shift in the exploitative mechanism of American capitalism. Mailer's essay reproduces an already widespread thesis amongst analysts of mid twentieth-century capitalism, namely that the primary terrain of contestation between classes has shifted from the realm of production to that of consumption, or, as Mailer has it, 'from the proletariat-at-work to the mass-at-leisure' (p. 355). Mailer goes on to argue that the health of the economy is now (in 1958) more parasitic on the psychic exploitation of leisure time by the State and monopoly capital, by means of the creation of new, 'psychically disruptive needs', than on 'forcibly subjecting the working classes to its productive role' (p. 355). This transfer of focus from labour to leisure had of course been anticipated both in the rather more developed positions of the Frankfurt School and in the 'cultural turn' of postwar French Marxism.[19] What Mailer's more impressionistic theoretical sketch brings to this analysis, however, is the novelist's descriptive eye, conveying potently the ways in which the logic of mass consumption impacts upon lived experience. In particular, he posits the new sovereignty of consumerism as the primary determinant of the spreading American 'cancer', generating a range of pseudo-physiological tropes to convey its effects.

Significantly, in the context of the present discussion, these effects would appear to be experienced foremost at the level of vision. Thus, Mailer denounces the carefully sustained proclamation of a 'healthy' economy by the State as 'an elaborated fiction whose bewildering interplay of real and false detail must devil the mass into a progressively more imperfect apperception of reality and thus drive them closer to apathy, psychosis and violence' (pp. 354–5).

The American plague's most apparent symptom, then, is a 'blunted apperception of reality', an erosion of the eye's capacity to engage its lifeworld actively and critically, generating a collective malaise whose apocalyptic consequences Mailer augurs in his conclusion. The essay's preceding companion piece, 'A note on comparative pornography', identifies yet more explicitly the primacy of the visual in consolidating the emergent power structures of Cold War America.[20] Here, his focus is on the 'pornographic' logic of advertising, its progressive colonisation of the unconscious by means of an elaborate fetish of surfaces. Where advertisements ten years ago (in 1948) 'sold the girl with the car' in order to invest the commodity libidinally, today,

> A car is sold not because it will help one to get a girl, but because it is already a girl. The leather of its seats is worked to a near-skin, the colour is lipstick-pink, or a blonde's pale-green, the tail-lights are cloacal, the rear is split like the cheeks of a drum majorette. (p. 351)

Here, then, is an exemplary projection of Buci-Glucksmann's allegorical feminine; Mailer sees the feminisation of the car's form as fracturing its functional meaning. It is in this sense that consumer culture, as I have argued in the previous chapter, works to erode the visual authority of the masculine subject, in its penetration of 'organic' femininity with the logic of the commodity. Mailer's late 1950s car thus becomes a new mutation of the Baudelairean prostitute, in the face of which, we recall, 'Baudelaire's poetic Ego is exploded by the allegorical impulse to destroy the appearances of nature and the social order' (Buci-Glucksmann, p. 97). For Mailer, similarly, the diffusion of the feminine into the space of consumer capital is an assault on the masculine eye, engendering 'the symbolic redistribution of relations between the feminine and the masculine' (Buci-Glucksmann, p. 97). In particular, this interpenetration of woman and machine produces a sinister redirection and transformation of 'authentic' masculine desire: 'the consumer is beginning to leave his desire to mate for the desire to hunt down his happy and faithful fetish' (Mailer, *Advertisements*, p. 351).

The proliferating dead objects of consumer spectacle, then, function as a perpetual drain on the perceptual capacity of the masculine subject, on his optic mastery of the feminine. Mass culture, for Mailer, can only be conceived conspiratorially, as the demonic, feminised other of the authentic self. The commodity image, despite being the determinate product of a specific historical condition, is nevertheless impermeable to the critical gaze, in its autonomous and self-perpetuating logic.

Mailer's critical project to renew the primal experience of the body precludes any apprehension of what Benjamin terms the utopian content of the mass cultural image.[21] Where the latter sought to locate, in the routinised visual experience of the commodity, a kind of 'profane illumination' that would reveal the subversive energies buried beneath its degraded surface, Mailer's perception of the spectacle would appear to be unrelievedly antagonistic. Monopoly capital's visual forms – most especially architecture and television – resurface throughout his non-fictional writings as the demonic and unremitting Other of the existential hero.

Mailer's prologue to an unwritten 'heroic cycle' of novels, 'Advertisements for myself on the way out' conveys palpably this hypertrophied hostility towards modernity's visual culture.[22] Casting a kind of pastiche decadent's gaze on the landscape of Cape Cod, the unnamed narrator fulminates against, '... the arterial highway with its savage excremental architecture of gas stations, chromium-panelled diners, souvenir traps, fruit stands, motels, blinker lights, salt-eroded billboards, all in cruel vision-blunting pigments ...' (p. 428). Douglas Kellner's description of Baudrillard's simulationary universe as 'an object world ... completely out of control' could apply equally to this breathless montage of images.[23] Just as Baudrillard posits the sovereignty of the object and the correlative dissolution of the subject in the space of the hyperreal, Mailer's 'vision-blunting pigments' serve as ominous signs of the absorption of the eye into the fractured spectacle of the postwar American landscape. At this stage in his career, however, Mailer's critical relation to this landscape could hardly differ more from Baudrillard's later injunctions to yield to the 'fate' of reality's dissolution into the simulationary. Mailer's engagement with late capitalism here is a profoundly polemical one, premised on a vision of the authentic, drive-ridden body, relentlessly assailed by 'the subway rails of an evening's television', which 'batter into stupidity the sense of the sensual' (p. 430). Mailer is motivated foremost by the impulse to explode the American fetish of visual surfaces, to restore vision to its rightful place within the body's sensory network. *Advertisements for Myself*, then, can be read as a kind of chronicle of Mailer's developing 'allegorical impulse', insofar as it unfolds the drama of his mounting anxiety towards the unremitting proliferation of spectacular signs that marks his historical moment.[24] His writing is charged by a splenetic 'bile' (to invoke Benjamin's Baudelairean vocabulary) in the face of the pervasive artifice and opacity of consumer culture, and in particular its inexorable penetration of sensory experience. Moreover, he repeatedly brings into play what Craig Owens terms allegory's 'counternarrative' drive, in his fixation on those transformative moments of immersion in the body's primal flows and intensities (orgasm, excretion, 'existential' violence), which 'arrest narrative in one place' (Owens, p. 30), interrupting the rigidly linear logic of technological 'progress'. In such novels as *An American Dream* and *Ancient Evenings*, digressive meditative passages on the sensual quality and significance of particular experiences work both to arrest the progress and to inflect the meaning of the narrative itself.[25] These are moments in which Mailer's 'primal' dialectic comes into play, a form of what Christine Buci-Glucksmann, following Benjamin, terms '*dialectics at a standstill*, frozen, fixed in images' (p. 103).

Mailer's extensive corpus of non-fictional writings after *Advertisements* continues to foreground the privileged status of vision as a primary site of contestation in Cold War America's cultural and political 'war' on the embodied self. The twin forces that lead this totalitarian front are, of course, architecture and television. It is against the 'severe eye-strain' induced by these forces that Mailer defines his ongoing existential struggle.[26] The ninth of Mailer's *Presidential Papers*, 'On totalitarianism', provides a succinct diagnosis of the American 'cancer' which is particularly attentive to its visual manifestations.[27] If totalitarianism can be defined as the erosion of all dialectical tension, as that which 'beheads individuality, variety, dissent, extreme possibility, romantic faith', and which 'blinds vision, deadens instinct, obliterates the past' (p. 201), then it finds its apotheosis in modern architecture. Mailer is careful here to distinguish between the subtle interplay of form and function that characterised early architectural modernism's challenge to aestheticism, and the collapse of modernism, during the second half of the century, into a kind of structured 'monotony'. The 'faceless plastic surfaces of everything that has been built in America since the war' (p. 194) serve as a pervasively visible paradigm of totalitarianism's drive to 'obliterate distinctions': 'It makes factories look like college campuses or mental hospitals, where once factories had the specific beauty of revealing their huge and sometimes brutal function – beauty cannot exist without revelation ...' (p. 201).

The somewhat Heideggerian concept of 'beauty as revelation' invoked here serves to underline the allegorical sensibility at work in Mailer's polemic. If what Heidegger terms 'unconcealing', that is, the unveiling of a being's essence, defines beauty, then the nature of postwar American architecture's ugliness is correspondingly illuminated.[28] The buildings in question 'blind vision' in that they erode the eye's capacity to read their meanings; in the built environment of Cold War America, as in the fractured universe of the German baroque dramatists, 'any object ... can mean absolutely anything else' (Benjamin, *Tragic Drama*, p. 175). The factory becomes charged with an ambiguity that conceals its place in the power structures of American capitalism. Moreover, the new architecture further effaces its own historicity: 'It is an architecture with no root to the past and no suggestion of the future, for one cannot conceive of a modern building growing old' (p. 194). Wrenched from the dynamic of lived history, the building disavows the temporal processes to which it is subjected, fetishising instead its appearance in an abstracted present, and so rendering itself illegible to the temporally and spatially situated gaze.

Mailer's response to this erosion of visual agency is to reclaim the eye from its insidiously enforced absorption into the totalitarian spaces of technological rationality. Tellingly literalising this posited condition of visual domination, Mailer answers his 1962 interviewer's objection to his use of the term 'totalitarianism' on grounds that the consuming masses are not 'drafted' like soldiers, by rhetorically demanding, 'And you're not drafted – your eye is not *drafted* when you turn on that TV set?'[29] It would appear that visual agency can never be activated *within* the spaces of mass culture. The television viewer will necessarily play 'object' to the TV 'subject', in a process that precludes dialogic exchange between the two. The eye can regain its subjective mastery only by withdrawing into the visceral experience of bodily impulses. I shall come to address this recourse to a trans-historical model of resistance at greater length, via a reading of Mailer's existentialism in relation to his European counterparts. For the present, it suffices to point to the effectively conspiratorial theory of mass cultural spectacle this model engenders; conspiratorial, that is, insofar as mass culture will always, for Mailer, elude the critical gaze of the historically and spatially situated subject, and can be countered only within some imagined space beyond the contingencies of everyday life.

The productive paradox of this rather paranoid relation to mass culture, however, is that Mailer nevertheless continues to insist, at least implicitly, on the efficacy of Marxism's critical tools in conceptualising American consumerism. His next volume of non-fiction, *Cannibals and Christians*, periodically articulates a materialist perspective on American conditions in the early 1960s. In a characteristic anticipation of his room in the Los Angeles Hilton during the 1964 Republican Convention, he explicitly theorises the 'torture of molecules' by America's omnipresent plastic structures in terms of the 'promiscuous' nature of American capitalism: 'It had won the war. It had won it in so many places you could picture your accommodations before you arrived.'[30]

The lived experience of American culture, then, is structured at every level by this victory, with the rather perverse consequence that Marxism is made, effectively, to theorise its own demise as a mode of praxis. For received notions of praxis, so the argument continues, are predicated on a 'dialectical' relation, that is, an unambiguous antagonism between subject and object, of which capital and labour remain the paradigm case study. Once capital's exploitative mechanisms diffuse into extra-economic spheres (culture, sexuality, language and so forth), however, this agonistic relation collapses into the pervasive sovereignty of one of its poles, and the correlative disempowerment of the other. It is this process that Mailer terms the 'anti-dialectical' drive of postwar American capitalism, which is everywhere visible.

Architecture, of course, embodies the erosion of the dialectic as the primary motor of American life. Its synthetic materials – 'fibreglass, polyethylene, bakelite, styrene, styronware' – provide no resistance to the machines that mould them into buildings, which consequently serve as 'the record of a strifeless war, the liquidation of possibilities'.[31] Indeed, any cultural form, Mailer claims in this pastiche, self-conducted 'interview', is 'the record of a war' (p. 236): what the proliferating artifice of the American built environment records, however, is a war divested of the 'heroism' conferred upon it when 'the environment resists mightily' (p. 237). Mailer thus bears anxious witness to the mounting optic impotence of the American subject, in the face of the totalitarian object-world of feminised spectacle which the new architecture represents. The mass media's proliferation is conceived as a process of feminisation: 'the mass media ... television first, movies second, magazines third, and newspapers running no poor fourth – tend to destroy virility slowly and steadily'.[32] This projection of 'the womanisation of America' once again enacts the fear of Woman as the illegible disruption of a dominant masculine optic, identified by Buci-Glucksmann as well as by Andreas Huyssen.[33]

If architecture embodies the anti-dialectical logic of corporate capitalism, then it is television most of all that helps produce the new consciousness that this logic brings into being. The emergent subjectivity of the American under Cold War conditions is described in his brief allegory of the formation of two dominant American typologies, 'Cannibal' and 'Christian'.[34] The latter are the dominant constituency of Midwestern agrarian culture, characterised by 'the boot-licking pieties of small-town newspaper editors and small-town educators, by the worst of organized religion ...' (p. 88). Cannibals, in contrast, are typified foremost by the 'sons of immigrants' who came to shape America's urban culture from the latter half of the nineteenth century. Driven by a deep-rooted hostility towards the Christian domination of America, they appropriated and expanded the cities geographically, politically and culturally. This process culminated with the spread of suburbs 'like blight on the land', following which the urbanites 'piped mass communication into every home ... they were cannibals selling Christianity to the Christians' (p. 88). At this point, 'an electronic nihilism went through the mass media of America and entered the Christians and they were like to being cannibals', whilst 'the cannibal sons of immigrants were like to being Christians ... and the collision produced schizophrenia in the land' (pp. 88–9).

Mailer's narrative is the by now familiar one of the growing illegibility of American culture. The dominant antinomies of American culture during the greater part of the nineteenth century, for all the reactionary force they released, nevertheless had the virtue of fostering and perpetuating meaningful conflict. Once the discrete identities engaged in this conflict are penetrated by the spreading 'electronic nihilism' of mass communications, purposive consciousness gives way to 'schizophrenia', or unreadable duality.

The dialectic is valorised by Mailer more for the revolutionary potential it releases than for the possibility of its successful resolution; indeed as Richard Poirier astutely remarks, 'no successful revolution is possible in the terms set by him', precisely because 'success' implies antagonistic forces being held in abeyance.[35] Existential 'heroism' is brought into play only when it can confront a clearly delineated object to which it stands in dialectical relation. Television culture, with its fetish of surface detail, obscures this relation of subject to object in rendering the identity of each ambiguous ('Christians ... were like to being cannibals ... and the cannibal sons ... were like to being Christians'). Mailer's collective schizophrenia can thus be defined as the absorption of dialectical clarity into mass cultural opacity.

Arguably, the theoretical position within the Marxian paradigm that this diagnosis most strongly evokes is Guy Debord's, whose *Society of the Spectacle* was published within two years of *Cannibals and Christians*.[36] Debord similarly equates mass cultural spectacle with an impermeable structure of domination, and the attendant eclipse of collective agency, as his dictum that 'the unification [spectacle] achieves is nothing but an official language of separation' (Debord, para 4) indicates. For Debord, the logic of spectacle works to draw the masses into a lifeworld of illusory relations that becomes their lived reality. Mailer comparably suggests, in a 1967 essay, that TV's primary 'danger' is that 'the mode by which we perceive our reality can indeed become our reality'.[37] Debord further echoes Mailer in identifying temporality as the category through which this structural deception is lived: Debord's claim that 'spectacular time is the time of self-changing reality, lived in illusion' (para 156) dovetails interestingly with Mailer's preoccupation with time as a key site of existential conflict and resistance. For Mailer too, the time of technological capitalism is an illusory one, in which living beings are subjected to the synthetic temporal regime of the dead objects that dominate both labour and leisure. This temporality gives rise to the condition he had described in his seminal 1957 essay, 'The White Negro' as 'a crisis of accelerated historical tempo and deteriorated values' in which 'neurosis tends to be replaced by psychopathy ...'.[38]

The existential cure: Hip vision

In this same essay can be found Mailer's first sustained attempt to prescribe a 'cure' for the cancerous condition of American consciousness. As I have already indicated, the cure is rooted in sensual experience, in an existential reclamation of the body from its abstraction by the forces of technological capitalism. The figure that Mailer famously posits as realising this mode of being is the 'Hipster', the streetwise hero of the American margins (Hip's prototype is the black jazz man), whose rebellious and unrelenting pursuit of existential fulfilment is articulated through both his (Hip is explicitly masculine) physical and his linguistic being. Thus, in an elaborate extrapolation of one of Hip's most significant phrases, Mailer claims that, 'To be with it' is to be 'nearer to God which every hipster believes is located in the senses of the body, that trapped, mutilated, and nevertheless maniacal God who is It, life, sex, force ...' (p. 283). The Hipster, then, is the American reinvention of the existentialist, assimilating the concepts of his European counterparts to the nihilistic conditions of Cold War America. He lives in dangerous proximity to precisely those primal mysteries of sexuality, violence, and, above all, mortality on whose denial the 'Square', representative figure of technological America, is parasitic. Central to the Hipster's world view is a temporality alternative to the synthetic time of America's dominant culture. In particular, truth is no longer conceived as a static agglomeration of facts, but as 'ambivalent and dynamic', subject to the play of time: 'truth is no more nor less than what one feels at each instant in the perpetual climax of the present' (p. 286). Hip, that is, involves an attentiveness to the radical temporality of being.

It is the experience of bodily intensities that most enhances this temporal awareness, as a fragment from Mailer's projected cycle of novels, 'The time of her Time' demonstrates.[39] In this story, Sergius O'Shaughnessy, running a bullfighting school out of his Greenwich Village studio, recounts his epic struggle for sexual mastery over 'a Jewish girl ... one of those harsh alloys of a self-made bohemian from a middle-class home' (p. 400). The story reads as an extended elaboration of Sergius's insight at the conclusion of The Deer Park, that Sex is Time, and Time the connection of new circuits. Mailer fleshes out this equation via Sergius's charac-terisation of his sexual life as an ongoing phallic quest 'to call forth more than one becoming out of the womb of feminine Time', and more specifically, to initiate Denise into 'the time of her Time' (p. 409). Orgasmic Time, then, is that time of 'becoming', of being in dynamic motion, which comes into play when the body overcomes its own alienation by modernity's abstracting logic. The 'connective time' of sexual experience, then, dovetails interestingly with Benjamin's 'projective time' as outlined in the previous chapter, insofar as it is similarly predicated on a refusal of the hegemonic time of progress.[40] Where, however, Benjamin looks to history itself as the ground of this redemptive time, Mailer's alternative temporality can be accessed only by recourse to the trans-historical terrain of the body's primal impulses. Moreover, it is dependent on a gendered opposition between phallic subject and uterine object; 'feminine Time' is activated only when its 'womb' is engaged in primal conflict with its masculine other. Mailer's dialectic is thus revealed once more as parasitic on the objectifying drive of a 'heroic' masculinity, deployed against, rather than in exchange with, the feminine. Conflict alone can cultivate the existential self, conflict generated by a kind of mystical physiology, and flattened by the contingencies of everyday life.

Mailer's conception of time, then, is bound intimately to his figuration of the 'White Negro'. In particular, the organic time of the body is thoroughly inscribed into the language of Hip. Mailer's exploration of this idiom, born out of black urban experience and made available to the white via rebel icons such as James Dean, draws out its 'pictorial' character. In the context of the present discussion, this pictorialism can be read as a kind of oppositional visuality, a counterforce to the proliferation of the illusory logic of the spectacle in everyday American life. As Mailer describes it,

> It is a pictorial language, but pictorial like non-objective art, imbued with the dialectic of small but intense change, a language for the microcosm, in this case, man, for it takes the immediate experiences of any passing man and magnifies the dynamic of his movements, not specifically but abstractly so that he is seen more as a vector in a network of forces than as a static character in a crystallized field. (p. 280)

Mailer's rather vague invocation of 'non-objective' art as a point of reference for this repertoire of verbal imagery nonetheless tellingly illuminates the privileged categories of his writings on Hip, as well as the ways in which they are registered visually. Valorising the mobile over the static, the situated over the transcendent, and the reversible over the fixed, he posits a critique of objectivist visual perception, whose implicit counterpoint is the embodied eye. Embodiment brings to the Hipster's vision an awareness of being as relational, of the self's status as 'a vector in a network of forces', and as such overcomes the constant elisions of everyday seeing. For the Hipster, as Mailer suggests in one interview on the subject, 'objects and relations that most people take for granted become terribly charged'.[41] If Mailer polemicises against the 'vision-blinding' ambiguities of Cold War American culture, then, he does so not in the name of some unproblematic 'transparency' of vision, but rather in order to reclaim for the eye that complex interpretative capacity eroded by modernity's spectacular logic.

Mailer invokes this heroic eye throughout his non-fictional writings of the period. The frequent point of entry for this conception of vision is Picasso's painting. What is perhaps most intriguing about the various fragments on Picasso is that they explicitly valorise those very qualities of opacity and ambiguity which, when deployed in a mass cultural context, Mailer so thoroughly demonises. Thus,

> He is the first painter to bridge the gap between the animate and the inanimate, to recover the infantile eye which cannot distinguish between a pitcher and a bird, a face and a plant, or indeed a penis and a nose, a toe and a breast. Tearing through all the obsidian flats of surface, the gargantuan anomalies of his figures return us to the mysteries of form.[42]

The evocation here of the above-cited description of the commodity (the car as girl) is not lost on Mailer himself. Picasso, he goes on to claim, 'is the modern creator of the visual symbol, the father of all advertising art' (p. 377). What enables Mailer to make this association, whilst nevertheless claiming Picasso for a paradigm of existential vision, is his insistence that the latter's imagery is produced by a heroic fusion of warrior's and infant's eye. Picasso, that is, is led by his proximity to the unalienated, perpetually creative vision of the infant, as well as to the 'monomaniacal' instincts of the warrior, to submerge the legible content of the symbol within its fluid, shifting forms. If his symbol thus anticipates the advertisement in its superabundance of interpenetrative meanings, it also distinguishes itself from the latter in penetrating 'the mysteries of form'. For the advertiser, form's ambiguities have a strategic value, insofar as they can be employed to exploit the associative mechanisms of the consumer's 'optical unconscious'. Thus, to take Mailer's own example, the car's play of functional and sexual connotations, whilst opening up the primal depths of the mind's eye, does so only to appropriate the ambiguity for the imperatives of capital. As such the commodity image's opacity generates less an awareness of form's mysteries than a fetish of its surfaces. Like Benjamin's allegorical object, it lends itself to a multiplicity of readings, each of which, however, is subsumed under the ultimate sign of capital itself. Picasso's object, in contrast, is possessed of a fecundity of meaning whose grounding in the primitive vision of the warrior-infant refuses any such subsumption.

This distinction between Picasso and the commercial forms he spawns should bring into focus Mailer's conscious inversion of the primitive–modern binary. In Mailer's scheme, the 'primitive' is defined precisely by the dialectical qualities of dynamism, mobility, and complexity conventionally associated with modernity, whilst, as we have seen, the latter is marked, at least after 1945, by the totalitarian impulse to standardise and rationalise all visible distinctions out of existence. Picasso's signal achievement, one to which Mailer himself perpetually aspires, is to infuse the experience of the modern with the vision of the primitive, and so to open up the possibility of their creative interpenetration.

It is this peculiarly inflected definition of the primitive that informs Mailer's wry claim that examining Picasso's work is a remedy for the 'severe eye-strain' induced by a split between the physiological and psychic parts of the visual mechanism. The modern eye is able to retain sight in the face of the physiological demands to which the proliferating culture of spectacle perpetually subjects it, only at the expense of effacing their attendant psychic demands. If, that is, the eye elects to engage the abundance of meanings with which it is constantly confronted, it risks a diremption of physiological and psychic functions, whereby, as Mailer describes it, 'My eyes begin to feel like an automobile driven by a man who has one foot on the accelerator and one foot on the brake' (p. 302). Picasso's images restore this lost equilibrium, in accommodating a gaze which is as psychically as it is physiologically active.

In Picasso, then, can be glimpsed an exemplary existential mode of vision that actively embraces the dynamic incommensurabilities of meaning born out of 'the mysteries of form'. Despite its apparent affinities with the visuality of mass culture, in particular its 'allegorical' impulse to explore the profusion of possible readings opened up by the visual symbol, it can in fact come into effect only outside the 'vision-blinding' spaces of television, architecture and the like. It is in this respect, as I have argued, that Mailer's conception of postwar visuality is so redolent of Debord's. For both, the spectacle functions as an impermeable machine, an object-world that structurally refuses any point of entry to the critical active eye.

Existentialism goes West: Mailer and the Europeans

It is the struggle to reclaim the body as a site of primitive excess that defines Mailer's revisionary existentialism. This struggle demands a recognition of the European existentialist insistence on mortality as the ultimate meaning of life.[43] In Heidegger and Sartre, he argues, death is understood only as the other of Being, leading to a kind of imaginative paralysis, 'a halt on the imaginary terrain of the absurd.' For Mailer, in contrast, 'Existentialism is rootless unless one dares the hypothesis that death is an existential continuum of life' (p. 232).

Mailer's distinction between himself and his European counterparts on this question points to a more general contrast regarding their respective conceptions of the body. Where Heidegger and Sartre each see the body's mortality as an index of its necessary historicity and finitude, for Mailer, the body is a site of mystic energies and primitive drives that exist outside of historical time. This peculiarly ahistorical conception of the body is at the heart of his project of resistance, developed over the ten years following 'The White Negro'.

This project differs in significant ways from each of the three key thinkers (Nietzsche, Heidegger, Merleau-Ponty) in the trajectory of existentialist thought discussed in the previous chapter. Thus, both Mailer and Nietzsche employ the hyperbolic language of the seer in order to articulate the vision of a potential hero of modernity. Moreover, both Nietzsche's Zarathustra and Mailer's Hipster valorise risk, dynamism and proximity to bodily intensities as the bases for a new form of subjectivity that would counter the spiritual violence wrought by modernity.[44] Yet in Nietzsche, these forces can be activated only *within* the historical time of modernity. A position outside modernity would reinforce, rather than disrupt, the *'immaculate* perception' of the transcendent eye. Mailer, in contrast, cannot conceive of modernity and its 'totalitarian' logic as conditions of the activation of an oppositional vision. Moreover, whilst both posit truth as relative and contingent, for Nietzsche it is history that opens up this relativity, whilst for Mailer truth is contingent less on history than on bodily instinct, on 'what one *feels* at each climax of the present' (Mailer, *Advertisements*, p. 246, my emphasis).

Arguably, Mailer's diagnoses of, and prescriptions for, the conditions of modernity dovetail more with Heidegger than with Nietzsche. Both, certainly, are concerned with the erosion of lived, authentic time by the forces of technological rationality. Both conceive of resistance more in terms of the recovery of a lost authenticity, than of an active intervention in a specific historical condition. Heidegger repeatedly charged Soviet communism and American capitalism with the same blind subservience to the logic of technological domination.[45] Mailer, in turn, charges the strategic and rhetorical manoeuvres of the organised American Left, in texts varying from *Barbary Shore* to *Armies of the Night*, with being more symptomatic of, than oppositional to, the instrumental logic of Cold War totalitarianism.

However, where Heidegger would extend this critique to a philosophical refusal of any form of subjective mastery, Mailer would wish to recover such mastery.[46] For postwar modernity, in his view, far from producing mastery, erodes it, in divesting cultural and political conditions of 'dialectical' conflict, and so rendering the subject a mere object of the spreading totalitarian 'cancer'. Immersion in the realm of bodily excess enables a recovery of existential energy, and consequently provides a perspective from which this cancer can be resisted.

The third of our representative triad of European existential thinkers, Merleau-Ponty, brings into more exact focus the aporias at the heart of Mailer's Americanised existentialism. Merleau-

Ponty's visual ontology, we recall, posits the grounding of perception in embodied, spatio-temporally situated experience.[47] It describes an active visual agent, engaged in an ongoing 'subject–object dialogue' and aware of the finitude, contingency and reversibility of this dialogue. Viewed in the light of Merleau-Ponty's phenomenology, Mailer's grounding of existential vision in primitive bodily experience is thrown into relief. Both thinkers, to be sure, identify embodiment as the basis for a dynamic mode of vision, which would recuperate the lived experience of time from its rationalistic abstraction by modernity's hegemonic cultural, political and economic formations. Yet where Merleau-Ponty insists on the historicity of the body, and therefore on the necessary finitude and reversibility of its objective horizon, Mailer wishes to take the body out of the play of historical forces into some imagined space of sensory transcendence. This fetish of the primal works to reproduce the very binarism of subject and object that Merleau-Ponty systematically dissolves.

I have drawn attention above to the intriguing sleight of hand by which Mailer inverts the distinction between primitive and modern, so that the latter emerges as the 'anti-dialectical' force against which the dynamism and complexity of the former is defined. This strategic move has the curious effect of extricating the dialectic from the material forces of modernity and transposing it on to the terrain of the senses.

Mailer's tendency to abstract dialectical relations from the historical conditions in which they are embedded is most clearly demonstrated by his treatment of gender relations. I have pointed above to his figuration of mass culture as a constitutive force in the spreading 'womanisation' of America, and its attendant fracture of the masculine ego's integrity. The 'feminine' object-world of the electronic media corrodes the dialectical tension on which authoritative masculinity depends. Mailer's polemic against this process, then, is centred on its reversal of the 'authentic' dialectic of gender that would pertain in some putative primitive state. As the above reading of 'The time of her Time' should indicate, sexual life, for Mailer, is authenticated foremost by dialectical interaction, by the literal and figurative interpenetration of masculine and feminine, the apotheosis of which is reached at the moment of conception. Because this dialectic is situated outside historical time, however, its polarities (masculine and feminine) are to be defined in absolute terms. The existential sexual encounter is one in which both participants embrace an identity, which, being defined *a priori*, eludes the contingencies of history. Mailer's notorious and recurrent example is the rejection of contraception, a means of defying the penetration and erosion of the sexual dialectic by technological rationality. His description of 'heterosexual sex with contraception' in *The Prisoner of Sex*, his 1971 broadside against the women's liberation movement, graphically distils his objections:

> Heterosexual sex with contraception is become by this logic a form of sexual currency closer to the homosexual than the heterosexual, a clearinghouse for power ... in which the stronger will use the weaker, and the female in the act, whether possessed of a vagina or phallus, will look to ingest or steal the masculine qualities of the dominator.[48]

Contraception, then, is charged with reversing the established dynamic of the sexual act. Its currency is 'homosexual' in that it renders indeterminate the function and meaning of its participants: divested of its teleological resolution in birth, the relation of masculine and feminine becomes ominously reversible. The apparent domination of the male conceals the mounting power of the female, her compensatory ingestion of masculinity in response to the contraceptive's effective annihilation of the womb's function. Indeed, 'male' and 'female', once infused with this ambiguity, cease to signify stable biological meanings; subject and object of sex may as likely be possessed of a vagina as of a phallus. In this, the sexual organs become exemplary allegorical objects: penetrated by history, in the form of contraception, nature (the vagina and phallus) is divested of its transparency, confounding Mailer's prized visual authority. It is just this reversibility, this 'symbolic redistribution of relations between the masculine and the feminine' (Buci-Glucksmann, p. 97), that Mailer is attempting to counteract when he insists that 'a man can become more male and a woman more female by coming together in the full rigours of the fuck ...' (p. 171). The 'full rigours of the fuck', that is, help to sustain that legibility of gender identities, of masculine subject and feminine object, threatened by technology's 'vision-blinding' logic.

Filmic existentialism?: a conceptual turn

In the years following the publication of *An American Dream* in 1966, however, Mailer's writings appear to undergo some important, if uneven, conceptual shifts. It is of course the late 1960s which have been identified by a number of theorists (see Chapter 1) as the moment at which the 'postmodern turn' redraws the political, economic and cultural coordinates of the West. Mailer's writings of this period stand as intriguing attempts to articulate and negotiate the experience of this transformation. Across a range of writings, including his essay on film-making, his book on the Apollo 11 moon landing, and, most important, his brilliantly sustained parody of America's collective schizophrenia, *Why Are We in Vietnam?*, he registers the increasing untenability of his sensory metaphysics in the face of the inexorable penetration of lived experience by late capital.[49] In postmodern America, these texts suggest, there can be no space, internal or external, which eludes the logic of technological capitalism, and so no unambiguously primal experience of the body. Consequently, Mailer finds himself attempting to transpose his model of existential resistance on to the terrain of technology itself, dramatising the interpenetration of body and machine that has superseded their clearly delineated opposition. This transposition enables the body's relation to the material forces of (post)modernity to be conceived historically rather than abstractly.

Despite these evident shifts in Mailer's perception of his own history, however, I do not mean to imply that a conscious and fully realised break can be identified in his work after 1967. Texts such as *The Prisoner of Sex* and his 1983 epic, *Ancient Evenings*, read as retrospective attempts to renew his model of existential primality, to recuperate it from its absorption by the logic of modernity. Indeed, as Christopher Walker has remarked, the latter text engenders Mailer's retreat into the ancient, as if its systematisation of his ongoing preoccupations with scatology, sexuality and reincarnation can be contained only within the unsullied historical space of the premodern.[50] My intention here, however, is to focus on those texts which anxiously dramatise the erosion of his sensual, and, in particular, visual master-subject, within the fragmentary and spectacular condition of postmodernity.

Mailer's 'Course in film-making', an account of the making of his 1971 film *Maidstone*, and of the ideas that informed it, provides my point of entry in tracing this shift. Its significance, in the present context, lies in its focus on film, apparently the constitutive force of the Cold War's landscape of mass cultural spectacle, as the terrain on which a new existential visuality might be forged. This involves bringing his dissident visual consciousness to bear on the established mechanisms of cinematic production. As Mailer himself, in characteristically bombastic terms, conceives his project, 'he believed he had come upon a way to smash the machine which crushed every surface of cinematic reality ...' (p. 118). The dominant narrative mechanisms of Hollywood cinema ('plot, dialogue, sets' and so forth), the main constituents of this machine, wreak a kind of aesthetic violence on film, effacing its buried and unique capacity to articulate Mailer's familiar existential thematics. If capitalism, then, appropriates film in order to transmute reality into artifice, to impose narrative order on the diversity of lived experience, in the name of the commercial imperative, it is to be negotiated by a counteracting violence, which would explode its temporal and visual hegemony.

The founding assumption of the film industry, Mailer argues, is that 'movies were there to tell a story' (p. 119), that is, to transpose to another medium the functions of literature and the stage. Inverting this logic thus constitutes the first step towards recovering the 'cinematic reality' that the movie-making machine has 'crushed'. What is also required, however, is a delineation of what this 'cinematic reality' consists of. Mailer's contention that film provides a point of entry into an alternative temporality, in particular into the time of mortality, provides a partial response:

> *Film is a phenomenon whose resemblance to death has been ignored for too long.* An emotion produced from the churn of the flesh is delivered to a machine, and that machine and its connections manage to produce a flow of images which will arouse some related sentiment in those who watch ... Film seems part of the mechanism of memory, or at the least, a peculiar annex to memory ... The psyche has taken into itself a whole country of fantasy and made it real ... (p. 125, Mailer's emphasis)

Mailer rehearses here a number of familiar Proustian notions concerning time; the past exists as a modality of the present in the form of involuntary memory traces, so that the relation between past and present is now perceived more as interpenetrative and disjunctive than as linear and continuous. Thus far, this departs little from Mailer's description of 'authentic' time as 'the connection of new circuits'. What seems like an unprecedented, if subtle, shift in the film essay, however, is that this temporality is conferred upon a technologically generated, 'inauthentic' mode of visual expression. Film is not simply a means of reproducing and projecting this interruptive time, but of actively producing and articulating it; as Mailer puts it, 'in every home movie there is a sense of Time trying to express itself as a new kind of creation, a palpability which breathes in the *being* of film' (p. 127). Deployed in the form he prescribes, film enables a new form of visual experience, one that rehearses for the film viewer the processes of death, and that consequently dissolves the subject–object binary. The viewer, that is, is positioned in relation to the film neither as objectifying subject nor as reified object, but as a participant in its excavation of a primal time-consciousness, correlative to the time of memory. Film activates the eye's most deeply buried associative mechanisms, he posits, in a passage that would serve as a succinct encapsulation of the central surrealist tenet: 'One can put anything next to anything in film – there is a correlative in some psychic state of memory, in the dream, the *deja vu*, or the death mask, in some blink of the eye or jump of the nerve' (p. 141). A further Benjaminian passage sees Mailer describe the heightened visual stimulation induced by his first film: 'The camera moved with the delicacy and uncertainty, the wariness before possible shock, that the human eye would feel in a strange situation' (p. 137). The camera eye, that is, far from being the optic master-subject of its objectified lifeworld, is situated in an anxious, reversible relation to it, which Mailer likens to 'a fifteen-year-old entering a room rather than a Mafia overlord promenading down a corridor' (p. 137). The characteristic analogy underlines the reversible, mobile character of the mode of seeing that he is attributing to filmic being.

Thus, if the technological age which Mailer so repeatedly figures as a demonically self-perpetuating cancer nevertheless possesses its own concealed existential core, it is to be found in the experience of film. Indeed, film is projected as the force that mediates, in the age of technology, the 'existential river' of the 'ultimate psychic states'. That river, he posits, no longer flows in the sequence of 'sex – memory – dream – death: but now flows through the technological age and so has to be described by way of sex – memory – film – dream – death' (p. 127). Film, that is, has literally inserted itself into the flow of existential consciousness, to become one of its constituent forces. The significance of this theory of film within the broader context of Mailer's writings lies in its refiguring of visual technology; no longer the demonic Other against which the authentic existential subject defines itself, it emerges as an actual *site* of contestation. In transposing his disjunctive optic on to the terrain of film, then, Mailer suggests a way out of the closed circuit of the 'primitive' in which his earlier concept of existential resistance was locked.

The body allegorised: Why Are We In Vietnam?

If the essay on film enacts a transition in Mailer's relation to the culture of late capitalism, however, it nevertheless leaves unaddressed the historical shifts which produce this transition. Perhaps his most sustained exploration of the emergent condition of postmodernity, in contrast, is his earlier novel, written in 1967, a crucial juncture in recent American history. *Why Are We In Vietnam?*, in the course of its deliriously digressive narrative, diagnoses the changing relations between nature and history, between the body and capital, and between consciousness and ideology, as they emerge during the momentous escalation of the Vietnam War.

In tracing the war's development in correlation with the growth of the space programme, Dale Carter makes explicit the logic of the Cold War's military, economic and cultural projects. The military containment of communism in Southeast Asia, he argues, requires the cultural apparatus of the space programme as a means of converging state and popular interests, and so of absorbing the potential for dissent at home. The unifying narrative of the Rocket State's programme works to reduce individual consciousness to 'the socially determined functions of consumption, spectatorship and passivity ... that is, to behaviour sanctioned by class rule in the interests of the development of existing relations of production, consumption, and exchange' (Carter, p. 145).

Arguably, however, Carter's account of the interlocking mechanisms of the Cold War during the late 1960s, in focusing largely on the homogenising function of the State, elides the crucial fragmentations of economic and cultural interests generated by the military escalation in Vietnam. As Anthony Woodiwiss's sociological perspective makes clear, 'the degree of political, ideological and economic strain created by the war in Vietnam' is the central determining force in the 'downward trend in profits' that marks the late 1960s.[51] The specific crises that attend these downward trends include liquidity crises, the collapse of the housing market, and massive trade deficits culminating in the dissolution of the Bretton Woods system of fixed exchange rates in 1972. For David Harvey, it is the collapse of Bretton Woods, with its consequent severing of the fixed relation between gold and the dollar, which constitutes the inaugural moment of the condition of postmodernity.[52] It is at this point that commodities, to shift terminological register, cease to be readable according to a universal monetary code, yielding instead to the fragmentary, unstable and ephemeral logic that will come to characterise the postmodern aesthetic.

It is in this context of capital's accumulation crisis and the various 'illegibilities' it engenders that Richard Godden reads *Why Are We in Vietnam?*. Godden's emphasis is on the growth of a permanent arms economy, actively stimulated by the alliance of state and corporate finance. It is this emergent mutation in the mechanism of accumulation that provides a precarious 'fix', both economic and ideological, for the seismic disturbances in the structures of capital: as Godden puts it, 'What "desire" was to the economy of the twenties, "destruction" is to the economy of the fifties and sixties' (p. 175). 'Destruction', the motor of the American defence economy, proves the ultimate unifying force in the consolidation of Cold War anti-communism. It provides the corporatist state with a rationale for marshalling labour into subservience to its own imperatives. Specifically, the Kennedy and Johnson administrations, executing their proclaimed project of securing labour 'peace', succeed in substituting grievance arbitration for the right to strike. Labour's recognition of this ideological strategy was registered by way of a postwar record in wild cat strikes by 1968, and the increasing ferment of that 'Other America' which the corporatist state had failed to integrate into its high-wage economy.

Godden reads Mailer's novel as a complex intervention in this newly emergent structure of class and racial fragmentation, fuelled by crises of overproduction and inflation. In taking up Godden's reading, I wish to extend the more general engagement with his book, staged in my first chapter, to the more specific context of a single text. In particular, whilst acknowledging my debt to his acute identification of the key political and economic crises of the late 1960s, I want to contest his reading of the novel's figurations of incest, miscegenation and other transgressive 'penetrations' as metaphorical displacements of unprecedented economic penetrations. Rather than equate the novel's narrative perspective with a determinate class-position, I suggest that the novel expresses a crisis of seeing engendered by the cultural logic of an emerging structure of late capitalism. This crisis is articulated foremost on the terrain of masculinity. The integrity of the masculine subject is here subjected to the destructive impulses of postmodernity's allegorical forms, made visible in the deliriously hybridised idiom forged by D.J.'s narratorial voice. It is, then, in the linguistic and visual impurities of the novel that the sexual and economic crises of its historical moment are laid bare.

D.J.'s manically rendered account of a corporate bear-hunting trip in the Brooks mountain range of Alaska is preceded and regularly punctuated by digressive analepses, descriptions and theories. In a characteristic example of the last, early in the novel, D.J. posits that 'America is run by a mysterious hidden mastermind, a secret creature who's got a plastic asshole installed in his brain whereby he can shit out all his corporate management of thoughts' (p. 27). The 'secret creature's' local representative is D.J.'s father, Rusty Jethroe, head of a subsidiary of the Dallas-based 'Central Consolidated Combined Chemical and Plastic', or '4C and P' (p. 22). The plastic fusion of the excretory and intellectual organs that defines the corporate American mastermind duly penetrates Rusty's physical being, and, in particular, his eyes:

> ... that's what you get when you look into Rusty's eyes. You get voids, man, and gleams of yellow fire ... in a photograph or just shaking his hand, Rusty's eyes are okay, sort of dead ass and dull with a friendly twinkle – typical American eyes – and when he's turned on ... why then Rusty's eyes are like yellow coals, liquid yellow fire ready to explode in its own success. (p. 27)

I have pointed earlier to Mailer's analysis of the interpenetrations of cannibal and Christian in the American consciousness, and in particular to the ways in which the mass media rendered these identities interchangeable, and consequently unreadable. Rusty's eyes are living embodiments of this irresolution: the Christian 'void' alternates with the cannibal's 'gleams of yellow fire'. In each case, his eye, betraying either no internal life or a surfeit of it, resists deciphering and so remains impermeable to the vision of the other. The description, of course, evokes Mailer's image of Hollingsworth's eyes some fifteen years earlier. In both cases, the ominous infiltration of all social and cultural experience by America's totalitarian corporatist state is figured via the representation of an opaque gaze. This opacity, then, serves as the marker of the creation and exploitation of new markets, or, to reiterate Benjamin's terms, of the penetration of nature by history.

In his focus on the commodification of the body's interior space that the novel both chronicles and interrogates, Godden is attentive to this shifting relation between nature and history. His first potent example is D.J.'s digression on 'Pure Pores', the corporate subsidiary headed by his father, a passage which demonstrates how, at points of accumulative crisis, 'non-capitalized parts of social life and of the human body are perversely interesting to industry' (Godden, p. 187). D.J. informs us that 'Foreseeing Plastic' is manufacturing a super-absorbent plastic cigarette filter 'which offers more pores in it than Sponge Valley, in fact if you perspire too much you can tape one of these cigarette filters to your armpit ... Pure Pores is the most absorptive substance devised ever in a vat ... Pure Pores also causes cancer of the lip but the surveys are inconclusive, and besides, fuck you!' (p. 23). Here, of course, we are witnessing the subjection of the body's flows to the discipline of the commodity, capital's unprecedented erosion of previously autonomous spheres. This is a peculiarly resonant observation in 1967, when the process of extending consumer culture into every corner of the private sphere, inaugurated in the 1950s (Godden's examples are the transformation of the collective space of cinema into the privatised space of TV, and the mutation of the traditionally patriarchal ritual of the family meal into the TV dinner), has become thoroughly entrenched.

For Godden, D.J.'s resounding 'fuck you!' to those who question the imperative of the commodity is unambiguous evidence of his class-based perspective: 'The old alimentary joke, about the body under consumer capital being no more than a conduit for commodity, is told from the particular perspective of the finance capitalist' (p. 188). In ascribing the joke to 'the particular perspective of the finance capitalist', Godden effectively represents capital, in the form of its representative D.J., as the novel's narrator. In so doing, he threatens to elide the crucial duality of D.J.'s subjectivity, his status as Mailer's familiar Hipster hero, guardian of sensory experience, as well as of capital's interests. The disparate idiomatic fragments of D.J.'s speech register – techno-jargon crossed with the vocabulary of existential dread, Southern Gothic fused with Hip obscenity – are, I would argue, demonstrative of his doubled relation to capitalism and its crises. Godden views this doubleness and the fractured vision that accompanies as a mere effect of capital. I would insist rather that D.J.'s split narrative perspective admits of no such dialectical resolution. If D.J., as he himself proclaims, 'suffers from one great American virtue ... or ocular dysfunction – D.J. sees right through shit' (p. 35), he nevertheless remains implicated in that very same 'shit'. Put another way, D.J.'s eye is situated not at some transcendent vantage-point above corporate capital's excremental logic, but is rather fully implicated in it. Embodying in hypertrophied form the existential masculine identity Mailer has repeatedly valorised elsewhere, his subjectivity is nevertheless simultaneously constituted by those very categories of mass culture and technology that have, so Mailer once claimed, 'womanised' American culture. As such, D.J. enacts the eclipse of the existential body as a means of defying the imperatives of technological capitalism. If, like Mailer the film-maker, he transposes this primal struggle on to the plane of (post)modernity itself, he nevertheless changes the rules of engagement in the process. The White Negro's existential heroism was premised on a sensory authenticity, rendered meaningful only in opposition to the totalitarian modernity it resisted; D.J., however, cannot partake of this oppositional relation to (post)modernity insofar as he is so thoroughly inscribed by the latter's logic. Neither its subject nor its object, his relation to corporate capitalism is reversible, that is, a peculiar hybrid of subversion of its imperatives, and collusion with them.

To reiterate, it is in the representation of the various masculinities in the novel that this crisis-ridden subjectivity is made most fully visible. D.J.'s projection of the sexual future as seen through Rusty's eyes is exemplary here:

> Yeah, the time is soon coming, thinks Rusty, when fornication will soon be professional athletics, and everybody will watch the national eliminations on TV ... well, shit-and-sure, fifty thousand major league fuckers will be clawing and cutting to get in the big time to present their open flower petal pussy, or hand-hewn diamond tool and testicles by Color Vision RCA. (p. 76)

It is perhaps unsurprising to find Rusty's anxieties about his own waning sexual potency articulated, at least in D.J.'s imagination, in the form of a fear of a more general diffusion of sex into the space of privatised consumer spectacle. Mailer interestingly inflects this anxiety, however, by plugging it into the specific historical conditions of late 1960s America, as documented in a subsequent list of seventeen indicators of national decline, amongst which are: 'The women are free ... The niggers are free ... The adolescents are breaking loose ... The products are no fucking good any more ... The Jews run the Eastern wing of the Democratic party ...'

(pp. 76–7). Rusty, Southern white male representative of corporate culture, reads the late 1960s' shifts in racial, gender, political and economic power relations into his own loss of visual authority. Unable to be a participant in the emerging spectacle of sexual and racial liberation, he is reduced to the role of its passive spectator, an impotent object of the television 'subject'. His previously unquestioned place in the hegemony of social and cultural power, his status as a narrator of capital's 'progress', is called into question by the pervasive black and feminist ferment that promises to transfer the narration of history to other voices. Thus, the proliferating 'object-world' of American spectacle is almost coterminous, for the Rusty of D.J.'s projection, with the decline of corporate white masculinity as the stable locus of political and economic power. These correlative phenomena, then, account for the urgency of Rusty's seventeenth and last indicator, namely that 'He, Rusty is fucked unless he can get that bear, for if he don't, white men are fucked more and they can take no more' (p. 77).

It is on the reassertion of his power over untamed nature that Rusty thus depends for the symbolic restoration of white male supremacy. Yet this proposition is predicated on a misleading assumption about the Alaskan mountains as an unsullied repository of the primitive, outside the reach of global capital. As the novel demonstrates, the bears of Brooks Range can hardly be defined as the unpenetrated Other of modernity. The infiltration of the Alaskan wilderness by hunting tourism, and the consequent omnipresence of airborne military technology, ('Sam Sting Safari, and other Safari Counters, with their respective airplanes, Cop Turds...' (p. 78)), has generated an implosion of the natural environment. In particular, 'the grizzers had gone ape ... now the psychomagnetic field was a mosaic, a fragmented vase as Horace said to Ovid ... too many grizzers were charging the hunter before the first shot' (p. 78). Nature, then, once subjected to the dynamic processes of historical, and particularly technological, change, is shattered into 'allegorical' fragments. The bear's relation to the hunter is no longer transparent; vulnerable to the new forces of technology that surround it ('Cop Turds are exploding psychic ecology all over the place' (p. 79)), it responds by rendering its own behaviour perilously unreadable.

On this fractured natural–historical terrain, then, D.J.'s encounter with the distorted consciousness of the bear is staged. Disgruntled by the protective mediation of the hunting by Luke Fellinka's veritable armoury of technological support, Rusty and D.J. contrive to lose the rest of their party in order to find and confront a bear by themselves. After shooting one mortally, D.J. steps edgily towards its dying body. He describes the subsequent visual encounter thus:

Yeah, that beast was huge and then huge again, and he was still
alive – his eyes looked right at D.J.'s like wise old gorilla eyes,
and then they turned gold brown and red like the sky seen through
a ruby crystal ball, eyes were transparent, and D.J. looked in ...
and something in that grizzers eyes locked into his, a message
... an intelligence of something very fine and very far away, just
about as intelligent and wicked as any sham light D.J. had ever
seen in Texan's eyes any time ... (pp. 100–01)

For Godden, this encounter is the metaphorical displacement of
a much broader confrontation between American geopolitical
power and the Russian 'bear' (sovereign over Alaska until the
American purchase of the territory in 1867). D.J., that is, 'eye-
wrestles with a summation of the USA's enemies' (Godden, p. 196),
in a space whose deepest memory is Russian. Godden's commentary
here is useful in deflecting the passage's sly invitation to read it as
an account of some putatively 'authentic' confrontation between
man and nature. In proffering such a metaphorical interpretation,
however, he implicitly confers an unambiguous victory on the
American hunter. As such, D.J. is once again identified as a
representative of corporate capital's interests, rather than as a
product of its crises. If D.J. succeeds in slaying the bear, the 'eye-
wrestle' in which they subsequently engage reads nevertheless
more as a complex and reversible visual exchange, than as the
triumphalist domination of one gaze by another. D.J.'s account draws
out his own inscription by the bear's eye, when he refers to it
'singeing him, branding some *part* of D.J.'s future' (p. 101). Thus,
if he and the bear represent the antagonistic forces of the Cold War,
D.J. nevertheless cannot be said to stand in an unproblematically
dominant relation to his symbolic counterpart. Rather, his
consciousness is formed by the complex interplay of ideological forces
that marks the Cold War world, a condition articulated by his
schizophrenic narrative perspective.

Indeed, my engagement with Godden's reading of the novel finally
hinges on the question of narrative perspective, and in particular,
on his theorisation of the tantalising narrative device at its heart.
The 'Intro Beeps' that punctuate D.J.'s account of the hunting trip
periodically raise the spectre of his possible blackness; as he
rhetorically demands of the reader, 'what if I'm some genius brain
up in Harlem, pretending to write a white man's fink fuck book in
revenge ... ' (p. 20). The novel itself leaves open the question of
the narrator's true identity, concluding that 'You never know. You
never know what vision has been humping you through the night'
(p. 143). Godden's historicist hermeneutics, however, painstakingly
resolve the ambiguity. D.J.'s narrative double, the 'spade gone
ape', can be understood as the gorilla ('ape')/guerrilla whose

ferment threatens to destabilise American capitalism during the late 1960s. If this is the case, however, then 'why', Godden asks, 'should D.J. adopt a voice from the social and political tradition of his enemy?' (p. 193). He locates the answer in Mailer's earlier conceptualisation of the American cannibal. Pointing to an afterword to his account of the 1964 Republican Convention, Godden notes Mailer's acknowledgement of an error of judgement regarding the likely outcome of the 1964 election.[53] Mailer has come to realise, in 1966, that 'the real possibility of what [Barry Goldwater] had to offer would not appear until Vietnam' (Mailer, *Cannibals*, p. 76). Once Vietnam, that is, has generated an inflationary crisis and a timebomb of social unrest, Goldwater's 'cannibalistic' fiscal and social conservatism will begin to resonate more deeply in America. Thus Mailer, Godden argues, constructs D.J.'s voice as an implicit critique of a New Left rhetoric which, in its faith in its own oppositional strategies, fails to recognise the emergent cannibalisation of blacks by the white Right. D.J.'s doubled persona is in fact the literal and metaphorical enactment of this process, a sign of corporate capitalism's new 'diet' of indiscriminate consumption. If this diet is cancerous, Godden adds, we have evidence from Rusty that cancer itself is profitable.

The New Left, then, is unable to grasp the logic of late capital, and in particular its relentlessly indifferent ingestion of all spaces that claim to be 'outside' of its reach. Indeed, capital's seemingly limitless penetrative capacity, Godden's reading of the text suggests, is metaphorically enacted on the place of sexuality as well as race. D.J.'s intense regime of transgression finds its apotheosis (like Fitzgerald's Rosemary), in incest. Yet in Mailer's mutation of the incest plot, the child becomes the aggressor, as evinced by D.J.'s vivid projections of maternal penetration and paternal cuckoldry. This engenders a proliferation of sexual roles (D.J. as son, lover and father, Alice as mother, mistress and adulteress and so forth) amongst the three members of the Jellicoe family, articulating 'a disintegral selfhood in which self-diffusion mirrors accumulation's post-war problematic of self-transgression (where capital must seek unrealized relations and forms)' (p. 195).

In Godden's reading, then, the novel's various crises of racial and sexual identity can ultimately be attributed to the disintegrative logic of capital itself. The transgressive projections of D.J.'s narrative become metaphors for the accumulative strategies of postwar American capitalism. My objection here is that Godden is ascribing to capital the very capacity for stable narration that is being eroded, within the text, by the emergent postmodern condition. What the novel dramatises, that is, is the *failure* of the logic of capital to explain and resolve the irreducible ambiguities of racial and sexual difference. Indeed, I would suggest that Godden is insufficiently attentive to the ways in which Mailer inflects the meaning of the term 'cannibal'. By 1967, we recall, American mass culture has made the antinomy of cannibal and Christian profoundly unstable, until each term inheres in the other. D.J. surely exemplifies this instability, insofar as his linguistic, sexual and, it would appear, racial being is constituted, as we have seen, by the schizophrenic interpenetration of cannibalistic and Christian elements. The novel's refusal to resolve the question of narrative authority bespeaks its allegorical impulse: the integrity of white masculinity shatters into unreadable fragments. The consequent proliferation of racial and sexual identities cannot be reduced to a mere effect of the economic; rather, these unstable identities form one of postmodernity's most central sites of social and cultural struggle. D.J.'s indeterminate identity as both corporate son and 'crippled Harlem genius' is not simply, to use Godden's own term, one of capital's privileged narrative options, but a palpable means of articulating the lived experience of postmodernity.

Why Are We in Vietnam?, then, constitutes an important transitional moment in Mailer's engagement with the 'totalitarian' logic of postwar America. It enacts a shift in his conception of the mode of seeing available to the subject in the lifeworld of Cold War culture and society. That subject can no longer situate his vision in the transhistorical realm of bodily experience as a means of resisting the mass cultural 'womanisation' of American consciousness. I have tried to demonstrate that for Mailer, the body, and in particular the eye, have been inescapably penetrated and transformed by the technological and spectacular apparatuses of late capital, and as such, mass cultural spectacle now constitutes a crucial site of social, political and economic contestation. The proliferation of allegorical signs that attends the fracture of both the collective and individual agent (satirically figured in D.J.'s images of blacks and women fornicating competitively on television) will become, from this point in Mailer's career, a fact of lived experience with which he is repeatedly forced to contend.

Allegorical history: Harlot's Ghost

Harlot's Ghost constitutes Mailer's most explicit engagement with the condition of Cold War since *Armies of the Night* in 1969. Much of the intervening work – most notably *The Prisoner of Sex* and *Ancient Evenings* – sees him develop and systematise the network of transhistorical ideas around bodily experience, gender difference and mortality, made familiar by his non-fictional writings of the 1950s and 1960s. *The Executioner's Song*, his exhaustive novelistic reconstruction of Gary Gilmore's murderous spree and subsequent trial in Utah, explores the appropriation and distortion of existential violence by the proliferating American 'mediascape', and as such addresses the social conditions generated by what Dale Carter, we recall, has identified as the sovereignty of the 'illusionist' in Cold War culture.[54] *Harlot's Ghost*'s concerns, however, are focused squarely on the intricate geopolitical relations and ideological dilemmas brought into being by the Cold War, questions that have not been directly addressed in his fiction since his first two novels.

Those early novels, I have argued above, attempt to forge a political perspective from which the spreading 'no man's land' of bipolar ideological illusionism might be critically contested. The protagonists of *Harlot's Ghost*, in contrast, divested of any material or internal space outside the logic of the Cold War State, find themselves immersed rather in the unreadable labyrinth of secrets that this State brings into being. As agents for the CIA, their lived experience is marked by an indeterminacy which appears perpetually to elude perceptual control. Every apparent fact of their lifeworld and most notably, as the title indicates, the pivotal figure of Harlot himself, is tantalisingly doubled by its spectral Other. Confronted by this proliferating object-world of political simulation, Harry Hubbard, the novel's narrator and central protagonist, finds himself unable to activate his own visual agency, to render its 'vision-blunting' stratagems transparent. The novel's painstakingly constructed world of espionage transforms its apparent subjects into objects of an always more expansive and indecipherable ideological machine. As Kittredge Montague, CIA psychologist and wife of the titular Harlot has it, 'whatever we are, we are never protagonists' (p. 559). The novel's dramatisation of Cold War espionage, then, is profoundly allegorical, insofar as it envisions a landscape of doubled signs in which, to reiterate Benjamin's dictum once more, 'Any person, any object, any relationship can mean absolutely anything else' (*Tragic Drama*, p. 175).

Historically, of course, the CIA proves fertile ground for exploring the reign of illusion in American geopolitics since World War II. As Victor Marchetti and John D. Marks explain in their history and critique of the Agency, the CIA enjoyed exemption from the established norms of political accountability in America, as a consequence of the legal precedent of the 1947 National Security Act.[55] Allan Dulles and William Donovan succeeded in persuading President Truman of the need for an intelligence agency that could attain foreign policy goals inaccessible to conventional diplomacy, and that would require the protective armour of secrecy. The Act consequently enabled the Agency's founders to construct an ideological space, outside the general imperatives of American politics, which would shadow the visible activities of the State. Protection from the scrutiny of the public gaze thus became the guiding imperative of the CIA. Technological devices, from the formation, in 1950, of a Cable Secretariat to ensure the controlled passage of communications within the Agency, to the development of supposedly undetectable forms of electronic intelligence collection, were employed to help entrench the principle of invisibility.

Harlot's Ghost, then, is concerned quite explicitly with the interplay of the visible and invisible as a primary constituent of American geopolitics. Its figuration of Cold War espionage as governed by the reign of illusion, simulation and doubled identity brings Mailer closer to Baudrillard than to existentialism, enacting a shift in his conception of visuality correlative to the postmodern turn of French theory. Baudrillard's concept of simulation, we recall, extends to the electronic age Benjamin's theory of the artwork as liberated from the 'aura' of authenticity by new techniques of mechanical reproduction.[56] He posits that postmodern cultural forms are 'conceived from the point of their very reproducibility' (p. 100), dissolving the categorical distinctions, such as 'true' and 'false', 'real' and 'imaginary', through which we come to know the world. Baudrillard likens this cultural condition to the psychosomatic development of symptoms that cannot be medically traced to the disease they signify. The analogy could be productively applied to the ceaseless proliferation of signs generated by the CIA in its espionage and counterespionage operations, as represented by Mailer. Like the Baudrillardian simulation, the various fictive identities assumed by agents and operatives in the course of their assignments are never unproblematically 'false' insofar as they effect actual consequences and so take on 'symptoms' of the real. This calculated interpenetration of truth and falsehood, with its accompanying disjunction of ideological sign from its material referent, becomes the means by which power articulates itself in the covert world of Cold War geopolitics, generating an ideological opacity which effectively paralyses the subject's critical gaze. It is in this sense that Mailer diverges from Baudrillard, identifying simulation as a historically specific strategy of the American State's global hegemony, rather than as a generalised cultural condition that inherently eludes historical interrogation. The first section of the novel potently evinces the CIA's simulationary logic, by way of Harry's recollection of Hugh Montague's extravagant take on Watergate. Montague posits that the intelligence community was bugging Watergate in 1972 to glean confidential information not from the Democratic campaign office, but the Federal Reserve office above, information that could be deployed to procure surplus finance for covert operations: 'Advance information on when the Federal Reserve is going to shift the interest rate is worth, conservatively, a good many billions' (p. 30). This new theory of the labyrinthine network of conspiratorial forces behind Watergate dovetails particularly closely with Baudrillard's own commentary on the affair. For Baudrillard, Watergate is an exemplary simulation of scandal, generated 'to conceal the fact that there is none' (p. 28). In other words, media condemnation works only to imply an exceptional violation of some putatively universal code of political conduct and consequently to efface the entrenched corruption of contemporary political and cultural institutions, demonstrated not least by the *Washington Post* journalists' deployment of very similar strategies, in investigating the affair, to the Watergate burglars themselves.

Hugh's theory, moreover, renders the affair yet more illegible, in positing that the conspiracy offered up to the public gaze is a mere media spectacle, conjured up to conceal a far more intricate one. Indeed, a surveillance operation against the Federal Reserve, far from being the 'exceptional' scandal of electoral duplicity disseminated by the media, would remove any economic constraints on the National Security State's capacity to perpetuate itself. Vision, then, emerges once more as a primary terrain on which the struggle for global power is enacted. The related forces of State surveillance and media spectacle fuse to wrest control of the visual realm from the public, by way of a doubled strategy of concealment and display: whilst the CIA conducts the material business of geopolitics in an invisible space, the media generate a proliferation of ideological signs that is all too visible and all too unreadable. The political autonomy enjoyed by the CIA as a result of its inaccessibility to the public gaze has been well documented by Marchetti and Marks, who suggest that a self-perpetuating surfeit of information, obtained by the Agency via technical collection, was a conscious and deliberate means of consolidating its power. They point to a review of intelligence collection authorised by DCI Richard Helms in 1967, in which Hugh Cunningham, the officer commissioned to head the review, came to the conclusion that, 'the glut of raw data was clogging the intelligence system and making it difficult to separate what was really important and to produce thoughtful material for the policy makers' (p. 96). The report, however, having caused much internal consternation, had none of its recommendations implemented, leading Marks and Marchetti to conclude that the ceaseless proliferation of intelligence is integral to the Agency's very structure. The CIA's power elite, it would appear, requires this supposedly unworkable excess of information if its political objectives are to remain unreadable to those outside it. This predicament of informational surfeit, with its attendant danger of entropy, is nicely dramatised by the novel's early 'Berlin' section, which recounts Harry's work and tutelage under Chief of Station Bill Harvey. An incident immediately preceding the Berlin section sees Harvey demanding of the Washington office, in which Harry is working as a filing clerk, information concerning a suspected

East German subversive named Wolfgang. Harry responds by requesting a more specific address, in order that he be spared the task of sifting through a vast backlog of intelligence, and consequently incurs Harvey's formidable wrath. Harry, however, is protected from discovery by the cryptonym of KU/CLOAKROOM and subsequently by a sympathetic Hugh Montague's dizzying manipulation of the CIA's international cable system. The attempt to conceal Harry's identity is sent into overdrive, however, when Harry is assigned to Harvey in Berlin, who, in a frenzy of conspiratorial speculation, confers on him the task of 'discovering' the real identity of KU/CLOAKROOM.

Harry's increasingly convoluted efforts to dissimulate his own identity generate a spiralling network of simulated informational trails, each of which provides Harvey with a 'reading' of KU/CLOAKROOM's status and motivations. These include the possibilities that he is a senior agent in liaison with MI6, that he is part of an internal conspiracy to unseat Harvey, and that he is an ally of Wolfgang. This latter scenario develops a kind of self-perpetuating internal logic, which coheres in spite of the theory's evident absurdity. Indeed, the imagined plot takes on rather Baudrillardian 'symptoms' of self-referential truth, when Harvey finally accuses General Gehlen, head of the BND, of conspiring to subvert his underground surveillance in front of Harry, in order to gauge whether the latter is linked to Gehlen. Once Harvey finally extracts from the proliferation of self-generating narratives the fact of Harry's identity as KU/CLOAKROOM, he is prevented from revealing it by Hugh's threat to expose devastating information concerning Harvey himself, namely that the latter, as the novel's conclusion discloses, is doubling for the FBI.

The Berlin plot, then, comically enacts the tendency of the CIA to function as a proliferating object-world of informational signs, which eludes any attempt to make sense of it. Harvey's hypertrophied quest to bring to light the true identity behind the cryptonym brings into play a seemingly limitless procession of spectral identities, bogus narratives and doubled motivations. In attempting to render transparent a concealed identity, Harvey succeeds only in intensifying its opacity, as truth is subjected to the relentless play of interpretation, generating a surfeit of allegorical readings, rather than a single authoritative one, around the cryptonym. Furthermore, Harvey's only opportunity to assert his interpretative and political authority is cancelled out by the revelation of his own doubled agency (as an informer for the FBI), in an exemplary demonstration of the logic of the CIA's closed circuit of informational signs. The figure who most acutely articulates this condition of ideological opacity is, of course, the titular figure of 'Harlot', or Hugh Montague. If it stretches credibility to invoke the Baudelairean 'harlot' as his

KING ALFRED'S COLLEGE
LIBRARY

genealogical predecessor in the allegorical disruption of the eye, it is nevertheless worth noting that his codename suggests just that synthetic identity that the French poet ascribes to prostitution. Montague constitutes in many ways a revealing transformation of Mailer's familiar existential hero. As Harry's recruiter and mentor, he provides for the novel a means to vocalise the philosophical basis for the CIA's existence. Most notably, in communicating the most deep-rooted meanings of the Agency's work, he tellingly employs the terminology that irresistibly evokes Mailer's prose writings of the 1950s and 1960s. This self-conscious device on the part of the latter works to transpose his earlier definition of the dialectic as an ongoing struggle between God and the devil on to the historically specific plane of the Cold War.

Montague's apocalyptic accounts of American–Soviet relations, periodically offered to Harry as part of an ongoing course of avuncular personal guidance, work to allegorise the Cold War spiritually. In so doing, they attempt to fix the play of allegorical interpretation, to provide absolute clarification of the moral and spiritual polarities that the two powers supposedly represent. Indeed, for Montague, it is this existential struggle, rather than the material contingencies of facts and figures, that constitutes the real and universal significance of the Cold War. Hugh is happy to acknowledge to Harry the 'all-out slovenliness in the Russian military machine' (p. 355), since the actual state of the Soviet armoury has little bearing on American foreign policy. It is in the interests of the American State to protect this information from the eyes of the American people, Hugh insists, because the latter, unable to apprehend the latent teleological dimensions of the Cold War struggle, will fix on its surface appearances, and consequently 'go soft on Communism' (p. 355). To counteract this danger, the CIA agent must develop an apocalyptic conception of the super-power confrontation. In Hugh's words,

> Communism is the entropy of Christ, the degeneration of higher spiritual forms into lower ones. To oppose it, we must, therefore, create a fiction – that the Soviets are a mighty military machine who will overpower us unless we are more powerful. The truth is that they will overpower us, if the passion to resist them is not regenerated, by will if necessary, every year, every minute. (p. 355)

Hugh, then, vindicates the proliferation and dissemination of 'fictions' as a necessary tool in the defeat of communism. In so doing, he condones a kind of limitless play of allegorical interpretation, that is, the ceaseless production and reproduction of 'readings' of the Cold War for public consumption, into which material reality (namely the Soviet's military impotence) will be absorbed. At the same time, however, he seeks to fix this play for Harry by invoking the teleological absolutes that underlie it. The counterpoint to the opacity engendered by the simulationary logic of the American State and mass media, into which the vision of the collective subject is assimilated, is the transcendent vantage-point of the 'teleological mind'. From this perspective, the subject–object binary ('The Reds, not us are the evil ones' (p. 361)) that constitutes the apocalyptic 'reality' of the Cold War can be clearly discerned, and visual authority consequently restored. As the novel potently demonstrates, however, this restabilising 'teleological' vantage-point is itself another fiction, ingeniously forged by Hugh as a means of dissimulating his own position in the intelligence community. Far from operating at one pole of an ideological opposition, Hugh is the author of perhaps the most tantalising of the novel's many baroque conspiracies. The central narrative of Harry's career in the CIA is framed by a present-day plot which gradually reveals the possibility that Hugh's 'death' at sea was a staged-managed event, engineered by himself in order to conceal his defection to the KGB. This possibility, of course, crucially inflects, and perhaps transforms, the meaning of his lofty ideological pronouncements as to the Cold War's 'teleological' nature. Most important, it disables the reading of Cold War geopolitics through a single, apocalyptically coloured lens. Hugh's perceptual mechanism is reversible rather than fixed, situated not at the transcendent vantage-point of American power, but, so it would appear, in the indeterminate and shifting space between the superpowers. In its availability to a potentially limitless range of readerly appropriations, his political identity exemplifies the allegorical impulse to destabilise the subject's interpretative perspective.

Hugh implicitly reveals this impulse to destabilise in his lecture to the CIA trainees on Feliks Dzerzhinsky, founder of the KGB (then Cheka), and of the modern practice of counterespionage. Hugh recounts the history of the operation engineered by Dzerzhinsky, to weed out '*rediski*' (radishes), or covert monarchists, from the new secret police, by way of an alliance with one of the leading members of the restorationist circle, Alexander Yakovlev. Appealing to his patriotism and political moderacy, Dzerzhinsky lured Yakovlev into a 'pact' to bring off a bloodless coup, which involved ridding the Cheka of those more extreme monarchist elements who threatened a bloody counterrevolution. In so doing, he persuaded Yakovlev to help curb the sabotage of the British Secret Service on grounds that the latter's activity might lead to an indiscriminate crushing of *rediski* by the Cheka's more punitive elements. This opportunistic alliance resulted in '"the largest neutralization of an enemy brought off in the history of counterespionage"' (p. 402).

Hugh provides the following commentary on the 'seductive' relation at the centre of this operation:

> When seduction is inspired ... by the demands of power, each person will lie to the other. Sometimes, they lie to themselves. These lies often develop structures as aesthetically rich as the finest filigree of truth. After a time, how could Yakovlev and Dzerzhinsky know when they were dealing with a truth or a lie? The relationship had grown too deep. They had to travel beyond their last clear principles. They could no longer know when they were true themselves. The self, indeed, was in migration. (p. 403)

Seduction, we recall, is a term deployed by Baudrillard to diagnose the logic of postmodern culture. It designates the 'feminine' reign of appearances, the privileging of reversible, rather than fixed, relations of power. As such, it dovetails interestingly with Hugh's use of the term, which similarly refers to the disappearance of truth into a labyrinthine network of fictions. Hugh figures the relation between Dzerzhinsky and Yakovlev as a kind of endless play of performance and interpretation, in which the self's integrity gives way to a 'migratory' condition of perpetual fracture and transformation. This condition, then, effectively disables the transcendent perspective of 'teleology', insofar as Hugh's teleological politics is revealed as yet another fiction, generated by him to dissimulate his own defection.

Hugh's Dzerzhinsky lecture, then, unbeknownst to its audience, figures his own unreadable and shifting subjectivity as much as its subject's. It is only at the novel's conclusion in Moscow that Harry is able to recognise this affinity of consciousness. Having flown to the Soviet capital in search of his mentor and godfather, after a year of writing, in hiding, the history of his CIA career, he finds himself standing in the middle of Dzerzhinsky Square. It is here, appropriately enough, that Harry recalls Hugh's fanciful hypothesis that the physical world's evolutionary traces constitute part of God's campaign of disinformation, calculated to prevent man from penetrating the mysteries of Himself and His Creation. For Harry, '*A man who could conceive of the universe as a distortion fashioned for the purposes of self-protection by God was a man to live in monumental double dealings he had created for himself*' (p. 1167, Mailer's emphasis). It is this doubled selfhood that binds Hugh so inextricably to Dzerzhinsky. Both conceive of the universe as a kind of cosmic simulation whose foundational origins must remain forever invisible and inaccessible, and construct their own identities according to the same logic. Harry wants to ask of Hugh Lenin's famous question, ' "*Whom? Whom does all this benefit?*" ' (p. 1168, Mailer's emphasis), in the hope that he might extricate from his mentor's labyrinthine network of contradictory motives and fictive identities a cohesive narrative subjectivity. Any such quest, of course, must result in frustration, insofar as Hugh's subjectivity consists precisely in what Craig Owens terms the counternarrative impulse. In rejecting the evolutionary account of the universe, in favour of his jocose ascription of creation to a divine conspiracy, he inserts the most fundamental of narratives into the indeterminate play of simulation. Within this space, the origins of the universe are subject to limitless allegorisation, a process which counters the narrative of evolutionary progress, in calling into question the authority of the Darwinian eye.

Hugh, then, is a tantalising figuration of the 'harlotry' that haunts the Cold War American State's most invisible geopolitical apparatus. His doubled identity resists reading through a privileged conceptual lens, including that of the economic. Where Godden might identify his 'disintegrative' subjectivity as a metaphorical displacement of capital's latest accumulative crisis, I would want to insist on its irreducible indeterminacy, and on its consequent resistance to resolution in terms of the logic of capital. Harlot's unstable ideological gaze, rather than being an epiphenomenon of the economic, embodies the actual lived experience of the postmodern condition. His biography exemplifies, and throws into intense relief, the postmodern subject's necessary occupation of what Homi Bhabha terms the 'in-between space, which invalidates all subject-centred vision'.[57] As such, it enacts just that model of postmodern narrativity I have attempted to set out above. Chapter 1 argued that such a model was premised on the interruption of the objectifying gaze of modernity with a new reversibility and fluidity. In continuously frustrating the intelligence community's attempts to fix and render transparent his visual subjectivity, Harlot surely performs just such an interruption. The teleological narrative of political and spiritual conflict he articulates in one place, is tantalisingly reversed in another by the counternarrative of his apparent KGB defection.

Once again, however, it is on the plane of gender, as much as politics, that the drama of shifting and unstable relations between subject and object is played out. This is particularly significant, we recall, in the broader context of Mailer's writings, insofar as his early work notoriously posits 'primitive' masculinity as the modality through which existential agency might be renewed and activated. *Harlot's Ghost*, in contrast, appears to enact the fate of fixed categories of gender and sexuality in the disjunctive time and space of postmodernity.

The novel's first foray into this emergent indeterminacy of sexual identity centres on the figure of Dix Butler, one of Harry's fellow

Agency recruits. Possessed of prodigious physical strength and magnetic sexual presence, Dix is revealed in the novel's initial present-day narrative frame as the lover for whom Harry's (and previously Hugh's) wife Kittredge deserts her husband. As such, he appears to embody precisely the kind of hypertrophied masculine consciousness made familiar by Mailer's earlier writings on Hip, boxing and the mass media. Given this context, his attempt to seduce Harry in Berlin (the first Agency posting for both men) is all the more unsettling. Offering him his 'powerful buttocks', he implores Harry, '"Goddamit, I need it tonight. I need it bad, Harry, and I love you"' (p. 292). Harry finds himself heavily disconcerted by his response:

> 'I love you too, Dix,' I said, 'but I can't.' The worst of it was that I could. An erection had risen out of I know not what, from puddles of urine on a cellar floor and a fat German slobbering his beer, from the buried loves of my life, from bonds of family and friends and all the muffled dreams of Kittredge ... (p. 292)

Confronted with the unexpected reversibility of Dix's sexual identity, Harry attempts to disavow the resonance this ambiguity has for himself. In so doing, however, he succeeds only in articulating a similar crisis of sexual consciousness. His erection emerges not out of the command of a defined object of desire but, on the contrary, out of an associative montage of transgressive images from his unconscious. Similarly, his declaration of love to Dix seems bereft of intentionality, an involuntary revelation of his fluctuating sexual being. This, then, is the context in which Harry is initiated into sexual life, after hurriedly taking leave of Dix. Venturing on to the Berlin streets, he encounters Ingrid, a 'companion for hire' at a Berlin nightclub, and is soon locked with her in a frenzied sexual embrace, culminating in his loss of virginity. Harry's first foray into what Mailer has previously termed 'the dialectic of sex' thus emerges more from a crisis, than a conscious activation, of masculine identity.

Harry is induced to confront this crisis further during his assignation to Uruguay, when he is introduced by his operative, the high-ranking communist Chevi Fuertes, to 'an angel with a heart like a honeycomb, full of sugar and greed' (p. 584): this is Fuertes' lover, a former prostitute, whose memorable sobriquet is Libertad La Lengua. Harry's lusty appreciation of this apparent apotheosis of femininity is enhanced after 'Libertad conferred on me one of her royal gifts – fellatio' (p. 589). This apparent boon to his masculine identity, however, is rendered ambiguous by Chevi's subsequent disclosure that Libertad is a transsexual: writing of the revelation to Kittredge, he tells her, 'I swear I could feel the simultaneous existence of Alpha and Omega, yes, Alpha, our manly

case officer ... had to wonder: Was he, himself a homosexual?'
(p. 608). The categories to which Harry refers have been formulated
by Kittredge as the theoretical basis for the CIA's psychological
warfare strategies, and designate Mailer's familiar binary of the
rational (Alpha) and its disruptive Other (Omega). Yet where
earlier writings projected these forces as polarities of an ongoing
dialectical conflict, they are now felt to be locked in 'simultaneous
existence', to inhere within one another. Put another way, the
transsexual seems to function as the latest, 'postmodern' mutation
of Buci-Glucksmann's allegorical feminine, whose disjunctive effect
on masculine integrity brings about 'the symbolic redistribution of
relations between the feminine and the masculine' (Buci-
Glucksmann, p. 97). Like the prostitute (which Libertad is also),
the transsexual signifies the penetration of 'organic' femininity by
technological modernity, engendering a crisis of masculine identity
anxiously articulated by Harry's question about his own sexuality.
Harlot's Ghost, then, narrates the penetration of the primal masculine
subject and his feminine counterpart by the shifting and destabilising
logic of postwar American history. The 'interstitial' position into
which the subject of this history is inserted is made visible by the
novel's engagement with gender, as well as with politics. As such,
Harlot's Ghost reads as a kind of culminating point in Mailer's implicit
history of visuality since the war, a history which this chapter has
attempted to draw out.

Always attentive to the lifeworld of mass cultural and propagandistic
spectacle brought into being by the Cold War, Mailer's earliest
responses to this condition involve an attempt to imagine a political
'third way' that would counter the binary logic of the warring
superpowers, a response exemplified by *Barbary Shore*. From the
mid 1950s, this historically conditioned mode of resistance gives
way to the formation of an informal system of existential vision,
rooted in the restoration of the eye to the primal experience of sensory
excess, and an outright withdrawal from the 'womanising' impulse
of mass culture. *Why Are We In Vietnam?*, in turn, reads as a kind
of satirical autocritique of this system, dramatising as it does the
creeping penetration of the embodied eye by the logic of late
capital. Finally, *Harlot's Ghost* posits this disruptive interplay of vision
and history as an irreducible fact of Cold War life, demonstrating
the eye's inescapable assimilation into postmodern time and space.
Mailer's welcome attentiveness to the historical forces which have
appropriated those primal spaces he had once valorised as sites of
existential resistance, however, is accompanied by an important
imaginative problem. Specifically, having both placed his critical
faith in a transhistorically conceived body, and disavowed the

American mass cultural landscape as itself a site of contestation, he is unable to envision any activation of the critical eye within the disintegrative simulationary space of the intelligence community. For Mailer, it would appear, the disappearance of the heroic masculine subject into the spectral logic of the postmodern portends the eclipse of visual politics as such.

3

In camera: the allegorical impulse of cinematographic fiction

The previous chapters have identified a postmodern aesthetic of fracture and discontinuity, expressing a crisis of seeing in which, as Walter Benjamin has it, 'ideas evaporate in images'; images, that is, articulate the destabilised mode of vision generated by the condition of postmodernity and, more particularly, by the society of the spectacle.[1]

The present chapter will explore the centrality of film to postmodern culture's 'allegorical' impulse, identifying in it an embodiment of the disruptive force of the image. The first chapter, we recall, signposted this conceptual transposition, in invoking Craig Owens' assertion that 'Film composes narrative out of a succession of concrete images, which makes it particularly suited to allegory's essential pictogramism.'[2] Film's 'pictogramatic' foregrounding of the image, Owens suggests, in opening up a potentially limitless range of readerly interpretations, produces a fluid relation between the eye and its object. This fluidity counters the narrative resolution which American mass culture's dominant cinematic genres ('the Western, the gangster saga, science fiction' (p. 80)) seek to contrive.

Film, in its privileging of the image, brings into being a new set of spectatorial relations between narrating subject and narrated object, one which exemplifies the reversible optic of postmodernity. As such, it is interruptive of a narrative authority grounded in an objectifying vision and a linear temporality. In what follows, I want to explore the destabilising force of the filmic as it operates in the context of recent American fiction. By way of readings in three writers (Jerzy Kosinski, Robert Coover and Stephen Dixon), each of whom seeks to dramatise and negotiate fictionally the penetration of lived experience by cinematographic modes of perception, I shall argue that the filmic constitutes an exemplary expression of the allegorical in postmodern American fiction. My point of departure here will be to extend the theoretical framework set up in Chapter 1 to the more specific context of film theory. In so doing, I hope to identify some revealing homologies between film theory and cinematographic writing, in the ways in which they represent visual experience.

Film and the agency of the eye: a theoretical interlude

One of the central questions raised across the trajectory of twentieth-century film theory concerns the critical power of the spectator. In particular, French film theory, the dominant tradition in this field, is perpetually engaged with the degree of agency the film viewer can exert in the face of film. Thus, the leading figure of mid twentieth-century film theory, Andre Bazin, provides one of the earliest attempts to theorise the agency of the spectator, identifying in film the potential for a new liberation of sight.

Presiding over the tradition that Martin Jay has termed 'phenomenological realism', Bazin posited cinema as the apotheosis of a timeless idealism that sought to produce 'the perpetual illusion of the outside world in sound, colour and relief'.[3] This illusion would make available to the eye new visual horizons, most specifically in its enactment of movement, throwing into intense relief the presentness of lived experience. Bazin finds this illusion most fully realised in Italian neorealism, of which he remarks that 'It is from appearances only, the simple appearances of beings and of the world, that it knows how to deduce the ideas it unearths. It is a phenomenology.'[4] Bazin's phenomenology is an idealised one, however, for he conceives of the relation between spectator and film not as spatially and temporally situated, but as grounded in timeless, quasi-Platonic illusion, which eludes the contingencies of history.[5] Unlike Benjamin's allegorical signs, Bazin's cinematic signs appear to be possessed of a mythic, fully readable transparency.

This idealising tendency became the focus of a seminal break with Bazin within *Cahiers du Cinema*, the journal around which his project was mostly organised. *Cahiers* was to undergo a transformation by the intellectual shifts of the 1960s, wrought by the work of Lacan and Althusser. Bazin's idealism was subjected to systematic 'scientific' critique, first of all by Christian Metz, whose semiology of film, developed during the mid 1960s, described cinema as a system of signification with specific codifying practices, analogous (though not identical) to the system of verbal language. By the end of the decade, the descriptive method of semiology had been absorbed into the politically charged vocabulary of structural Marxism and Lacanian psychoanalysis. *Cahiers* reflected this methodological shift in film theory, along with a network of journals, including *Cinethique* and, in Britain, *Screen*, dedicated to the excavation of cinema's ideological function. Jay terms this project 'apparatus theory', in reference to its overriding concern with the nature of the cinema as an instrument of ideological control, rather than the specific products (i.e. films) of that mechanism.

One of the most definitive and influential elaborations of apparatus theory was produced by Jean-Louis Baudry, in his essay 'Ideological effects of the basic cinematographic apparatus'.[6] Cinema, he claims, deploys a model of visual perspective which has its philosophical and ideological roots in Renaissance painting, which reproduces a centred space whose focal point coincides with that of the viewing subject. This centred perspective is collusive with the dominant conception of the subject as an individuated and autonomous being. Cinema is an apparatus in that the mechanism of projection works to counteract the potentially disruptive effects of camera movement. Where the camera's shifting gaze might break the illusion of the centred linearity of vision, that illusion is restored by the projector's screening of these fractured images as a continuous unity; the famous phenomenon of the 'persistence of vision' enables the eye to experience cinematic movement as 'real'. This cinematic denial of difference and discontinuity becomes cinema's organising principle: 'it is a question of preserving at any cost the synthetic unity of the locus where meaning originates' (p. 309).

Apparatus theory, then, polemicises against the 'violence' that cinema perpetuates against visual difference, in the service of preserving a narrative continuity expressive of the phallic order and the transcendent perspective of ideology itself.[7] If the camera has the potential to articulate a fractured discontinuity, it is counteracted by the unifying function of projection; the systemic relations of the various cinematic mechanisms thus work to disempower the eye as a critical agent.

If the moment of apparatus theory in this Althusserian form is largely over, a number of its assumptions continue to operate in the rather different discourse of postmodern cultural theory, most notably in Paul Virilio's work on the cinema.[8] The thesis that resurfaces throughout Virilio's corpus posits postmodernity as a culminating moment in the accelerating development, in conjunction, of cinematic and military technologies. It is at this moment that the technological appropriation of vision plays out its dangerous course, that we experience the eclipse of the individual eye's perceptual control over its visual environment. In Virilio's cinematised lifeworld, space is no longer delineated through the categories of human perception, but through the ubiquitous camera, or 'sight machine', for which the infinitesimally large and small, near and far, are equally accessible, so that, as Virilio has it, the distinction between 'here' and 'there' is obliterated.[9] Where for Baudry, the Euclidean perspective of Renaissance painting serves as the basis for the cinematic apparatus, for Virilio, cinema constitutes the disappearance of the universal quantification of space into the random, accidental movements of quantum space-time. As the disembodied subjects of this 'critical space', we can only witness, through a televisual window, the shifting organisation of our physical environment by cameras and transmitters oblivious to spatial limits.

Virilio diverges at a number of levels from the apparatus theorists – most notably, where the latter focus on the cinema's illusory transparency, he stresses rather the graphic fracture produced by the sight-machine's penetration of public space. Nevertheless, he shares with Baudry and Metz an underlying characterisation of cinema as a 'bad object' that objectifies and structurally paralyses visual agency.

As this cursory survey should suggest, theories of film since the 1960s have typically been saturated by the paranoiac trope of the spectator-as-victim. Baudry's apparatus theory and Virilio's 'aesthetics of disappearance' share a conception of the viewer as the victimised object of a tyrannical cinematic mechanism, entirely divested of critical autonomy and subjectivity. Unencumbered by material constraint, film has the capacity to invade the body of an empty-headed spectator, who necessarily collapses his or her visual activity into that of the film. At perhaps no other moment in intellectual history can the spectacle have been endowed with such systematically irresistible power. Yet, as I shall come to argue, this projection of cinema as a systemic divestment of visual agency is premised on a markedly abstract conception of spectatorship, one that reproduces the familiar subject–object binary by simply inverting its terms. The spectator, that is, becomes, in both Baudry and Virilio, a fixed and immobile object of the cinematic mechanism.

In a critique of Baudry and Metz (one that would apply with equal force to Virilio), Constance Penley aptly describes their theories as 'bachelor machines', invoking Duchamp's wry sculptural figurations of perpetual motion.[10] In characterising the eye as structurally impotent, these theorists reproduce the very effect they claim to unmask, namely visual domination. Moreover, Penley's term identifies the crucially gendered subtext of apparatus theory, its tendency to close off the very questions of sexual difference it claims the cinema itself effaces. In the thought of Baudry and Metz, cinema is a 'machine celibataire', that is, an anthropomorphised mechanism (her comparative examples are Shelley's *Frankenstein* and Lang's *Metropolis*) to be controlled by a masculine subject. This subject is motivated by the drive to eradicate friction, or difference from the machine, in order to maintain its homogeneity and internal efficiency. The question for film theory becomes that of how to 'debachelorise' the theoretical machine so as to readmit the seeing subject, and specifically the female subject, into this apparently impermeable mechanism. Rejecting apparatus theory's conception of the phallic law as the incontestable, 'natural' logic of subject-formation, she emphasises instead the arbitrary, culturally constructed status of the phallic sign, and the consequent 'bad fit' between the dominant sexual identity set up by the phallus and the concrete subjectivities of the women and men who must take up a relation to it. Her strategy of cinematic reading is based on the mining of this bad fit. The model for such a strategy is the psychoanalytic account of 'fantasy'. Spectatorship becomes a process of shifting amongst the wide range of 'fantastic' subject positions that cinema makes available to the viewer, 'in accordance with the mobile patterns of his or her own desire' (p. 80), and so breaking down the irresistible control of the eye posited by Metz and Baudry.

By way of an examination of Benjamin's and Merleau-Ponty's writings on film, I intend to elaborate a means by which the 'machine' of film theory might be 'debachelorised' and the critical agency of the eye reactivated. Unlike Penley, however, whose strategy of fantasy involves a refusal and transcendence of everyday time and space (as structured by the limits of phallic law), Benjamin and Merleau-Ponty each view everyday experience as a condition of resistance rather than confinement.

Benjamin's seminal essay on the subject constitutes one of film theory's most significant interventions in the visual politics of the medium.[11] Film, he argues, obliterates the 'aura' of inalienable uniqueness inscribed into the work of art, in being conceived in terms of its very reproducibility and its capacity for infinite circulation. The filmed object, in being dispossessed of its, his or her corporeality, is liberated from its immediate material context, to become a fleeting image of redemption. This account of the filmic image should evoke Benjamin's concept of allegory: the image is allegorical in its disintegrative effect on the transparency of the sign, which is here dubbed its 'aura'. The object's penetration by the camera can thus be read as a new stage in the allegorical process of the passing of nature into history.

Characteristically, then, Benjamin negotiates the cinematic spectacle internally, rather than externalising it as the eye's antagonistic Other. The cinematic lifeworld, rather than closing down critical modes of seeing, enables them, opening up a new and powerful perceptual acuity in the spectator. The camera explores the familiar sites of lived experience, and in doing so, 'manages to assure us of an immense and unexpected field of action' (p. 229). We are taken 'travelling' through this field of action, experiencing the expansion of space through the close-up, and the extension of movement through slow motion. The minutest interactions of everyday life, between, for example, a lighter and the hand reaching for it, are thrown into intense relief:

... we hardly know what goes on between hand and metal, not to mention how this fluctuates with our moods. Here the camera intervenes with its resources of lowerings and fittings, its extensions and accelerations, its enlargements and its reductions. The camera introduces us to unconscious optics as psychoanalysis does to unconscious impulses. (p. 230)

Michael Taussig's essay on Benjamin's 'unconscious optics' argues that the new sensory experience engendered by the camera is attended by a new subject–object relation.[12] Film endows the object of representation with what Taussig calls a 'contact-sensuosity', which engages the eye in a kind of perceptual dialogue with the image, 'merging the object of perception with the body of the perceiver and not just the mind's eye' (p. 208). Film enables a mode of seeing premised on dialogue rather than domination, the interpenetration of, rather than distance between, eye and object. In this respect, film is an augury of a new form of narrativity, one which divests the narrator of absolute visual authority, positioning him or her rather in a fluid perceptual relation to the world.

As the first chapter argued, it is in this emphasis on perception that Benjamin most suggestively dovetails with Merleau-Ponty. For Merleau-Ponty, as his one meditation on the subject demonstrates, film is remarkable foremost for the perceptual horizons it opens up.[13] Film distinguishes itself from other art forms, particularly the novel, by bringing to light not the interior life of beings in the world, but their mode of conduct as externally perceived. Movies, that is, 'directly present to us that special way of being in the world, of dealing with things and other people, which we can see in the language of gesture and gaze and which clearly defines each person we know' (p. 58). Film thus enacts some of the most fundamental elements of a perceptual phenomenology, in demonstrating the profoundly embodied, intersubjective nature of being.

The productive potential of Merleau-Ponty's engagement with the cinema has been more systematically elaborated by Vivian Sobchack.[14] Sobchack employs the concept of embodied experience as the basis for a sustained critique of apparatus theory and a consequent elaboration of a phenomenology of spectatorship. The spectator, far from being the victimised object described by apparatus theory, is seen as engaged in an ongoing exchange with the world of the film: 'the spectator's experience of the moving picture ... entails the potential for both *intentional agreement* and *intentional argument* with the film's visual and visible experience' (p. 278, Sobchack's emphasis). Cinema, unique amongst art-forms, can make visible and audible the subject's ongoing engagement with the world.

For Sobchack, however, this mode of engagement is threatened by the destabilising force of the electronically simulated culture of postmodernity, which engenders a new form of spectatorship. Digital technologies of motion place their spectators in what she describes as 'a spatially decentered, weakly temporalised and quasi-disembodied state', one that can't be inhabited by bodies 'as they are' (p. 300). Surprisingly, Sobchack fails to respond critically to this condition, taking refuge in a static conception of the body 'as it is', rather than reinventing her own conception of an embodied, historically situated subjectivity for the virtual world of late postmodernity. A new strategy of spectatorship, rather than Sobchack's implicit defeatism, is required in the face of electronic culture's decentring of the eye. Gilles Deleuze's work on the cinema, and in particular its discussion of cinematic framing, offers a point of entry into just such a strategy.[15] The filmic frame, Deleuze observes, appears to be spatially enclosed and fixed, only to have this fixity perpetually refused by the mobility which is the essence of the camera. This mobility signifies the presence of an 'out of field', an implied space outside the visualised frame that 'refers to what is neither seen nor understood, but is nevertheless perfectly present' (p. 16). The 'out of field', that is, is a visually absent signifier of the dynamic 'Whole' that keeps the parts in motion, a marker of the radical temporality of the filmed image, its refusal to be fixed in space. The spectatorial consciousness that recognises this mobility would be one that could map the discontinuous and disembodying space-time that Sobchack claims defines postmodern electronic culture.

However, just as the model of cinematic seeing I am deploying here is to be distinguished from Penley's activation of 'fantastic' subject positions that liberate consciousness from phallic law, so it poses a similar objection to Deleuze's concept of 'deterritorialised' consciousness. In keeping with this concept, Deleuze's mobile spectatorship seeks to be liberated from the concrete particulars of time and place. Derek Taylor has criticised Deleuze for just this 'transcendentalism'.[16] Deleuze's model of consciousness as 'phantasmatic uncertainty', resisting 'territorialisation', or spatial grounding, as Taylor argues, effectively removes itself from politics, insofar as politics is thoroughly contingent on time and place.

In contrast, I want to situate the mobility of the spectator within a strategy through which the embodied eye can operate critically at the specific historical juncture of an advanced, technologically mediated capitalist society. It is in these specific conditions that we can locate the point of departure, both for overcoming the 'bachelor machines' of film theory, and for reading the narrative strategies and crises of cinematographic fiction.

Cinematographic fiction and the question of narrative

As the privileged site of postmodernity's simulationary culture, America has been viewed with a persistent self-consciousness by its contemporary writers, which vacillates anxiously between self-valorisation and auto-critique. In examining recent American 'cinematographic' writing, I shall attempt to demonstrate the different ways in which the conception of a 'cinematised' America has been reproduced, negotiated and interrogated, both formally and thematically evoking the range of philosophical positions on film elaborated above.

It is worth prefacing these readings, however, with some methodological clarification as regards the category of 'cinematographic writing'. Stephen Kellman has noted a tendency to a somewhat cavalier deployment of this term in much criticism, which conflates unproblematically the devices of filmic and literary production.[17] The categories of film theory alone will not sufficiently illuminate cinematographic fiction, or, as Gavriel Moses defines it, fiction 'in which film is at the centre and in which the epistemological and existential repercussions of this new medium are explored through means of narrative'.[18] This kind of scrutiny requires the formulation of a schema that will demonstrate how different dimensions of filmic expression infiltrate fiction, to produce a diversity of literary effects and meanings.

A useful attempt at such a schema can be found in the work of Alan Spiegel. Spiegel argues that the central elements of cinematographic fiction come into being before the development of cinema itself. Cinema, that is, merely intensifies the condition of a kind of degraded perceptual authority produced by modernity itself and expressed for the first time in Flaubert. Thus, in Spiegel's schema of the development of cinematographic writing, narratorial consciousness from Flaubert onwards is progressively divested of moral and epistemological authority. The object of vision becomes increasingly resistant to the hermeneutic control of the writerly subject, who, like the camera, is reduced to the flat denotative function of recording the image. Spiegel identifies a range of characteristics specific to cinematographic fiction: the presence of 'adventitious detail', the random, unforeseen details that the camera eye records regardless of intentionality; 'anatomisation', a heightened sense of movement through space and time; 'depthlessness', a preoccupation with the flattened, derealised surface of the image; and montage, the process of editing the field of vision that produces filmic motion. Spiegel goes on to locate in what he calls the 'American Gothic' novel a frenzied intensification of these characteristics. The ur-texts of the tradition are Faulkner's *Sanctuary* and West's *Day of the Locust*, and the genre extends to contemporaries such as Ken Kesey and William Burroughs. In these texts, the object-world becomes a focus of intense anxiety, constantly threatening to develop an autonomy that will envelop, and, in later examples, destroy the seeing subject.

Spiegel's work is most productive, I suggest, in defining 'cine-matographic' fiction in terms of a general visual epistemology, insofar as this avoids the unproblematic assimilation of literary into cinematic categories. Like Spiegel, I am concerned less with the thematics of cinema *per se*, than with the ways in which filmic visualities inflect the narrativity of postmodern American fiction. As such, a number of the texts in question are concerned less with thematising cinema as a discrete medium, than with engaging the filmic as a paradigm of postmodern vision, manifest in television and the mass media as much as the cinema itself.[19]

However, Spiegel's narrative of this fictional tradition is, I believe, overly linear, charting as it does a neatly progressive divestment of visual agency in writerly consciousness, in correlation to the increasing dominance of the camera eye in American culture. As such, his characterisation of postmodernity seems to accord with Sobchack's in its pessimistic projection of the increasing disembodiment of the subject within a totalising cinematic space. Spiegel's account can be recoded as a map of the increasing penetration of narrative consciousness by what Owens describes as postmodernism's 'allegorical impulse'. The 'adventitiousness', 'depthlessness' and montage effects that he identifies in cine-matographic fiction are surely homologous with the aesthetic brought into being by the 'graphic fragmentation' which marks allegory. Cinematographic writing, that is, in dramatising the paralysis of the narrating eye's authority by the unreadable lifeworld it encounters, exemplifies the 'counternarrative' impulse which, as Owens has it, 'arrests narrative in one place' (p. 57). As I have argued following Benjamin however, this aesthetic need not presage the wholesale demise of visual agency that Spiegel appears to identify in cinematographic fiction.

To be sure, then, the filmic image is charged with an unprecedented ambiguity and opacity, which undercut the visual authority of the narrating subject over his lifeworld. Yet this displacement of narration from a privileged vantage-point enables the emergence of a new form of visual agency, premised on a dialogic and reversible relation to the object. Spiegel, however, in implicitly positing the transparency of the object as a condition for narrative authority, is able to perceive the cinematisation of narrative only in terms of the waning of visual agency. As I hope to demonstrate, however, the cinematographic narrator is by no means confined to the flatly denotative function with which Spiegel endows him. The readings below should reveal rather that narrative's relation to film, in the fiction in question, is negotiated in a range of complex and multivalent forms, which reveal a profound ambivalence towards postmodernity's filmic transformation of vision.[20] This ambivalence is registered most visibly on the plane of gender; film's capacity to rupture the authority of the eye is typically enacted as a crisis of masculinity before the flickering and unreadable spectacle of the feminine.

Optics of domination: Jerzy Kosinski's camera eye

Of the three novelists under discussion, it is perhaps Jerzy Kosinski whose narrative strategies are most flatly premised on an optic of domination which seeks to contain the instability of visual relations which marks the allegorical impulse. Kosinski's biography, of course, attests to a peculiar intimacy with relations of domination. From his childhood as an itinerant Jewish refugee in Nazi-occupied Poland (fictionally rendered in *The Painted Bird*), to his careful cultivation of the contradictory public persona that would shadow his novelistic career (both debonair socialite and traumatised survivor, anti-Soviet activist and sexual dissident), Kosinski's life story is shot through with the very stratagems of dissimulation and power that pervade his fiction.[21] His tendency to construct the relation between the narrating eye and its (feminine) object as irreducibly antagonistic makes him an intriguing point of departure for a discussion of the visualities of cinematographic writing. Against Kosinski's projection of a polarised field of visual perception, the contrasting ambivalence and complexity of both Coover's and Dixon's fictional engagements with the filmic will, I believe, be thrown into relief.

Despite his pervasive preoccupation with both the ontological and social nature of film, Kosinski's fiction, unlike that of the other writers in question, does not at any point engage the cinema as a discrete cultural form. This is perhaps because his notion of cinema suggests a totalising mode of perception rather than a spatially distinct and historically specific cultural form. Indeed, as Samuel Coale notes, Kosinski himself has identified the cinematic image as the paradigm of modern perception.[22] His fictional world is itself a kind of cinema, one conceived as a quasi-Sartrean realm of hostile gazes. It is a deeply universalist conception, which reduces lived experience to a site of perpetual reenactments of a brutally intense master–slave dialectic, consciously effacing any palpable sense of place and time. The binaries of modernity – East and West, urban and rural, work and leisure – function, in Kosinski's novels, as integrated modalities of this mythicised, systemic totality. His protagonists typically negotiate this totalising logic through a strategy of hypertrophied domination and cruelty. They construct the very presence of others as a conspiratorial erosion of the defined borders of self, and formulate bizarrely elaborate strategies to maintain the impenetrability of those borders. Not unexpectedly,

the Other which is opposed to the narrating subject of the novels
is repeatedly figured as Woman. The destabilising ambiguity of the
feminine threatens the intricately contrived transparency of vision
that the male protagonists strive to retain, by means of both optical
and physical violence.

I shall take the novels *Steps* and *Cockpit* as paradigm dramatisations
of Kosinski's narrative optic.[23] In each, the protagonist is engaged
in a sustained withdrawal from situation, from intersubjectivity itself,
and it is from this transcendent vantage-point that he meticulously
controls the objects in his field of vision. This objectifying relation
to the world is marked foremost by the heightened depthlessness
and descriptive precision of the prose, uninflected by the peculiarities
of personal history. To invoke Constance Penley's term, the
Kosinski protagonist is an exemplary bachelor machine, rigorously
denying entry to the play of linguistic difference, and of alternative
visualities, into its narrative mechanism. The narrator, that is,
forges a mode of seeing grounded in a fixed and polarised relation
between eye and object, which demands that the signs it confronts
be fully legible. Those 'allegorical' signs which attempt to resist this
regime of perceptual control, which display an indeterminacy that
challenges its absolute visual authority, as in the case of the women
portrayed in the novels, are eluded or relentlessly eradicated. The
allegorical feminine, then, is made visible in Kosinski by its
systematic repression. The narrating protagonists' conception of
the world as immutable, 'unchanged by any quest or struggle'
(Coale, p. 360), is premised on a refusal of the disruptive meanings
of the feminine. The form of seeing enacted by the novels is based
in the drive to protect the integrity of the subject, rather that to
alter its relationship to objects. A descriptive passage from one of
the forty-eight, loosely continuous episodes that comprise *Steps* will
show this disengaged consciousness, uncannily similar to the
camera-eye of apparatus theory, at work. The anonymous narrator
drives into a village, and comes across a barn from which a strange
sound emanates. He steps into the darkened interior, after which,
he informs us,

> Gradually my eyes made out two small plows with broken
> handles leaning against a wall along with an old harness and
> various hoes, rakes and pitchforks with splayed and crooked tines
> ... Still further on were rimless wheels, clusters of horseshoes,
> whips, buckles, and belts hanging on nails, and two axes driven
> into a short, thick tree stump. (p. 85)

This flat inventory of broken tools confers an irreducible objectivity
on the space of the barnyard. Countering Spiegel's insistence on
the 'adventitiousness' of cinematic detail, the pedantic precision
with which these objects are denoted betrays more a sense of

conscious purpose than of unforeseen accident. In the language of phenomenology, these are fully intended objects, whose existence is affirmed by the gaze of the seeing subject. Yet this is a subject that operates transcendentally, driven by a quest for a pure objectivity of perception, uninterrupted by the contingencies of embodiment. The few adjectives in the passage modify the nouns only to clarify their objective modalities of shape, size and number, never conveying meanings specific to this particular observing subject, or observed object. The protagonist negotiates the world's depthless surfaces, then, through the unyielding rigidity of his gaze, reifying, rather than reducing, his distance from the objects in his field of vision. Only by acquiring the optical control of the surveillance camera, by abstracting vision from the whole human sensorium, and divesting objects of any sense of tactility, can the subject penetrate the opacity of what he sees.

It is precisely through a strategy of surveillance that Tarden, narrator of *Cockpit*, navigates the world. A former Secret Service agent who has retired from espionage, the imperative to preserve his anonymity mediates foremost his relations with others, as the (again) episodic narrative demonstrates. He constructs these relations by establishing a clinically intimate knowledge of the person's everyday existence whilst painstakingly eluding counter-investigation. The opening paragraphs of the novel establish this method. He writes to an unnamed correspondent of his meticulous inspection of her bedroom during her party:

> I opened your closets and checked the proportion of evening dresses to sports clothes, noting their quality and condition. I examined your underwear and the heels of your shoes. Then I flipped through some of the letters on your desk, read a few, and glanced over your checkbook, telephone and hotel bills and airline ticket receipts. (p. 1)

This catalogue of violations is disconcerting because apparently unmotivated by subjective curiosity, as the unrelentingly affectless tone of address suggests. The contents of personal letters are consumed with the same indifferently imperial gaze as the telephone bills, collapsing the woman's personal and public being into the same abstracted inventory of information, and so flattening the apparent ambiguity of the feminine sign. Like the narrator of *Steps*, Tarden is driven by a desire for an absolute perceptual control, which abstracts the world to an objectively knowable quantity. Tarden's status as a former espionage agent, however, charges this impulse with specific historical meanings; like his counterpart in *Steps*, I suggest, he seeks to usurp the privileged vantage-point of the Cold War's hegemonic forces. Certainly, his figuration of visual power relations evokes Dale Carter's description of the Cold War American

State as 'one continuous no man's land, boundless in its domain but besieged at all times, ostensibly unrestricted and demobbed but potentially hostile at all points'.[24] The terrain on which Kosinski's fictional encounters are played out is similarly abstracted, divested of determinate historical or geographical meanings, and experienced as a state of perpetual siege by a 'potentially hostile' other. Thus, where Mailer's early novels attempt to forge a critical relation to this objectifying geopolitical condition, the micropolitics of everyday life dramatised by Kosinski seem merely to reproduce it. Confronted by a multiplicity of opaque signs, he takes up an observational perspective that paranoiacally refuses visual dialogue, that projects its object as irreducibly other. This position acutely articulates the perspective of the global superpowers, who each figure historically specific geopolitical relations as transhistorical oppositions. Kosinski's narrative eye is thus impelled by the need to exert power over the objects in its field of vision, as if to ward off any disturbance of the self's integrity.

This imperative of perceptual domination manifests itself most palpably, in each novel, in the narration of encounters with others, particularly women. In the earlier novel, the narrator recounts his persecution of an elderly nightwatchman in a disused factory where he has been hiding. He throws a battery of glass bottles, unseen, at the old man, until, having 'calculated the distance very carefully' (p. 105), he catches his target. The incident tellingly establishes the continuity of perceptual with actual violence, both of which are grounded in the calculated maintenance of 'distance' from the object. The account of the old man's consequent death comes to us through the secondary medium of a newspaper report, a barely distinguishable, fragmentary image; the impenetrability of the image to the collective gaze (its allegorical charge) is precisely what fuels the narrative impulse to objectify it. The same objectifying impulse informs the narrator's many sexual encounters. In one episode, he tells of his changed relation to a lover after seeing her gang-raped, blankly acknowledging his inability to separate his own vision from that of the rapists: 'She became an object which I could control or pair with other objects' (p. 58). The episode culminates in his 'donation' of the girl to the guests at a friend's party. In declining to participate in the rape himself, he affirms her status as object, and his refusal to yield to desires that elude his calculation. It is the willingness of women to surrender their sexual being to the masculine subject that determines their desirability. For the protagonist, then, as Paul R. Lilly remarks, 'the only way to defer vulnerability is to reduce his partner to the status of victim'.[25]

It is for this reason that the male interlocutor of the series of dialogues between nameless lovers declares his predilection for prostitutes. The prostitute is an ideal partner because she is an abstraction of sexuality, a universal representation of, rather than a concrete participant in, desire. in the male speaker's words, *'Since no man is excluded from having her, she appears to be not so much a woman as a desire that all men share in common'* (p. 61, Kosinski's emphasis). As a common signifier of sexuality, a commodified fetish that dissolves sexual organicity, the prostitute is a kind of template on which specific masculine desires and anxieties can be inscribed, whilst evading the counterinscriptions of female desire. This conception of the prostitute betrays a profound fear of the female object acquiring a parasitic will, a capricious autonomy that resists the controlling mechanisms of the bachelor's subjectivity.

Once again, then, the allegorical meaning of the feminine is realised in the form of the prostitute; Kosinski represents her as the apotheosis of the commodity's penetration of the organic. Like the money form itself, she is a 'concrete abstraction' in generalised circulation, a sign available to limitless forms of actual and metaphorical appropriation.[26] Kosinski's protagonist, however, is distinguished by his violent refusal to register the prostitute's disruptive potential. In embracing the abstract status that prostitution confers upon her, he positions her in a fixed optic of domination, and so effaces her ambiguity, rendering her a mere object in his contained field of vision. In *Cockpit*, the same impulse, to maintain the self's inviolability by way of a refusal of the Other, is thrown into yet greater relief. Tellingly, Tarden's will to dominate is frequently figured in his deployment of photography and cinematic devices. His most effective controlling mechanism, his infallible memory, is described in terms of 'a film ... that was being run backwards in slow motion' (p. 91), providing the same control over the internal life of his consciousness that he exerts over the world before his eye. Film, then, is explicitly invoked as the instrument of mastery that apparatus theory has so systematically described. It is only via this anthropomorphic reinvention of consciousness as cinematic machine that Tarden can resist the penetration of his own being by an object of vision. Photography, Tarden's original profession, extends this ruthless mechanisation of consciousness, transforming the photographed figure into an abstracted object of knowledge. Moreover, the figuration of his memory as a 'film ... being run backwards in slow motion' reveals an impulse to bring time itself into this mechanism, to render it a manipulable and quantifiable object. Thus, if some of the cinematographic writing discussed below releases what I have termed a 'counternarrative' temporality that resists the time of a narrating master-subject, Kosinski's fiction, it would appear, is premised on its relentless repression; time is perceived and experienced only through the lens of the narrating subject.

The camera's function as an instrument of perceptual control resurfaces throughout the novel. In the culminating episode, photography is employed in the humiliation of a female acquaintance, whose marriage to a wealthy industrialist and subsequent entry into high society he has stage-managed, on condition that she remain his mistress. When she reneges on the agreement, he pays three derelicts to rape her: 'They threw her down on the carpet', he recounts. 'All three of them swarmed over her, licking and squeezing. I climbed on the desk and took pictures from above ... the screams subsided into a gagged silence. I moved in for close-ups' (p. 224). Veronika is subjected to this sexual 'discipline' in order to reintegrate her into the sphere of control she threatened to escape. Photography bears witness to this reintegration, in the form of the ordered montage of images despotically constructed by Tarden, which violently counteracts the threatened illegibility of the feminine object. The camera as scientific mechanism of reproduction, apparently uninflected by the history of the subject that controls it, becomes Kosinski's paradigm of consciousness, just as 'science' functions as apparatus theory's privileged site of knowledge. In Kosinski's later novel, *Pinball*, the abstraction of the female body as filmic surface no longer functions as a marker of the protagonist's violently objectifying consciousness, but has become the text's habitual mode of description, as a series of increasingly tiresome soft-focus passages demonstrates.[27] Domostroy, one of the two wilfully anonymous composers at the centre of the novel, is seduced by Andrea Gwynplaine, a music student, in a ploy to make him help her trace the identity of an elusive rock star named Godard. In order to establish her beauty as Domostroy's motivating force, Kosinski consistently attempts to convey the allure of her body, as exemplified, for instance, by 'her calves, their roundness not marred by the slightest muscle bulge, their smoothness not disturbed by a single hair' (p. 64). Toward the end of the novel, Domostroy is drawn magnetically to a gifted black pianist, whose 'skin gleamed like polished bronze' (p. 225). What is most telling about these evocations of femininity is their anxious disavowal of the materiality of the body, their sense of the skin as a landscape unspoiled by signs of its own organicity (muscle, hair). Donna's 'polished bronze' body reflects light outward, its gleamingly impenetrable surface divested of particularity. Her skin's opacity is less interruptive than affirmative of the visual authority of the masculine subject. This is the feminine paranoiacally essentialised, then, effacing all evidence of embodiment as concrete being. Filmic consciousness produces not the surgically accurate perception of Benjamin's camera, nor the tactility invoked by Merleau-Ponty, but pure visual abstraction.

As I have suggested, the motor of this relentless strategy of objectification is a fear of the invasion of the masculine bachelor machine by the female object. Indeed, the transient realisations of this fear, the points at which the object threatens to elude the protagonist's apparently panoptic visual control, constitute these texts' most interesting moments of tension, revealing as they do the potential reversibility of the subject–object relation. In *Steps*, the protagonist recounts the failure of his attempts to seduce a fellow worker. When she becomes instead the lover of his friend, the latter arranges for the narrator a sexual encounter with her. The condition is that he remain anonymous to the woman, who will be blindfolded, in submission to the wishes of her lover. He recalls that,

> I was aware that to her I was no more than a whim of the man she loved, a mere extension of his body, his touch, his love, his contempt. I felt my craving grow as I stood over her, but the consciousness of my role prevailed over my desire to possess her. (p. 100)

The narrator's visual absence is a tantalising marker of his lack of control. Despite the woman's blindfold, he effectively experiences shame of being looked at, insofar as he has become an object rather than the subject of the scheme. His sexually debilitating self-consciousness is produced by the loss of his transcendental gaze, his reduction to a participant in another's design. It is just this experience of objectification, of inscription by another's intentions, that the narrator struggles to overcome throughout the novel. As in the early Sartre, the subjective nihilation of the Other is defined in relation to its opposite, namely nihilation as object by the Other.[28] No ambiguity interrupts this neatly binary conception of human relations, no reversible interaction between subject and object that might throw these fixed terms into question.

In *Cockpit*, Tarden's conspiratorial vision of the feminine object-world is even more uncompromising. In the episode alluded to above, in which he enables Veronika's entrance into high society on the condition that she be in sexual thrall to him, the threatened fracture of his control is tellingly bound up with the workings of the mass media. Veronika is absorbed increasingly into its glare as an international celebrity, 'photographed beside an antique car in Rhode Island, and dancing at an after-hours bar with a celebrated rock star ... She disclosed in a TV interview that she was working on an autobiographical novel' (p. 219). Tabloids and TV are the sovereign realm of the society of the spectacle, and it is through these hyperreal forms that Veronika precariously slips from Tarden's grasp. Veronika, that is, in being made visible to the multivalent gaze of the mass cultural collective, passes into that fractured realm of allegory which strikes at the heart of Tarden's masculine integrity.

Kosinski's most hypertrophied images of a menacing feminine object, however, are to be found in *Pinball*. The fearsomely doubled status of Andrea as, simultaneously, dazzling sexual object and manipulative parasite is encapsulated in Kosinski's description of her sexual behaviour: 'One minute she would be so aggressive as to suck up the strength out of him; the next, totally submissive, letting him sap her energy and use her body in whatever way he wished' (p. 28). This representation, of course, is thoroughly continuous with the trope of the allegorical feminine, 'dispenser alternately of perfume and poison, seraphic and hell-black by turns'.[29] Andrea's calculated doubleness, furthermore, is reproduced at the level of plot, in which she is gradually revealed to be mastering a plan to destroy both Domostroy and Godard, a plan motivated by the desire to see her own lover, Chick Mercurio, topple Godard's commercial supremacy in rock music. The novel's narrative thus contains her taunting illegibility by situating it within a familiar genealogy of the demonic feminine. Her climactic death at the hands of Domostroy's bodyguards further puts to rest this slippery force of both sexual deceit and mass cultural opportunism, and so dissolves the disruptive challenge to the integral masculine subject that she represents.

Kosinski's demonic characterisations of Others, then, perhaps accounts for the inability of his protagonists to negotiate the object-world through any strategy other than a withdrawal from the collective, from ethics, from their very historical situation, a withdrawal that can be enforced only through a perpetually activated optic of domination. Perhaps the most emblematic vision of this condition can be found in the culminating image of Tarden, enclosed within the integral space of the titular aircraft cockpit, gazing imperially down at Veronika on the runway, as he secretly bombards her with lethal radar beams. This moment is perhaps the most explicit enactment of the gendered binary that, for Kosinski, structures human relations. As such, it throws into relief that narrative contradiction which, for Craig Owens, characterises postmodernism's allegorical impulse in general, namely that 'the fragmentary, piecemeal combination of images that impels reading is also what blocks it ...' (p. 75).

Kosinski's narrative fragments, driven by an affectless perceptual 'bachelor machine', perpetually promise to make their doubled and ambiguous images of women fully legible. Paradoxically, however, his narrative mechanism is able to exert control over the female object only by retaining an extreme perceptual and emotional distance from her. Consequently, Kosinski's women remain thoroughly externalised, inaccessible to the interpretative gaze, attesting instead to the failure of both narrator and reader to penetrate their objectified surfaces. Veronika can be subjected to absolute perceptual control only by being objectified to the point of unreadability.

In Kosinski's most uncharacteristic novel, however, the fabulistic *Being There*, the question of the subject's relation to its object is dramatised rather differently.[30] Chance, the simple gardener at the centre of the novel, thrust accidentally into the public spaces of finance, politics and the media after a life confined to a millionaire's estate, epitomises most of all of Kosinski's protagonists the subject's estrangement from history. This estrangement, moreover, is effected by television, from which all Chance's knowledge and experience of the world, prior to his exit from the garden, have been derived. Chance's subjectivity has been left uninscribed by history, that is, because it has been constructed by a medium that systematically effaces it. Television, as figured by Kosinski, is governed by a logic of surfaces which privileges the transient and fractured image over spatially and temporally continuous narrative. This logic is dramatised by Chance's forays into the medium (which renames him 'Chauncey'), which succeed precisely because his own depthless and affectless subjectivity reproduces that logic. As Herbert B. Rothschild remarks, 'The absence of a real presence is what makes Chauncey possible as an image.'[31] Chance, then, is an effective object of television, insofar as it produces his identity, whilst he in turn is excluded from any active interpretative relation to it. *Being There*, in taking up the narrative position of the reified object, inverts the perspective of the master-subject through which the novels discussed above are visualised.

Chance's only material point of reference is the vegetable world of the garden, and it is precisely his references to the garden which throw themselves up for metaphorical appropriation by the mass media. The financier Benjamin Rand, the President of the United States and a voracious television audience each interpret Chance's references to the garden as an allegory of the state of the economy, that is, an allegory in the traditional sense, whose meanings are universally and transparently readable. I would argue, however, that the novel reveals Chance's elliptical pronouncements as allegorical in accordance rather with the definition offered by Benjamin. Rand's and the President's employment of Chance's narrative of the garden's seasonal cycle, in the service of finance capital and the State, exemplifies what Benjamin identifies as the slippage of nature into history.

Thus, Chance's remark, in the course of a television interview, that 'trees have to lose their leaves in order to put forth new leaves, and to grow thicker and stronger and taller' (p. 54), is offered as an unambiguous reference to the specific garden in which he has spent much of his life. Thrust into the collective gaze, however, it reveals its availability to allegorical interpretation. Whilst the President and the mass media are confident of having fixed the determinate meanings of the natural forces invoked by Chance, the novel plays on the sheer arbitrariness of their hermeneutic scheme; as the narrative develops, Chance's identity becomes increasingly indeterminate, resistant to the inquisitive gaze, as when extensive searches on his past by both American and Soviet intelligence, at the novel's conclusion, yield no information. Chance is a literal absence, an object inscribed by the multiplicity of subjective desires and anxieties (the allegorical impulses) of those who encounter him.

Rand's wife, Elizabeth Eve (known as EE), functions as the central actor in this allegorical reinvention of Chance's identity. She is the first to interpret his vacant pronouncements, a process which soon extends to her effective invention of a sexual understanding between them, which she sustains by transforming the absence of his visible desire into a sophisticated articulation of it: '"Do you know, that you're very brainy, very cerebral, really, Chauncey, that you want to conquer the woman within her very own self, that you want to infuse in her the need and the desire and the longing for your love?"' (p. 62). Once again, it is a woman who opens up the allegorical impulse of the narrative. *Being There* departs from Kosinski's other novels, in releasing rather than repressing this impulse; indeed, the novel, in being visualised from the perspective of the object, inverts the perceptual logic of those texts. Chance's subjectivity is produced by those very interlocking mechanisms of State, finance capital and, most important, the mass media, against which the likes of Tarden define themselves. The novel is seen not through the lens of a narrating master-subject, but through the range of incongruous gazes that (mis)interpret Chance. As such, Chance provides an exemplary enactment of Benjamin's contention that in allegory, 'Any person, any object, any relation can mean absolutely anything else' (*Tragic Drama*, p. 175).

Being There, moreover, provides a particularly cogent demonstration of the shift in narrative logic that, I have argued, attends the postmodern condition. Godden's readings in American modernism, we recall, designate fictional narratives as metaphorical displacements of economic shifts. This novel, however, enacts the very failure of Chance's pronouncements to represent the economic. Whilst the President is confident of having established the determinate metaphorical meaning of the 'garden', the ferocious interpretative play that his public appearances release (most notably the feverishly conspiratorial speculation about his real identity), finally work only to affirm Chance's irreducible illegibility; 'what initially impels reading is also what blocks it' (Owens, p. 75). The most visible causes of this crisis of interpretation are, of course, television and the mass media. Chance experiences himself as an object of the TV cameras, 'licking up the image of his body ... recording every image of his movement and noiselessly hurling them into TV screens throughout the world' (p. 52). In his transformation into an effect of television's fetish of surfaces, Chance surely brings into play Owens' counternarrative impulse, insofar as his consequent unreadability, his lost transparency, arrests the narrating eye, generating a range of arbitrary, spectral narratives. The novel, then, obliquely dramatises a historical condition in which, as David Harvey has it, 'images dominate narratives' and for which 'there is no question of a representation or even a master discourse that is fated to assume the logical centre of historical change'.[32] Chance's televisual consciousness, in other words, potently illuminates the emergent condition of postmodernity. The disavowal of the social that, for Kosinski's other protagonists, is uncompromisingly willed, is inscribed into Chance's existence. This produces significant contrasts in prose. Where the language of, say, *Cockpit* moves with a deliberately sustained flatness of tone, resolutely sealing itself off from subjective linguistic affect, the language of *Being There* produces unexpected and revealing tensions. Where, that is, the other novels articulate the perspective of a narrating subject bent on retaining his masculine integrity, *Being There* sets up the inherently unrealisable task of representing an absent consciousness, producing inevitable linguistic gaps between narrator and protagonist. For example, when we are told of Chance that 'to him, the viewers only existed as projections of his own thought' (p. 52), the intrusion of a writerly consciousness other than Chance's demonstrates the unrepresentability of a subject that cannot think the world. The disavowal of the social that characterises the likes of Tarden is here driven to its limit, exposing a fundamental mimetic aporia: the narrative is consequently forced to admit back into itself the very subjectivity that Chance apparently lacks. Kosinski, in short, is unable to divest the subject of consciousness, of a lived relation to the world. *Being There*, then, is distinct in Kosinski's corpus because its absurdly empty narrative perspective satirically interrogates the violent withdrawal from history that the other novels tend merely to reproduce. In releasing the allegorical force of the spectacular lifeworld of postmodernity, it reveals the reversibility of the gaze, and the unattainability of Tarden's panoptic vantage-point.

It is nevertheless significant that historicity can be made visible only through the perspective of the object. The Kosinski protagonist remains at base unable to think outside a transhistorical subject–object binary. Any intimation of mutuality or intersubjectivity exists only as a spectral illusion, masking the reality of what Tarden terms 'the estrangement that may lie underneath apparent mutual understanding' (p. 49). The figures at the heart of Kosinski's fictional world certainly live an existential relation to the world, outside any universal code of ethics or action. The bleakness of their dilemma emerges, however, in their projection of the social as an inherently parasitic drain on the autonomy of the subject, their inability to locate redemptive possibilities within others. Kosinski's corpus, then, emerges as an exemplary enactment of the rigid modernist dualism of visual subject and visible object, arguably thrown into starker relief by the narrative inversions of *Being There*.

Phantasmagoric optics: Coover and cinematic spectacle

If Kosinski's prose is distinctive for its static immutability of tone, Robert Coover's fiction strikes the reader first for the sheer excess of its linguistic texture. His sentences move with an almost orgiastic energy, marked by their breathless multiclausality, their irrepressible mining of semantic ambiguity, and their relentless traversing of different discursive registers. It is partly in this exhausting verbal play that the allegorical impulse of his fiction can be identified. Like the 'runes' of baroque culture excavated by Benjamin, Coover's figurations of postmodern spectacle project a world of objects endowed with an agency of their own, producing the 'fragmentation in the graphic aspects' which, for Benjamin, 'is a principle of the allegorical approach' (*Tragic Drama*, p. 186). The allegorical content of his writing is further articulated by his representation of the subject–object relations brought into being by this phantasmagoric lifeworld. Where, as we have seen, Kosinski's paradigm subject remains resolutely externalised, Coover's writing negotiates the postmodern object-world internally. His protagonists are situated in an intensely reversible relation to the mass cultural space that surrounds them, simultaneously resistant to and overwhelmed by it. Coover's prose is itself haunted by this reversibility, shot through by the visual and verbal signifiers of commodity culture, yet consistently appropriating, defamiliarising and reinventing those signifiers and igniting their sedimented meanings. This perpetually mobile narrative positionality works to demonstrate mass culture's status as a primary site of contestation within the postmodern, rather than a mere effect of its economic base. As I shall attempt to show, by way of a close reading of his short story, 'The phantom of the movie palace', from *A Night at the Movies*, this narrative strategy is made particularly visible in his figuration of cinematic spectatorship.[33]

Throughout his corpus, however, Coover's writing is informed by an understanding of the bizarrely spectacular character of the political, ethical and personal modalities of postmodern American experience. Where Kosinski's novels enact the imperative to withdraw from the collective gaze, every action performed in Coover's fictions is consciously thrown up for the visual consumption of others. This condition of specularity is nicely exemplified by one of the 'Seven exemplary fictions' of Coover's *Pricksongs and Descants*.[34]

In 'Panel game', a 'Bad Sport', reflexively identified as the reader of the story ('the Bad Sport you ask, who is he? fool thou art!' (p. 63)), is called upon to participate in the TV show of the title. The Participant's response is subjected to a range of intimidating gazes – of the ingratiating Moderator, the panel of hackneyed televisual caricatures (Aged Clown, Lovely Lady and Mr. America), the 'docile, responsive, good-natured, terrifying' Audience and, most important, the technological apparatus of television itself ('Cameras swing, bend, spring forward, recoil, Lights boil up, dim, pivot, strike' (p. 63)). The Participant begins the search for clues (Benjamin's 'runes' again come to mind) to a riddle buried within the various quips of the panel. Thus, on hearing the Aged Clown refer to a 'stickleback', he releases a stream of semantic and assonant associations with the word: 'Stickleback. Freshwater fish. Freshwater fish: green seaman. Seaman: Semen. Yes, but green: raw? spoiled? vigorous? ...' (p. 63). Yet this surreal activation of possible meanings does little to produce the required response for the Moderator, Panel and Audience. The Moderator, on failing to extract an answer from the Participant, warns him irritably that '"Muteness is mutinous and the mutable inscrutable".' Despite this rhetorical fulmination against the 'inscrutable', however, the logic of the panel game itself renders the riddle 'mutable'. The game, generating an overabundance of ambiguous signs, divests the Bad Sport of visual authority.

The overdriven triviality of the game quickly takes on a Gothic menace, as the encroaching failure of the Participant prompts a series of apocalyptic variety acts. The Lady bellydances to the rhythm of a limerick, recited by the Clown, which tells of a bellydancer's death by cancer, aped grotesquely by the Lady. The climactic set-piece, as 'Cameras crouch, pounce, jab, retract' (p. 68), is the hanging of the Participant for his failure to solve the riddle (whose solution, significantly, is 'much ado about nothing' (p. 69)), performed with titillating panache by the Lady. As the text's parting words, 'So long, Sport' (p. 69) remind us, this execution is equally a figurative dispatch of the reader.

The positioning of the reader in this victimised relation to the hypertrophied logic of mass culture reveals much about Coover's conception of the lifeworld of spectacle at this early point in his career. The story is premised on the projection of a demonically feminised mechanism of entertainment absorbing the agency of the seeing subject. The Bad Sport's crime is, in effect, to demonstrate a tenuous grasp of dominant cultural codes, and an inclination to think independently of them. As Paul Maltby argues, meaning within this cultural space turns on a power to uphold the fixed regulations of communicative interaction.[35] It is worth noting that Coover is writing at a time (1969), when America is very forcefully preoccupied with the imposition of its own political and cultural logic on those who attempt to challenge it. Arguably, Coover's bellicose characterisations of the camera are informed by his nation's ongoing military campaign against the Vietnamese. The televisual apparatus 'boils up', 'strikes', 'pounces', 'jabs', metaphorically echoing Paul Virilio's arguments concerning the convergence of the technologies of war and cinema in their drive to dominate space telescopically.[36] Virilio contends that the unlimited speed engendered by this telescopic function produces the crucial capacity for surprise, as manifested by the cinematic jump-cut. It is this same specular violence that assaults the Participant of 'Panel game'. Moreover, many of the stories in *Pricksongs and Descants* dramatise the same conflict between a cybernetic visual order and a deviant other. In 'Morris in chains', a dystopian telematic order employs every available mode of surveillance to entrap a fugitive shepherd whose mock-pastoral, sub-Joycean ramblings and blatant libidinal energy threaten the repressive order of technological rationality.[37] In another of the 'Seven exemplary fictions', 'The wayfarer', a sadistic policeman shoots a vagrant to death for his indecipherable silence.[38] In this collection, then, the autonomous male subject is repeatedly confronted by indeterminate signs that threaten to reduce him to the status of object.

Indeed, 'Panel game' pointedly evokes Nietzsche's figurations of an emergent culture of the masses.[39] This Audience constitutes a kind of collective embodiment of the Last Man, in hysterical subservience to a pseudo-theology of entertainment. Their response to the television show recalls, albeit parodically, the degraded spectator of apparatus theory, its eye ensconced within the despotic cinematic mechanism. Furthermore, the 'Eye of the World', before which the Participant crumbles, becomes increasingly bound up with the eye of the Lovely Lady, directed at the Participant in the bellydance that precedes his execution. As his hangman, the Lady is the instrument of the Participant's visual objectification and destruction, the allegorical Woman whose sexuality lures the unwitting masculine Self into her dazzling, deceitful, and parasitic sphere of control. Coover, then, appears to invert the condition of totalised subjective control portrayed by Kosinski, dramatising rather the phantasmagoric reign of the mass cultural object. To this extent, his early writing appears to reproduce, within the emergent context of postmodernity, the paranoiac terror of the object on which, as Peter Nicholls has shown, a significant strand of Anglo-American modernism is premised.[40] Coover's writing diverges from the objectifying optic of High Modernism, however, in positioning the narrative eye not at some putative vantage-point outside mass culture, but in a reversible relation to it. Because, that is, his writerly consciousness is so emphatically situated within spectacular culture, he is able to intensify its logic, to draw out its sedimented meanings, and to locate positions internal to it that refuse objectification. The reader of 'Panel game' is invited to view television from the perspective of the reified object, rather than that of the transcendent subject. From this position of visual objectification, as the later 'Phantom of the movie palace' implies, one might negotiate a new form of agency, which disrupts the 'stereotomy' of seeing subject and visible object, and which activates the fecundity of meaning in mass culture's phantasmagoric codes. In 'Panel game', however, this position can only provide glimmers of an active visual consciousness (for example in the associative linguistic play of the Participant), before submitting to the violent logic of spectacle.

A spectacular execution is, of course, at the centre of Coover's most ambitious work, *The Public Burning*, a bizarre fictional reinvention of the Rosenbergs' last days.[41] The dual narrative structure traces both the build-up to the public electrocution of the couple in Times Square, and, in alternate chapters related by Vice-President Richard Nixon, the catalogue of mishaps to which the latter is subjected in his struggle to prevent a stay of execution by the Supreme Court. The execution, produced by the specific historical conditions of the Cold War, is framed by the American State as a chapter in the eternal conflict between the 'Sons of Light' and the 'Legions of Darkness'. The novel thus satirically interrogates the hypertrophied rhetoric of postwar anti-communism, its imperative to reduce the specific geopolitics of the Cold War to a static binary, manifested as a spectacular confrontation between 'Darkness' and 'Light'.

The national media function as crucial instruments in this rhetorical apparatus. Coover figures this subservience by way of a surreal device of estrangement, in which *Time* magazine becomes the National Poet Laureate, its propagandist vocabulary transformed into modernist verse form. Thus, the magazine's actual report on the battle over a Korean hill appears as:

> during the night
>> twenty thousand shells
> exploded in an area
>> smaller than times square
> but the hill remained
>> in u.s. hands (p. 323)

Coover's strategy here is to draw out the uncannily ritualistic character of the interlocking systems of the Cold War propaganda machine. He demonstrates not only the comic incongruity, but also the curious affinity between propaganda and modernist poetry, their common impulse to transform material reality into a fractured clutter of emblems, which frustrates the inquisitive gaze; both forms, that is, work here to render the reader subservient to their impenetrable logic.

The Rosenbergs' execution, as the microcosmic enactment of superpower confrontation, is projected as the performance that will consolidate this mass spectacular relation to the American State. As such, it releases the 'static, ritualistic, repetitive' counternarrative impulse which, as Craig Owens has it, 'arrests narrative in one place' (p. 57). The execution, that is, reproduces the propagandistic representation by the American State of the Cold War as an eternal conflict between the forces of Darkness and Light. This hegemonic representation absorbs the subjective into the overarching visual mechanism of the State. Thus coopted, the eye is made a passive object of the violent mythic recoding of geopolitical relations. The apparent transparency of the Cold War landscape is thus contrived only by inverting the eye's perceptual control over its object.

This optic is further enforced by the State's employment of the representational mechanisms of Hollywood cinema in staging the Rosenbergs' execution. As Maltby observes, 'the danger of superpower confrontation can only be grasped through the discourse of Hollywood films' (p. 119). Thus, the public execution is preceded by a series of routines in which America's cinematic and televisual comedy icons (Jack Benny, Laurel and Hardy, the Marx Brothers) stage the electrocution in their trademark styles. The final appearance of the pre-execution programme, however, is made by the apotheosis of American iconography, Uncle Sam himself, figured as a kind of psychotic superhero, a master of the most extravagant rhetorical gestures of every regional American idiolect.

One of the elaborate turns of the plot, however, has Uncle Sam's entrance upstaged by the unexpected entrance of Dick Nixon, pants at his feet, '"I AM A SCAMP" lipsticked on his butt' (p. 469). The entrance is the culmination of a frenzied rush to the execution after a picaresque sexual encounter with Ethel Rosenberg, during which she has, unbeknownst to him, written the phrase on his buttocks. Nixon, desperately seeking to save face, succeeds in persuading his fellow Americans, including the amassed luminaries of political life, to take down their pants in a ritual of collective patriotism that will demonstrate their pride before the world. Buoyed by his triumph, he attempts to extend the ritual to Uncle Sam himself. Just as the latter is about to comply, enragedly, with the demand, the mass audience experiences a terrifying blackout. An apocalyptic terror strikes through them, in the grip of the belief that '"THE PHANTOM'S KILLT UNCLE SAM!", "HE'S STOLE THE LIGHT!"' Mass hysteria, however, is finally curbed by the aerial approach of a beam of light: "'IT'S A FLYING SAUCER!", "IT'S A BOID!", "ISSA PLENN!", "NO! IT'S ... IT'S UNCLE SAM!"' (p. 493). The terrors of Uncle Sam's destruction are cathartically revealed as phantasms, "'the illusory marvels and disasters of Cinerama and 3-D, th-th-that's all, f-folks! Light up and laugh!"' The cinematic force of the spectacle is intensified again by the projection of 'Uncle Sam's film on the Rosenberg boys' (p. 511) on to the Paramount Building by Cecil B. DeMille, in conjunction with Julius's actual execution. State power is thus figured in terms of the cinematic control of the fundamental modalities of vision, darkness and light, assimilating the perceptions of the mass into the logic of entertainment.

In its dazzling reinvention of this pivotal moment in Cold War history as a cinematic spectacle, to which the American masses hysterically yield their collective visual agency, *The Public Burning* seems in a sense to be transposing the central conceit of 'Panel game' on to the terrain of Cold War politics. 'Cinerama and 3-D' apes the totalising function of TV in the earlier story, absorbing the transgressive Rosenbergs into its despotic mechanism. The novel marks a new moment in Coover's writing, however, insofar as the cinematic objectification of the eye is explicitly identified as an historical imperative of the American State. Spectacle is the means by which the material origins of the Cold War are effaced, along with the agency of the collective eye. The unlikely figure to discover the historical meanings elided by spectacle is, in fact, Nixon himself. During his hazardous journey to Times Square, he recognises that the narrative of inevitability projected by the execution is in fact illusory:

> Them were no scripts, no necessary patterns, no final scenes, there was just *action*, and then *more action*! Maybe in Russia History has a plot because one was being laid on, but not here – *That was what freedom was all about!* ... Act – Act in the living present! (p. 362, Coover's emphases)

This curiously existential vision of history as made directly counters the mythic codification of history by State-managed spectacle. His absurd encounters with both Ethel Rosenberg and the American masses, moreover, each affirm the contingent and discontinuous logic of history. In his buffoonish attempts to consummate his repressed sexual yearnings for the former, he is made to confront the power that his apparent object yields over him. Similarly, in his unintentionally slapstick entrance into the public glare of Times Square, he is positioned as the victimised object of a collective gaze.

In both cases he is forced into an awareness of the reversibility of spectatorship; despite Uncle Sam's attempts to secure the American State's function as subject of history, Nixon's confrontation with the feminine, manifested as both the wily, elusive role-playing of Ethel, and the hysterically 'feminised' spectatorial mass, conspire to render him history's object. Nixon's anxiety before his encroaching loss of subjective mastery is thus registered as a crisis of masculine integrity.

Coover's Nixon, then, unwittingly discovers the new conditions of political action brought into being by the emergent logic of postmodernity, in which history can no longer be narrated from the perspective of a privileged master-subject. Assailed at all times by the superabundance of images generated by both mass culture and the State, the postmodern eye experiences a crisis of visual authority, a shift in status from subject to object of its lifeworld. Nixon's epiphanic recognition of contingency as the primary motor of history, however, momentarily provides a glimpse of the new form of seeing that this crisis might open up. The allegorical world of cinematic signs, once read as a historical, as opposed to a universal, space, can become a condition for the activation of visual politics by a situated and embodied, rather than transcendent, eye.

It is just this possibility of visual agency activated within the cinematic object-world that Coover attempts to explore in his later short story 'The phantom of the movie palace'. In terms of the story's premise, he once again reproduces Virilio's conception of the disembodied and decentred subject of cinematic space, in the narrative of a cinema projectionist assailed by the phantasmatic spirits of the cinematic figures he has unwittingly liberated from the screen. The opening paragraphs, for example, transcribe a bewilderingly random succession of cinematic moments, palpably realising Fredric Jameson's description of postmodern experience as 'a rush of filmic images without density'.[42] What emerges is a kind of generic shape-shifting that breathlessly traverses sci-fi horror, gangster, backstage musical, situation comedy and religious musical (*Going My Way* transposed to a unisex toilet), an exemplary realisation of what Owens terms 'allegory's essential pictogramism' (p. 80). This immaterial world of cinematic bodies gradually but terrifyingly envelops Coover's protagonist, the projectionist.

We first find the projectionist yearning nostalgically for days past, when the teeming auditorium constituted a sensuous and sensible force in opposition to the ephemeral space of the screen, when material reality and immaterial fantasy could be firmly distinguished. This leads into a kind of parodic jeremiad for the absent traces of human activity:

> All that human garbage ... sticky condoms in the balcony, sprung hairpins, stools clogged with sanitary napkins ... Even excrement in the bridal fountain or hair grease on the plush upholstery. He feels like one of those visitors to an alien planet,

stumbling through endless wastelands in the vain search for life's telltale scum. (p. 15)

Despite their gruesomely textured and odorous materiality, these objects, like the audience that discards them, exist only as the residual dregs of the projectionist's memory. He is to find, instead of the visceral testimony of human presence, simply more phantasmatic images, as if the totality of the human sensorium has been obliterated by technologically generated sight and sound. Indeed Coover's description of the projectionist's experience as a traumatic filmic invasion of the body brings the language of apparatus theory, and of Virilio, irresistibly to mind: 'he can feel his body, as though penetrated by an alien being from outer space, lose its will to resist' (p. 30). His body, as a consequence of his experiments in splicing filmic images together, is thrust into a Gothically comic world of cinematised bodies, made all the more menacing by their immateriality and consequent defiance of the conventional logic of bodily form. These experiments reveal the 'softness' of cinematic forms, their availability for technological manipulation. Thus, as he 'slides' a line of chorus girls into the barroom of a Western, the grizzled, brawling prospector of the Western finds himself undergoing a bizarre bodily fusion with the chorus line ingenue: 'his knees buckle, suggesting a curtsy, even as his testicles, dangling out of the showgirl's briefs like empty saddlebags, seem to float upward toward his mouth' (p. 26). The image graphically enacts the loss of masculine bodily integrity engendered by the 'feminised' lifeworld of cinematic signs.

As the story drives relentlessly towards its mock-apocalyptic conclusion – the projectionist about to experience dematerialisation himself by way of a filmic executioner and his guillotine – he finds his anchoring in defined space-time inexorably, and quite literally, stripped away. For having been released from the spatial limits of their celluloid frames, the marauding phantasms proceed to roam the picture palace, transforming its very structure in their wake, in accordance with the crazed quantum logic of a dematerialised cinematic space capable of transformation without reference to human intention. Thus, attempting to make his way through the suddenly unnavigable territory of the movie palace, the projectionist finds himself peering over an abyss down which he narrowly missed falling, and where he had previously known a staircase to be. Shortly after, he attempts to recover his grip on the material in the unpromising form of the underwear of a cinematic orphan girl – underwear that may have a number of holes in it, or may be covered in celluloid waterspots:

He climbs upward reaching for them, devoted as always to the passionate seizure of reality, only to have them vanish in his grasp, the ladder as well: he discovers he's about thirty feet up the grand foyer wall, holding nothing but a torn ticket stub. It's a long way back down, but he gets there right away. (p. 33)

It would appear, then, that the projectionist's predicament of entrapment in the phantasmagoria of immaterial bodies surreally enacts Virilio's description of our own condition in a space-time organised by advanced cinematic technologies, and is to this extent continuous with the blackly comic pessimism of 'Panel game'. The relation between subject and cinematic space, however, is rather more fluid here than in the earlier story. Where the Bad Sport has participation in the television show forcibly imposed upon him, the projectionist, in his experiments, is consciously engaged in the drive to open up new horizons of meaning. This drive can be read productively, via Sobchack's model of cinematic vision, as a struggle to forge a dialogic relation to the disembodied images he produces with his equipment, to exert, that is, a kind of perceptual control over their narrative composition. In splicing cinematic images together, he takes physical and generic transformation to its frenzied limit – at which point he is robbed by those same images of the very control he has tried to exert. Nevertheless, the apocalyptic cinematic implosion that gathers force during the course of the story is generated initially by a situated, embodied visual consciousness making specific, visually creative choices (as in the sliding of the chorus girls into the barroom), and consequently liberating the cinematic bodies on the screen, not only from their spatial confinement on the celluloid reel, but equally from the tired generic prescriptions of Hollywood cinema. The orgiastic anarchy of these newly formed filmic scenarios, in fact, evokes Coover's earlier call (in the 'preface to the 'Seven exemplary fictions'), to reanimate the mythic sediment of American culture.[43] As Coover's narrator remarks of the projectionist, 'He knows there's something corrupt, even dangerous, about this collapsing of boundaries, but it's also liberating' (p. 23). Cinematic vision, amplified by the technology of projection, reveals unprecedented horizons of meaning – so that the story's apocalyptic enactment of cinematic dematerialisation comes into subtle tension with a valorisation of the cinematic imagination. Put another way, the story is less about a crisis of seeing *per se*, than of a particular kind of seeing, namely one which defines itself transcendentally. This crisis, however, itself provides the condition for a new form of seeing, characterised by a fluid and reversible relation between eye and image. The story is significant foremost, then, in projecting the allegorical universe of cinematic signs as a terrain of contestation for, rather than the demonically impenetrable Other of, the seeing subject.

Immersed within the cultural forms his stories explore (the hyperbolic language of the movies, the flattened vocabulary of the bureaucrat, the excessive ramblings of the deviant), Coover's is very much a situated authorial consciousness, in contrast to the externalised subjectivity that marks Kosinski's narrators. His prose expresses this internality, in being simultaneously shaped by mass culture and explosive of its established meanings. The commodified sphere of the image is conceived (as in Benjamin) as the condition of both the repression of the mass and the release of new cultural and political possibilities.

Coover's vision of the cinema departs from Benjamin, however, in its ultimate capitulation to technological paranoia, as marked by the culminating 'execution' by the cinematic guillotine and executioner. Where his reinvention of the Rosenbergs' execution figures an actual historical act as public spectacle, the projectionist's beheading has no material status whatsoever. Rather, it enacts the absorption of an acting subject into an immaterial cinematic space. The liberated filmic phantasms of the movie palace have been disembodied, severed from any specific spatiotemporal grounding, transformed into a marauding and uncontrollable object-world.

This conspiratorial vision of cinematic technology developing its own murderous logic, furthermore, is very much bound up with Coover's representations of the mass cultural sign of the feminine. In 'The phantom of the movie palace' the figure of the chorus girl 'ingenue' reprises the function of the Lovely Lady in 'Panel game' as the emblematic force of the assault on masculine vision. The projectionist hears another cinematic phantasm speak of her: "'Her pearly teeth, when she smiles, are marvelous. And she smiles often, for life seems to her a constant film of enjoyment.'" Her smile widens even as her eyes glaze over, the glow in them now burning like twin projectors' (p. 35). This smile is thus a mark of the deceptive feminine artifice that threatens to explode the integrity of the masculine eye. The feminine sign, for Coover, is that which eludes critical consciousness, and as such is bound up with the irrational force of filmic technology. Coover's disengagement of the cinematic feminine from history finally closes off the active vision opened up in the first part of the story.

Thus, where Kosinski reifies the cinematised society as the modern mutation of a timeless, unchanging ontology of hostile gazes, Coover is deeply conscious of its culturally specific character, and consequently of its ceaseless capacity to generate new conjunctions of meaning. This consciousness is particularly evident in *The Public Burning*, in its excavation of the underlying political content of the mythic spectacle of postwar America. In its fascination, however, with the ways in which mass cultural spectacle develops its own hyperreal logic, Coover's fiction tends to project an explicitly

feminised phantasmagoria that eludes its own history. This severing
of the cinematic sign from its own historicity finally reaffirms the
experience of cinematisation as a paranoiac one.

Reversible optics: Stephen Dixon's Movies

Coover's central preoccupation, then, is with the construction of
American public life through the codes of mass culture, and of
cinema in particular. As such, the panoramic terrain of his writing
seems far removed from the intimately mundane spaces shared by
the figures who populate the short fiction of Stephen Dixon. A prolific
contributor for some twenty-five years to the American literary
subculture of highbrow, low circulation prose journals and small
presses, Dixon's public profile at least until 1997, when his most
recent novels began to achieve successful U.S. sales figures has been
as removed from the collective gaze as the claustrophobic domestic
settings that his stories repeatedly explore. Dixon's sphere of
concern properly defined, however, is less the 'private', than with
the complex ways in which the private is mediated by different, often
competing, modes of perception. In particular, he interrogates the
cinematic character of modern perception, as it penetrates the
lived experience of personal relationships. *Movies*, that is, deploys
the mobile camera as its mode of narration, transposing its effects
to the medium of writing.[44] Spiegel's category of 'anatomisation'
an intensified consciousness of movement through space and time,
is particularly applicable here. Constructed predominantly through
dialogue, and lacking any descriptive interventions outside the
lived time of the text, Dixon's stories resist even momentary
narrative fixing in space. As Jerome Klinkowitz has put it, 'there
are no *conventions* in his stories, because everything is happening
quite literally for the first time'.[45]

This absence of a privileged narrative perspective evokes the
Deleuzean definition of the frame as a dynamically shifting whole
kept in motion by the visually absent signifier of the 'out of field'.
His male protagonists, however, are perpetually engaged in the
struggle to maintain a perceptual grip on this mobile visual horizon,
to order the instability of that horizon by assimilating the figures
they encounter to their own interpretative logic. Their complacently
overarching gazes are repeatedly destabilised by the unexpected
verbal and physical gestures with which contemporary urban life
confronts them, particularly in the form of women's responses to
them. The women of these fictions typically break out of the object
status conferred upon them to reveal themselves as living subjects.

A story in a slightly later collection neatly exemplifies this
perceptual interruption. 'Meeting Aline' is an inconclusive anecdote
narrated by Ty, recounting a chance meeting in the park with a

former girlfriend.[46] The story opens with an disconcertingly pedantic account of an erotic dream of Aline, which leads abruptly into his startled recognition of her, as she passes him with a friend, during the lunchbreak of the following day. The following pages recall his painstaking projection of alternative scenarios and responses that might follow from his approaching her, which rapidly take on absurdly precise inflections:

> If they decide to sit against the wall, wave to her as they approach, if it's this wall, and if it's the other wall, go over to them without your sweater and jacket, and food if you haven't finished by then, and ask if she'd mind you joining them. If she does mind, say sorry and leave. If she doesn't mind, go back to where you were sitting, get your things and sit with them. (p. 22)

The illusion of filmic motion is unmistakable here, refracted through the eye of a kind of pastiche auteur, striving to account for every possible contingency of space and time. Bound up with this anxious impulse to total perceptual control is a desire to foresee every narrative alternative his encounter might produce, as indicated by her prescribed range of possible responses. Aline thus becomes a calculable object of Ty's imperial mind's eye, a character in a movie he has already scripted, edgily striving to avoid unexpected improvisation. Having apparently sealed off this encounter from contingency, then, he is suitably taken aback to find his greeting met with undiluted horror. Covering her eyes and exclaiming that she doesn't want to see him, she implores her companion frenziedly to walk her away, declaring that she had promised herself at the end of their relationship to avoid him for ten years. Her parting words to him are an injunction to 'remember this' (p. 26) as she points to her nose. As she takes her leave, he strives anxiously to interpret her apparently hysterical response. The recollection gradually surfaces that 'I hit her the day I left ... Probably in the nose' (p. 26). The revelation works to recast radically the preceding events both for Ty, and for the reader whom Ty has carefully positioned at his vantage-point. Aline, to deploy Benjamin's terms, is blasted out of Ty's carefully ordered image sphere, transformed from abstracted object of his vision, into a concrete subject situated in a specific relation of power to him. His (initially literal) dream state, in which men and women function in a state of blissful sexual intersubjectivity, is awakened by an image of the actual condition of gender relations and his active complicity in enforcing that condition. 'Meeting Aline', then, establishes the complex, shifting perceptual relations between masculine subject and female object explored further in *Movies*.

'The moviemaker' can be read as a comic dialogic enactment of a rather Baudrillardian 'seduction'.[47] It consists of a single telephone conversation, during which a male novelist is manipulated by his ex-lover into surrendering to her the film rights to his latest novel, a fictionalised account of their affair. The exchange follows the increasingly outlandish transformations to which she subjects the narrative, in the service of commercial viability. The novelist emphasises his text's resistance to filmic adaptation, its three hundred pages, '"some very thickly written"', its lofty thematics of '"language and love"' (p. 82). Yet the scriptwriting ex-lover's response to this avowal of the book's aesthetic integrity is to intensify her fictional reinvention of their experience, so as to draw out its adaptability to mass culture. She relocates the affair to California in order to enable the insertion of '"a racy hot tub scene or just a quick almost subliminal shot of one if we want the rating to be PG"' (p. 79). After proceeding to change in addition the novel's title, the characters' names and occupations and their various familial situations, as well as divesting the text of the '"arts and crafty tricks" of the novel that '"movies aren't about for sure"' (p. 82), she extorts the film rights out of the hapless novelist by threatening legal action for violation of privacy if he refuses to issue them to her for the fee of a dollar.

The ex-lover, then, 'allegorises' her relationship with the novelist subjecting it to potentially limitless interpretative play, undermining the novelist's visual authority in the process. In her cinematic reinvention of the novel, characters and events are available for constant transformation in accordance with the imperatives of commerce, so that 'Any person, any object, any relationship can mean absolutely anything else' (Benjamin, *Tragic Drama*, p. 35).

In making the apparently inviolable masculine preserve of high culture malleable to the simulationary artifice of commercial cinema, reducing its dense texture to the skeletal palimpsest of an 'hour and a half' movie, the tellingly feminised 'moviemaker' mercilessly exposes the guilty secret at the heart of the modernist aesthetic sensibility; namely, as Andreas Huyssen puts it, that 'mass culture has always been the hidden subtext of the modernist project'.[48] If the female screenwriter represents the reversible logic of the mass cultural object world, however, she does so in a very different manner to the cinematic phantasms of femininity that haunt Coover's story of the movie palace. The 'feminine' logic of cinema, in this story, is identified not as a floating signifier, unmoored from any determinate historical situation, but, on the contrary, as thoroughly inscribed by history. In self-consciously playing out the role of Woman as shadowy object feeding on masculine creativity, the screenwriter effectively demonstrates this conception of the feminine to be more rhetorical strategy than eternal truth. She operates with a hard-headed commercial logic that both expresses her position within a specific cultural and economic formation, and reveals the hyperreal space of the cinematic as an effect of that formation.

'My dear' dramatises a very different confrontation between masculine subject and feminine object. It is centred on a woman who enters her husband's study whilst he is working, only to tantalise him with her inscrutable stares and silences.[49] The story's narrative perspective reproduces the frustrated attempts of the protagonist to exert interpretative control over his wife. The husband exasperatedly strives to order the relations between the parts in his visual frame, only to be perpetually destabilised by his wife's unaccountably shifting gazes. She becomes, in cinematic terms, an embodiment of the Deleuzean Elsewhere, the radically Other space outside the ordering gaze that refuses the frame's closure, integrating it into an ever-shifting whole. The motility of an exchange of looks and words based in communicative norms of rationality and consequentiality is disrupted by the wife's indifferent flow of silences, cryptic utterances and random glances, compounded by the husband's earnest requests for clarification and stillness. Her silent glances continue regardless: 'Ceiling. "Please don't." Still does. "Okay, what do you see up there? Our neighbours on the third floor? Bird or a few through the next two ceilings and roof? ..." ' (p. 59). Her elusive behaviour continues, culminating in his discovery, some time after she has left the study, of the destruction of most objects in the apartment, along with her announcement that she is about to leave. The unnamed wife thus emerges as an exemplary allegorical Woman, her impenetrable looks resisting her husband's attempts to read them.

The final paragraph, however, in which she returns home, apologising for having 'lost control' (p. 64), effectively contains the preceding disruption of the field of vision, accounting for it as a temporary, though recurrent, aberration. Of the stories under discussion, then, 'My dear' perhaps most unproblematically reproduces the trope of the irrational feminine object, reifying the inscrutability of the woman's behaviour, rather than, as in 'Meeting Aline', accounting for its political meaning.

I suggest, however, that one might excavate such a political content in the volume's shortest story, 'Joke'.[50] In this story, in which a woman removes and hides each piece of the male narrator's clothing and responds to his attempts to reciprocate by clubbing him with her shoe, the Deleuzean Elsewhere is now radically disruptive, resistant to mapping by the male narrator's framing mechanisms, and conveying the irreducible difference of the woman's gaze. It is worth noting that the woman ritualistically removing and making off with the narrator's clothes is named Dotty, precisely the name the novelist gave to the seductive 'moviemaker' female of the earlier story. The elusive, unfathomable movements of the woman disembody the gaze of the man. She operates as an object that frustrates his visual authority, and as such mimes the ungrounded motion of electronic culture that he so angrily attempts to resist: '"Don't make me even madder," I say, "Tough," she says, "You're making me much madder, Dotty," "Tough tough tough," she says and jerks her wrist out of my hand and goes down the hall with my underpants ...' (p. 128).

Dotty's elusive movements can be read in conjunction with the very material act of violence she carries out at the climax of the story. This motility, I would contend, becomes an articulation of the mobile spectatorship, as a strategic mode of embodiment specific to the historical juncture of postmodernity, that I have attempted to outline above. Within this context, her shoe takes on something of the explosive resonance of the Benjaminian object. A commodity wrenched from its conventional use and personal history, it becomes a means of violently refusing the visual order and narrative gloss of her unwitting male antagonist, providing a distorted, fragmentary glimpse of awakening and resistance. Benjamin, it is worth noting, refracted his conception of the mass-cultural dreamworld through Freudian dream theory. The joke, like the dream in Freud, is a distorted wish-fulfilment that emerges out of an unresolved ambivalence of feeling. The narrator has attempted to impose this resolution on the antagonistic gender relations expressed by the irresolvable capriciousness of his would-be lover, only to be violently awakened to the fact that, as he acknowledges following his vicious beating, this is no joke. My reading of the story, then, should demonstrate the possibility of activating the object as the condition of a specifically feminist, as well as more broadly critical, mode of vision. Whereas the resistance of the female object of vision is articulated as escape in 'Meeting Aline', and as aberrant irrationality in 'My dear', it takes the form of situated action in 'Joke'. The 'figural' narrative discontinuities of postmodern fiction, 'strongly marked by the historical ambiguities of the feminine', work here to shatter the binary masculine optic of domination.[51]

In the selection of writers discussed above, I suggest, can be traced an implicit narrative of both the subject and object of cinematic vision, premised on divergent responses to the allegorical charge of the image. In Kosinski, the object is figured as an abstracted image locked into an optic of domination, one premised on the male protagonist's impulse to protect the integrity of his gaze. Coover dramatises the eclipse of this transcendent spectatorial subjectivity, and the consequent 'revenge' of the phantasmagoric object-world, a historically produced force that nevertheless threatens, in its resistance to the critical eye, to elude history. It is in Dixon's fiction, however, that the reversibility of visual relations between subject and object is most fully articulated. In each writer can be identified different dramatisations of visual relations within the cinematic. This chapter should suggest which of those fictional negotiations might activate new forms of agency in the field of vision.

Allegorical city: Los Angeles in postmodern American writing

In the previous chapter, the fictions discussed were read as complex and differing negotiations of a crisis of visual authority, engendered by film's penetration of the postmodern lifeworld. One of the central observations to emerge from this discussion was that film, in postmodern American culture, is in no sense reducible 'to the locality in which it happens to be practiced'.[1] On the contrary, postmodern cultural theorists such as Paul Virilio have repeatedly insisted on the pervasiveness of cinematic ways of seeing within every sphere of contemporary experience. In particular, Virilio has focused on the ways in which the cinematic 'sight machine' has transformed the organisation of the city, and especially the American city.[2]

In the present chapter, I want to explore the ways in which this claimed 'cinematisation' of the urban is registered in two sets of literary representations of Los Angeles (those of Joan Didion and James Ellroy). I shall argue that the city functions within the postmodern imaginary as a kind of paradigm allegorical space, in which the displacement of the critical authority of the (masculine) eye is played out in everyday experience. Los Angeles' postwar history provides unprecedented testimony to the increasing symbiosis of political-economic development and mass cultural spectacle. Moreover, the intricate relations between capital and mass spectacle produce shifts in the city's visual landscape, which, as the writers in question should demonstrate, are reproduced in the landscape of power relations. In other words, the transformation of Los Angeles into a city of spectacle corresponds to a new instability of relations between subject and object of vision, a crisis of seeing. In both Didion and Ellroy, postmodern Los Angeles displaces the subject's vision from a privileged narrative vantage-point.

I want to begin by situating this displacement within the postwar history of the city itself, and so counter the tendency in much recent French theory to project Los Angeles as simply an immaterial phantasmagoria severed from material reality. At the same time, in keeping with the more general argument of this study, I shall read this history as disintegrative, rather than explanatory, of narrative; far from providing a ground of explanation for fiction, this history produces an ongoing preoccupation with narrative's failure to explain, to make sense of the profoundly unstable and indeterminate social, economic and cultural forces it struggles to represent.

Visuality and the city: a theoretical interlude

It is Virilio's work, and in particular his *Lost Dimension*, which most unambiguously conceives the postmodern city as a pure excess of signs, an object-world impermeable to the critical gaze.[3] In charting a radical shift in metropolitan life from 'urbanism' to 'cinematism', he implicitly defines postmodernity in terms of an irretrievable loss of historicity. Thus, where the modern city was founded upon principles of monumental architectonics, mathematically rationalised planning and centralised public space, the postmodern city is coordinated rather by a range of 'ethereal' technologies, including electronic surveillance, satellite communications and globalised telematics, to which material structures (buildings, roads, open spaces) are now subordinate. Cinematisation, then, produces a literally 'flattened' public sphere, in which the three-dimensional space of the city square has been absorbed into the surface of the televisual screen. This absorption is registered in Virilio's apocalyptic dictum that 'cinematism broadcasts the last appearance of urbanism, the last image of an urbanism without urbanity' (p. 19). The dissolution of a material urban life portends the eclipse of an active, resistant human eye. The city as site of both communal value and political-economic contestation exists only as a residual collective memory trace, its actuality eroded by the sovereignty of spectacle. This is a condition 'in which appearances are all against' (p. 78), in which the object has usurped the position of the subject.

Virilio's undiluted apocalypticism, I suggest, is a consequence of his insufficient attentiveness to the complex convergence of material forces that produces the contemporary city of spectacle. The transformation of urban life that he describes needs to be theorised without recourse to his technological idealism. Nevertheless, Virilio offers a number of useful diagnostic insights, the most immediately productive of which is the foregrounding of space as a constitutive force in postmodernity. As Edward Soja has argued, the broad tradition of Western Marxism has been prone to a kind of 'anti-spatialism', in which geography is a mere static backdrop to the unfolding dialectical drama of history.[4] The occlusion of space by critical social theory, however, has become increasingly untenable as spatial structures – nations, regions, cities – consistently reveal themselves as constitutive material forces in the shaping of modernity. No longer conceivable as an innocent container of historical progress, urban space in particular has emerged as a dynamic terrain of contestation over political power and control.

Merleau-Ponty's *Phenomenology of Perception*, and specifically its chapter on spatiality, directs us to the critical ontology of space that would enable the thinking of the city as just such a terrain.[5] Merleau-Ponty describes a relation between subject and space as one of reciprocal exchange and dialogue – based neither in the subject's rationalistic domination of space nor in his or her subservience to 'built' space. Space, that is, is not the empty terrain of abstract measurement and manipulation, but the very ground (the spatial terms are tellingly unavoidable) of social being. Moreover, vision itself is fundamentally spatial: insofar as 'the perceived world is grasped in terms of direction, we cannot dissociate being from oriented being' (p. 253). Temporal is thus always bound up with spatial experience; or, in more material terms, history is always geographically specific, as well as the reverse.

This phenomenology of space has clear implications for a theory of seeing in a specifically urban context. Imbricated in the embodied subject, visual perception is perspectival rather than transcendent; absolute visual authority over the city is untenable. It is precisely the positioning of the urban subject in an interpretative, rather than authoritative, relation to the city that opens up the possibility of a visual politics. The eye of the urban subject is neither the privileged '*dieu voyeur*', nor the disempowered victim of Virilio's sight machine; its agency is grounded rather in its dialogic relation to its environment.

It is this form of agency that forms the basis, in Walter Benjamin's writings, for an active critical engagement with the city. The metropolitan experience, for Benjamin, is defined foremost by the experience of shock, by the relentless bombardment of the human sensorium routinised by urban capitalism. This experience is first registered in Baudelaire's images of the degraded landscape underlying the dazzling surfaces of Hausmann's Paris.[6] Benjamin repeatedly attempts to forge an agency, and especially a visual agency, which, whilst informed by Baudelaire's conception of the city as a terrain of pervasive shock, refuses to yield to the latter's despair for the 'lost aura' of premodernity. The aura can be identified not only in the premodern artwork, but also in the intimacy forged between individuals in the mutual exchange of looks: 'The person we look at, or who feels he is being looked at, looks at us in turn' (p. 184). Metropolitan life, in contrast, overburdens the eye with the unceasing spectacles of crowds and commodities that it generates, divesting the human eye of 'its ability to look' (p. 185). This figuration of urban experience as a crisis of seeing extends Benjamin's concept of allegory into the era of modernity. The city's proliferating landscape of images is felt as an assault on the authority of the eye, inducing an anxious melancholy correlative to that of the baroque dramatists. Moreover, this historical transposition makes explicit, as Buci-Glucksmann argues, the status of the feminine's disruptive power as allegory's defining principle.[7]

Benjamin sought to wrest Baudelaire's insights into urban experience from the realm of impotent melancholy, and deploy them in strategies of critical negotiation. These strategies are elaborated in Benjamin's portraits of modern European cities, and in his uncompleted 'Arcades Project'.

Benjamin's early essay on Naples, cowritten with his sometime companion Asja Lacis, provides one of a network of concepts in this model of urban visuality, namely that of 'porosity'.[8] In the play of light on the craggy grey stone, in the anarchic play of architectural form, in the pervasive diffusion of music and dim light, and in the interpenetrations of night and day, 'noise and peace ... home and street' (p. 175), can be identified the porous character of Naples, its refusal of fixed visual definition; 'building and action interpenetrate in the courtyards, arcades and stairways. In everything, they preserve the scope to become a theatre of new, unforeseen constellations' (p. 169). This landscape is significant foremost in enabling the seeing subject to participate in the active making and unmaking of the city. Rather than being set in opposition to a disempowered urban subject, Naples is projected as a site of creative possibility, malleable to the activity of both the individual and collective eye.

This model of 'porous' visuality is further elaborated in Benjamin's descriptions of the restless participatory energies of Moscow's citizens, and of his own enhanced vision after smoking 'Hashish in Marseilles'.[9] Benjamin was to produce his most sustained exploration of the politics of seeing, however, in his intricately planned, largely unwritten project on the Parisian Arcades of the nineteenth century, which has been imaginatively reconstructed by Susan Buck-Morss.[10]

This project extends the question at the heart of Benjamin's writing on the city, namely whether 'the metropolis of consumption, the high ground of bourgeois-capitalist culture', could be 'transformed from a world of mystifying enchantment into one of metaphysical and political illumination' (Buck-Morss, p. 23). Benjamin's metaphor for this process of transformation was derived from natural history: just as that discipline sees in the fossil a visual encoding of the genealogy of a species, so the 'fossils', or defunct commodity objects of the cultural past, encode the origins of the commodity culture of Benjamin's (and our own) time, as 'archaic residues ... petrified ur-forms of the present' (p. 65).

This fossil, Buck-Morss explains, takes four broad forms in Benjamin's project. The first and most conventionally Marxian of these is the 'fetish', visible everywhere in Paris's phantasmagoric commodity culture, its 'magic-lantern show of optical illusions, rapidly changing size and blending into one another' (p. 81). In these optical illusions can be glimpsed the ur-forms of present-day mass cultural commodification.

Fetish images, however, do not hold impermeable sway over the city's consciousness; rather, their mystifying effects are everywhere shadowed by 'counterimages' of the degraded material realities beneath them. Benjamin locates the exemplary counterimage in the constructed femininity of modern fashions, in which the organic processes of bodily deterioration are absorbed into the perpetual imperatives of beauty and youth, 'the repetitive punishment of Hell' (p. 99). The feminised space of consumerism, in other words, is not simply an abstract force of disempowerment, but equally a disruptive and illuminating counterimage of the mystifying spectacle of the modern city.

A different source of 'dialectical illumination' is to be found in the 'wish image'. Benjamin points to the revival of the Classical tradition in the architectural and ornamental forms of Hausmann's Paris as an articulation of the unconscious utopian drive at work in modern urban life. Urban spectacle, even as it mystifies the social struggles that have produced it, simultaneously registers a collective impulse to resolve those struggles.

The last of the image categories is that of the 'ruin', the residual fragments of consumerism's earliest forms. As Buck-Morss shows, the ruin is the exemplary allegorical image, revealing the object's lost plenitude of meaning as it shatters into an 'arbitrary arrangement, as a lifeless, fragmentary, untidy clutter of emblems' (p. 173). Benjamin's response to these images of ruin is to activate them as sources of profane illumination.

The readings in this chapter will attempt to extend Benjamin's conception of urban spectacle as a contradictory site of hope and betrayal to the city that is arguably to the second half of the twentieth century what Hausmann's Paris was to the nineteenth – that is, a showcase for the logic of the contemporary city. This paradigmatic status has been confirmed by a range of work in urban geography. Thus, in the work of Edward Soja, Los Angeles most palpably demonstrates a distinctively postmodern pattern of urban development.[11] This pattern's more general features have been usefully outlined by David Harvey, for whom the postmodern city is defined foremost by the spectacle of consumer desire, as expressed by advertising, by newly prominent leisure spaces, by the rapid expansion of suburbanisation, and by the dazzling facades of the city itself.[12] The political–economic 'restructuring' of the postmodern city is expressed predominantly in its new visual forms. The restructuring process forges new fragmentations of consumption, residence and lifestyle along class and racial lines through the perpetual deployment of spectacle. Spectacle thus works to efface the seismic shifts in labour relations and in the shape of urban space, after the widescale abandonment of the inner cities to poverty and decay.

To recode Harvey's arguments in a very different terminology, the spectacle, in deflecting the interrogations of the critical eye, functions as a crucial instrument of urban power, forging a 'unification' that Guy Debord contends 'is nothing more than an official language of separation'.[13] Divesting the urban eye of power, the proliferating landscape of spectacle effects that eye's transformation from subject into object.

Rather than view urban spectacle through such a deterministic lens as a force of unrelieved domination, I want to deploy the texts to be discussed as a means of showing the diversity of ways in which the postmodern city can be negotiated. In exploring the narrativity of Los Angeles writing, that is, I aim to bring out a relation between the narrating eye and the city that is grounded as much in porosity as in domination. By way of readings in Didion and Ellroy, I will argue that the perpetually shifting landscape of Los Angeles denies any privileged vantage-point to narration. Whilst each writer negotiates this denial in very different ways, they share an explicit consciousness of the city's resistance to the authoritative gaze, of its 'allegorical' transformation of the urban eye from observer to interpreter of its proliferating signs. Of course, this displaced subject position, far from opening up the porosity of vision, often serves in the fiction under discussion as the basis for its closure, as Didion's melancholy resignation to the failure of the interpretative gaze in Los Angeles should demonstrate. In designating postmodern narrativity as porous, then, I am not offering a broad description of existing Los Angeles writing; rather, I am suggesting that the disruptive visuality of the postmodern city produces modes of narration premised on the partial and finite position of the narrative eye.

Los Angeles: the allegorical city

I want to preface my readings of these texts, however, by outlining briefly their more specific context, namely the postwar development of Los Angeles. This process has been vividly charted by Mike Davis, who sees in the city the ultimate trajectory of advanced capitalist urbanity made shockingly apparent.[14] Once again, it is in spectacle that this trajectory is displayed: a city 'infinitely envisioned' (p. 23), 'the most mediated town in America' (p. 20), Los Angeles' visuality is remarkable in functioning not only as a feature of, but as an actual constitutive force in its developmental logic. Hollywood, Disneyland, 'revivalist' and 'fantastical' architectural styles, the futuristic skyscrapers of Downtown, and the widespread deployment of electronic surveillance converge to form a showcase for the globalist logic of postmodernity whose organising principle is the simulation of reality.

This foregrounding of simulation as a strategy of urban development suggest some points of convergence between Davis's and Soja's materialist urban geography and French postmodern theory. Virilio describes Los Angeles as playing out the yielding of traditional urban divisions to a phantom landscape in which material and filmic reality become interchangeable.[15] Baudrillard, in turn, posits the city as the apotheosis of the floating hyperreal landscape of America.[16] Los Angeles, like America itself, is at the centre of a decentred universe, the site at which the collapse of reality into the 'reality-effect' is enacted. Its 'pure' indeterminacy is marked by its endless proliferation of images, sprawling outward with infinite license. Los Angeles is beautiful, for Baudrillard, in 'being in love with its limitless horizontality' (p. 61), that is, with the capacity of its signs to defy all spatiotemporal boundaries. The freeways are the most elegant expression of this defiance; these are spaces of pure motion, an integrated, collective network, in which the individualistic imperatives of European driving give way to a subordination of self to the demands of an intricate technological system. Baudrillard is here joining a tradition of near-rhapsodic visions of the freeways. Rayner Banham, for example, in his classic 1971 study of Los Angeles' architecture and 'ecologies', speaks of the freeways as 'a single, comprehensible place, a coherent state of mind, a complete way of life', prefiguring Baudrillard's images of seamless technological collectivity.[17]

Similarly, John Portman's Bonaventure Hotel, another object of much critical commentary, serves as an emblem of Los Angeles' spectral urbanity, with its glass facade reflecting its own environment, 'sending back its own image' (Baudrillard, *America*, p. 59). This erosion of the interior–exterior distinction appears to exemplify the allegorical impulse to opacity, to a refusal and absorption of the inquisitive gaze.

Fredric Jameson's analysis of the same building, in his now seminal *Postmodernism*, demonstrates how this pessimistic conception of Los Angeles' visuality has carried over into recent materialist accounts of the city.[18] Focusing, like Baudrillard, on the blurring of its interior and exterior boundaries, he points similarly to its reflective glass skin, repelling the city outside whilst obscuring any view of the interior, and so achieving 'a peculiar and placeless dissociation of the Bonaventure from its neighbourhood' (p. 42). The experience of this pseudo-Utopia once inside is even more dislocating, as a series of transportation machines appropriate the individual's mobility. This experience can be read as 'the symbol and analagon of ... the incapacity of our minds, at least at present, to map the great global network in which we find ourselves caught as individual subjects' (p. 44). In this context, Jameson adds, Benjamin's account of modern urbanity as a new experience of bodily perception becomes both 'singularly relevant' in its profound insights into the shock induced by the technological transformation of public space, and 'singularly antiquated' in its necessary inability to anticipate the degree to which postmodernity would naturalise that shock.

The conception of postmodern urban consciousness as impotent derives in large part, I suggest, from Jameson's failure to historicise his own descriptive perspective. This failure flattens the specific historical and geographical situations of all postmodern subjects to an undifferentiated experience of 'disembodiment' and 'decentredness'. Thus dislocated from any specific position in space and time, Jameson's subject is necessarily bereft of a point of departure for the 'cognitive mapping' of postmodernity. Moreover, his invocation of Benjamin misses the latter's insistence on the ways in which urban shock is inflected by one's specific position in history and geography. This is the significance of his 'typology' of modern urbanity, which posits 'flaneurie', prostitution, fashion and so forth, as different experiences and negotiations of shock, and hence of active, as well as degraded, relationships with mass spectacle.

As Mike Davis contends, Jameson's conception of the hotel as a microcosm of postmodern spatiality effectively elides the specific social and economic conditions that brought that spatiality into being.[19] The Bonaventure Hotel's simulated garden and 'street' spaces are not, as Jameson has it, 'signs of capital's drive to expand', but 'symptoms of global crisis' (Davis, p. 109). The hotel, that is, is an index of the attempts of corporate architects to protect downtown financial and other high property value districts from the tensions of the city, after the wave of urban insurrections between 1964 and 1969. In viewing postmodern spatiality as the product of a strategic response to crises in the political and economic organisation of the city, rather than the realisation of capitalist expansionism, Davis thus demonstrates that the spectacular facade of Los Angeles is more finite and contingent that absolute and impermeable.

It is this same impulse to 'excavation' that informs Davis's *City of Quartz*, a text that seeks to account for the incorporation of all oppositional political energies into the relentless process of urban development. Davis identifies in Los Angeles' spatial order a key element of this process, maintained as it is by a system of 'electronic

militarisation', the same overlay of 'special effects' described by
Virilio. This spatial order has to become an emblem of the dissolution
of any effective oppositional culture by the forces of technological
and economic fragmentation.

Spatiality, then, is a constitutive historical force in Los Angeles'
development. The city's unique source of wealth creation, namely
land development without a significant productive base, has
produced the effective decimation of cohesive communal space,
for the maintenance of land values demands the vigilant exclusion
of marginal populations. Indeed, the Downtown and Westside
elites' projects for architectural growth are effectively predicated
on exclusion: to generate more wealth, city government, in
conjunction with commercial developers, must find ways of
obliterating its material past and present, by creating hermetically
sealed zones of wealth and cultural homogeneity. Inflecting politically
a distinctively Baudrillardian set of terms, Davis describes the
Downtown financial district as 'a single, demonically referential
hyperstructure, a Miesian skyscraper raised to dementia' (p. 229).
Its immaterial form, cut off from the needs and aspirations of local
communities, is maintained by the enforced exclusion of the
homeless by the police, who remain confined to the degraded, violent
streets of Skid Row, their visibility an intrusion into the dazzling
semiotic landscape. In this apparently incontestable regulation of
urban space can be witnessed a particularly bleak vision of the fate
of Benjaminian 'porosity' as a mode of visual agency.

Davis's pessimism towards the possibility of cultural resistance
in postmodern Los Angeles can be understood as a result of his
rather too rigid definition of agency. His curiously moralistic
polemic against gangster rap, for example, as 'an uncritical mirror
to fantasy power-trips of violence, sexism and greed' (p. 87) is
symptomatic of a certain blindness to forms of resistance which
operate outside the mode of production. It is consequently difficult
for Davis to evade the charge of a nostalgia for the lost class
formations of modernity. His final invocation of Fontana, a decaying
industrial suburb, or as he puts it, 'junkyard of dreams', as an image
of the city's corrosive impact on the utopian impulse, points to an
implicit conflation of the 'dream' with a thriving productive base.
Yet, as his own account of Los Angeles' development indicates, it
is precisely such a productionist model of resistance that the city
has short-circuited. Its complex history of spatialised class, racial
and gender fragmentation displaces the subject from any privileged
vantage-point, demanding instead a mode of agency that is mobile,
situated and partial. As I shall argue, the crises of representation
enacted in Didion and Ellroy point to just this dissolution of
narrative authority.

Davis, then, in exhaustively documenting the political and economic forces underlying the visual politics of Los Angeles, has produced a kind of jeremiad for the erosion of oppositional energies. If French postmodernism tends towards the abstraction of visual phenomena for their historical and geographical contexts, Davis inverts this theoretical blindspot by viewing these phenomena exclusively from the perspective of the economic. Postmodern culture appears largely as a mere refraction of the fragmentary logic of late capitalism, and as such devoid of critical political content. Davis lacks Benjamin's sense of the doubleness of spectacle, its status as simultaneously a source of phantasmagoric mystification and utopian yearning. *City of Quartz* is heavily weighted towards the former pole of this dialectic, regarding urban spectacle as a force of unmitigated repression, impervious to resistance.

In this respect, Jameson's work can stand as a corrective to Davis's, as well as the reverse, in its capacity to see the images of postmodern urbanity as possessed of an autonomy that reaches beyond the history which determines it. Thus, where Davis sees the work of Los Angeles' most prominent architect, Frank Gehry, as reproductive of 'the underlying relations of repression, surveillance and exclusion that characterize the fragmented, paranoid spatiality to which Los Angeles seems to aspire' (p. 238), Jameson finds in its refusal of a privileged vantage-point a resistance to commodity fetishism, 'evading the image imperialism of photography'.[20] Jameson displays here a more acute sense of the visual as a terrain of continual contestation than Davis, who seems to perceive it as mired in its own bleak history. Only by thinking of Los Angeles as an ongoing site of 'resistance, rejection and redirection in the nonetheless structured field of urban locales' (Soja, 'It all comes together', p. 235), can this determinism be countered.

Los Angeles, fiction and counternarrative

Recent attempts to delineate Los Angeles' fictional tradition have tended to affirm the city's status as a phantasmagoria. This tendency is exemplified in the repeated invocation of Nathaniel West's *Day of the Locust* (also, in fact, a key text in Alan Spiegel's 'American Gothic' genre, outlined in the preceding chapter) as a paradigm text.[21] West's 'persistent pattern of imagery linking bizarre and inappropriate human costuming, absurd roleplaying, and eclectic, counterfeit design' is posited as the expression of a generalised dystopian vision of Los Angeles.[22] Moreover, as the protagonists of West's novel clearly demonstrate, the pervasiveness of mass spectacle produces, and feeds on, the degraded subjectivity of its typical inhabitant, whose consciousness has been absorbed wholesale into a mass cultural 'dreamworld', her potential for 'awakening' paralysed by the pervasive inscription of consumer desire. According to this account of a dominant strain in Los Angeles writing, the only force that might disrupt the spectacle is the apocalyptic moment (West's climactic riot, for example) which looms as a menacing counterpoint to the dazzling surface of artifice and glamour.

It is this tradition that Davis, in his survey of the cultural history of Los Angeles, terms 'noir', invoking the novelistic and cinematic genre most influential in the construction of its image. In the novels of Chandler and Cain, and the many movies they spawned and in their more recent progeny, can be identified the reinvention of Los Angeles as the dystopian site of deceptive visual surfaces perpetually disrupted by shady and violent undercurrents, that is, by a literal and figurative 'shadow world' of criminal pathology. The inheritor of Chandler's role as noir chronicler of Los Angeles, for Davis, is James Ellroy; the noir vision, however, penetrates well beyond these generic boundaries. In the long line of novels articulating what Charles L. Crow calls 'the rhetoric of apocalypse', this same dystopian impulse is clearly apparent.[23] For Davis as for many others, West's fiction stands as an exemplification of this impulse, whilst Bret Easton Ellis's *Less Than Zero* functions as its contemporary apotheosis. Ellis's more immediate precursor, however, is, for Davis, Joan Didion, who brings to bear her dark vision of American (post)modernity most potently on contemporary Los Angeles, in both her journalism and her novel, *Play It As It Lays*.

In the present discussion of Los Angeles writing, I wish to focus specifically on the dystopian sensibility that continues to characterise its representation, for it is this sensibility that releases what I have termed an allegorical impulse. Both writers under discussion extend to the context of Los Angeles the thematics of vision I have identified in previous chapters. Didion's Los Angeles, I want to argue, is imagined as the site at which the critically interpretative gaze of politics and ethics is refused wholesale. From the vantage-point of a perpetual present, Didion envisions an urban lifeworld closed off to historical interrogation, producing what I have termed a counternarrative temporality. Ellroy, in contrast, constructs his vision of Los Angeles via a reinvention of its criminal past. This disintegrative history, however, serves less as a ground of narrative explanation for his labyrinthine plots, than as the condition of that explanation's failure. Ellroy's detectives are locked into a crisis of seeing, engendered by the surfeit of urban signs with which they are perpetually confronted. This crisis frustrates the diegetic impulse of Chandlerian detective fiction, systematically undoing its stable epistemology. From the finite perspective of each writer, then, a particular view of the phantasmagoric lifeworld of urban spectacle, is implicitly articulated.

The melancholic gaze: Joan Didion in Los Angeles

Perhaps the most pervasive theme at work in Joan Didion's thirty-year corpus of journalism and fiction is that of the unremitting opacity of the historical present, its indifference to questions of determination and value. Her writing's resistance to either historical illumination or political judgement is, moreover, inscribed into the wearily disengaged tone and flatly denotative rhythms of her prose. I want to argue that this impulse to detachment is articulated foremost by her visual relation to the contemporary, and to the spectacular space of Los Angeles in particular. That is, it is from her *images* of the landscape of postmodern Los Angeles, that there emerges a vision of an opaque object-world, in which visuality is tantalisingly unmoored from any determinate origins, and objects, to borrow Hal Foster's term, 'seem agentless'.[24]

My reading of Didion will foreground, then, her impassivity towards the opaque and proliferating cultural signs that her gaze consciously fails to read. At the same time, I will suggest that this impassivity is produced by an inability to confront the historicity underlying these signs, a historicity on which Benjamin contrastingly insists. There is evident rather, in Didion, a tendency to take the impenetrable object as an affirmation of the inherent and eternal indeterminacy of existence itself.

As a number of critics have observed, the primary characteristics of Joan Didion's writing are, as she has said, an uncompromising pessimism, a 'predilection for the extreme', and a mind that 'veers inflexibly towards the particular'.[25] By way of an examination of a range of her essays, however, I intend to demonstrate how this particularising perspective becomes itself another form of abstraction. Indeed, Didion acknowledges the peculiarly generalised character of her eye for detail when she remarks that, 'I have always had trouble distinguishing between what happened and what merely might have happened, but I remain unconvinced that the distinction, for my purposes, matters' ('Notebook', p. 115). The particular, I want to suggest, functions in Didion not to ground her observations in the specificity of personal and social history but, on the contrary, to signify meanings that are almost consciously disengaged from that specificity. The 'inflexible' fetish of the particular that Didion attributes to herself is not to be taken as a marker of a historical sensibility, but rather as a way of expressing her very failure to penetrate the opacity of contemporary sociocultural life. Thus, the more apparently vivid and exact the image she invokes, the more curiously resistant it seems to critical engagement. Mark Z. Muggli, in his theorisation of the poetics of Didion's journalism, terms this metaphorical strategy 'emblematic', in its deployment of the image, or 'emblem', to evoke 'a large world of meaning beyond the confines of the particular story'.[26] The term tellingly evokes Benjamin's designation of the peculiarly visualised character of allegorical narrative, its fracture into 'emblematic' units. Objects in Didion's field of vision seem perpetually to elude and perplex her and are, as such exemplary allegorical objects, shot through with an irreducible surfeit of visual meaning.

Whilst Didion acknowledges the inevitability of the narrative organisation of experience as part of the impulse 'to live', she insists on the essentially fictive status of any such mode of explanation. In her own words,

> We live entirely, especially if we are writers, by the imposition of a narrative line upon disparate images, by the 'ideas' with which we have learned to freeze the phantasmagoria which is our actual experience.[27]

In this rather Woolfian account of lived experience, any framework of value or causal explanation becomes a form of, admittedly necessary, conceptual violence. The tellingly visual terms employed to render the subject's experience of the world ('disparate images', 'freeze', 'phantasmagoria') reinforce the sense of the autonomy of the object, its persistent tendency to withstand the inquiring gaze. The phantasmagoria of everyday life severely constrains the eye's critical power. In Didion, as Samuel Coale contends, there is a pervasive sense of 'immobility' 'stunned by the conscious contradictions of contemporary American society and its moral burdens'.[28] The resistance of experience to coherent conceptualisation is demonstrably intensified in contemporary America, primary site of an emergent condition whose description by David Harvey as one in which 'images dominate narratives' could scarcely be more apposite than in the context of a discussion of Didion.[29] A cogent example of this immobile sensibility is found in Didion's account of The Doors' studio session on Sunset Boulevard in 1968, in 'The white album', in which Didion's gaze lights upon the random details of the studio:

> There was the producer and the engineer and the road manager and a couple of girls and a Siberian husky named Nikki with one gray eye and one gold. There were paper bags half-filled with hardboiled eggs and chicken livers and cheeseburgers and empty bottles of apple juice and California rose. (p. 22)

A comparison with Kosinski's enumeration of objects in a room (in *Steps*, for example) is instructive.[30] Where his gaze is marked by the drive to order and dominate all objects that enter its field of vision, and by an uncompromising violence towards those that attempt to elude it, Didion's observations seem to be inscribed by a bewildered passivity before the sheer surfeit of 'agentless' signs that confront her. The repeated linking of objects with the 'and' conjunction conveys an anxious anticipation of their slippage from her visual control. Visual detail here, rather than clarifying a hierarchy of significance amongst objects, serves only to flatten them into an undifferentiated surface, on which the place of each individual within the studio remains resolutely unspecified. The exactitude with which the discarded rubble of food is recalled similarly succeeds only in affirming the unwieldy materiality of objects in the face of any attempt to elucidate their meaning. Like Benjamin's allegorical signs, the objects before Didion's eyes have been reduced to 'a lifeless, fragmentary, untidy clutter of emblems' (Buck-Morss, *Dialectics*, p. 173). Didion's invocation of the term 'catatonia' to describe the atmosphere in the studio aptly designates her own response to this spectacle of weary and indifferent excess. Consciously uninquisitive, she presents the scene as if it paralysed any interpretative gesture, rendering inevitable her silent and immobile perspective. The Doors, then, like the San Francisco hippies of her earlier essay, 'Slouching towards Bethlehem', exemplify the opacity of late 1960s Californian culture, short-circuiting by their very extremity the possibility of what Jameson terms 'critical distance'.[31] To analogise, The Doors seem merely to reflect back any gaze into their internal motivation or external determinants, rather as the Bonaventure Hotel's mirrored exterior will later more literally ward off visual scrutiny. Indeed, in this respect, Jameson's description of the disembodying experience of the hotel usefully diagnoses Didion's relation to the world she describes. Perhaps her own most chillingly incisive articulation of the image's capacity to immobilise the gaze comes when she recounts a moment of realisation in which

> I discovered I was no longer interested in whether the woman on the ledge outside the window on the sixteenth floor jumped or did not jump, or in why. I was interested only in the picture of her in my mind: her hair incandescent in the floodlights, her bare toes curled inwards on the stone ledge. ('The white album', p. 44)

The account of this flash of self-recognition is remarkable in that it reveals Didion consciously willing the abstraction of the object's visual surface from its determinate origins in space and time. The suicidal impulse to which the image bears uneasy witness functions simultaneously as a frozen encapsulation of a historical moment (1968) apparently driven by an uncontainable excess; and as a demonstration of that moment's paralysis of any mode of narrative representation other than the emblematic spectacle, a mode that repulses all but the aestheticising gaze she describes.

It is difficult, furthermore, to view as coincidental the gender of this spectacle. The 'incandescent hair' and 'bare toes' that stand glimmering against the sixteenth-floor ledge, evoke irresistibly a virtual canon of images of female hysteria. Christine Buci-Glucksmann's assertion that 'allegory is anti-dialectical or, to use Benjamin's terms ... is dialectics at a standstill, frozen, fixed in images' (p. 103) cogently illuminates this passage; divested of her situation within a determinate history, the woman appears to us blasted out of the dialectical continuum of time, her abstracted surface 'frozen' and 'fixed in images'. Yet where for Buci-Glucksmann this frozenness is produced by a disjunctive history, alternative to the narrative of historical progress, for Didion it belies the redundancy of history *per se*. In this respect, her writing exemplifies allegory's 'counternarrative' impulse, 'for it arrests narrative in one place'.[32] In Didion, narrative arrest marks history's failure to render the image determinate; the nihilistic excesses of 1968, emblematised by the suicidal woman, block, rather than facilitate, reading.

Given this association of the impenetrability of the present with the irrationality of the feminine, it is perhaps unsurprising that Didion's critique of the rhetoric of the women's movement centres on its tendency to flatten the ambiguities of gender in the service of contingent ideological imperatives. This tendency leads to the elision of the 'irreconcilable difference ... that sense of living one's deepest life underwater'[33] that, for her, constitutes feminine existence. The feminine, then, in its 'irreconcilable difference', implicitly refuses dialectical resolution.

For Didion, finally, the contemporary world in general remains indifferent to the active human agent, cruelly oblivious to the subjective demands of politics and ethics. Her melancholy conviction in the futility of convictions is perhaps the central theme of her writings, a theme occasionally expressed quite explicitly, as in her meditations 'On the morning after the sixties', which she concludes by declaring that 'If I could believe that going to a barricade would affect man's fate in the slightest I would go to that barricade, but it would be less than honest to say that I expect to happen upon such a happy ending.'[34] 'Man's fate' is, as it were, to be forever condemned to its own illegibility, and so to the futility of any conscious attempt to activate change within it.

Didion's writings on Southern California's perilous natural environment, identifying in nature an irreducible unreadability that penetrates consciousness itself, further underscore this distinctly Benjaminian melancholy. Thus, when the furious Santa Ana winds of Los Angeles blow, they cause the destruction not only of the built environment, but also of all notions of motivation and agency; 'nervousness', 'depression', violence and crime become mere effects of a malevolent meteorology.[35] The interpenetration of nature and history, then, and the consequent loss of the transparency of each, induce a melancholic resignation to the impotence of the interpretative eye. The conception of Los Angeles as a fragmented and indeterminate cityscape, whose logic evades the interrogative gaze, is played out once again in Didion's most recent collection of essays, *After Henry*. The city's radical divergence from conventional urban logic is based, she argues, in its 'absence of narrative', in specific contrast to the narrative sensibility that governs the everyday life of New York.[36] Again, then, Los Angeles is posited as the site of a counternarrative space-time, unassimilable to a normative linear time. It is in these terms that she views the phenomenon of the city's spiralling wealth base in real estate that Mike Davis has so exhaustively analysed as an effect of Los Angeles' unusual economic and urban-political logic. Didion, predictably, exhibits little of Davis's concern with the material determinants of the character of the property market, viewing it rather as one of the many signs of the city's detachment from identifiable trends. Thus, she recounts the fever-pitch of buying and selling that had been reached by June 1988: 'Multiple offers were commonplace, and deals stalled because bank appraisers could not assess sales fast enough to keep up with the rising market.'[37] The sentence is significant for the near-absence of human beings as grammatical subjects. The 'multiple offers' and 'deals' of the market panic are instead themselves conferred with the power of agency, as if operating autonomously of the people who make them ('lifeless objects ... may speak and act', Benjamin, *Tragic Drama*, p. 186). Indeed, when human subjects ('bank appraisers') are invoked, it is only to affirm their incapacity to function, to maintain any correspondence between their activity and the speed of the 'rising market'. The peculiar logic of capitalism in Los Angeles, then, enacts a reversal in which the human subject is rendered the market's object. The indifference of the urban landscape to conventional modes of narrative explanation is subsequently made explicit when she remarks that Los Angles is 'in many ways predicated on the ability to deal with the future at a rather existential remove' ('LA days', p. 151). Thus, where New York's property market felt the impact of the October 1987 stock market crash directly and immediately, the same event 'seemed in Los Angeles, not to have happened' ('LA days', p. 151). In this apparently inexplicable violation of the broad trends of contemporary capitalism, can be seen the real estate market's compliance with the principle of opacity that governs existence in Los Angeles. The spectacle of land development is somehow self-generating, producing relentless spatial expansion and inflationary pressures that seem impervious to subjective control) as well as to narrative representation. In the capacity of its objects and relations to stand for 'anything else', Los Angeles constitutes perhaps the paradigm allegorical space of postmodernity. Once again, however, this insight is achieved at the expense of a kind of blindness to the historicity of that space, as if the experience of Los Angeles constituted a kind of wholesale flight from history itself.

Underpinning this condition is the absence of any point of continuity, or collective meaning, in the city: 'there is in Los Angeles no memory everyone shares, no monument everyone knows, no historical reference as meaningful as the long sweep of the ramps where the San Diego and Santa Monica freeways intersect ...'.[38] The sprawling, dispersed and ceaselessly mutating urbanity of Los Angeles, constantly renegotiating its historical and geographical coordinates, disables the formation of a consciousness informed by collective historical experience or a common visual environment.

For Didion, Los Angeles is the ultimate realisation of a spectacular object-world, before which the subject's only appropriate response is a surrender to the disembodied state of 'rapture-of-the-freeway', to the bewilderment of the bank appraiser. It is just this degraded visual subjectivity that seems to characterise Mariah Wyeth, the protagonist of *Play It As It Lays*.[39] The novel begins with the retrospective observations of three of its central figures on the events documented in the remaining pages. Mariah, a burned-out actress, opens the novel with a stark disclaimer of interest in questions of motivation: 'What makes Iago evil? some people ask. I never ask' (p. 1). This disengagement from the impulse to understand, in favour of a willed acceptance of the existential irreducibility of things clearly evokes, of course, Didion's own journalistic voice. 'I am what I am. To look for "reasons" is beside the point' (p. 1), Mariah contends, going on to insist on the same disavowal of causality in the consideration of all phenomena, including that of her own daughter's mental illness ('Kate is Kate', (p. 3)), which seems to defy all the attempts of institutional psychology to diagnose or cure it. Countering the abstractions of those who 'look for "reasons"', Mariah states her intention 'to throw the I Ching but never read the coins, keep my mind in the now' (p. 6). She embraces a kind of perpetual present, refusing both the visualisation of the future (the I Ching coins) and the interrogation of the past. Again, somewhat resembling the writer who brings her into being, Mariah fetishises the particular and immediate as the only available truth. The hummingbird before her, on which she attempts to concentrate, reveals a stubbornly visible facticity which, like Benjamin's allegorical object, refuses the easy ascription of abstract significance. Mariah, then, is bent on annihilating meaning itself from experience; when asked by the suicidal BZ 'what matters', she baldly responds 'Nothing' (p. 201).

One of Mariah's more flippant self-descriptive remarks – that her name 'is pronounced Mar-eye-ah' (p. 2) – provides a telling insight into the character of her perceptual orientation. The 'eye' is at the centre of her identity, a visual mechanism abstracted from her bodily and affective experience, and determining the manner in which she articulates her being. The formal characteristics of the novel reinforce the notions of 'presentness', facticity and randomness that dominate at the level of content. Cynthia Griffin Wolf has pointed to Emerson's figuration, in 'Nature', of the self as 'transparent eyeball ... nothing' as a literary prefiguration of 'Mar-eye-ah's embrace of nothing.[40] For Mariah, the eye has been divested of its interpretative function, to become the abstracted, denotative mechanism that a number of critics have defined as 'cinematic'. Thus, Samuel Coale writes of 'the disconnected episodes with the ellipses between ... the carefully controlled point of view with the camera's precision' (p. 162) that accompany the reading of the novel. Spiegel's schema of 'cinematographic' fiction is also instructive here, insofar as Didion's novel seems to constitute an apotheosis of the progressive divestment of moral and epistemological authority that defines this genealogy. Furthermore, Spiegel's framework underscores the interpenetration of cinema and city as paradigm allegorical spaces.

Didion's vision of Los Angeles is indeed notably marked by its 'cinematic' rendering of the city's landscape, most notably its freeways. When Mariah begins to drive the freeways some time after the breakdown of her marriage, they represent for her the possibility of a transcendent space, removed from the painful, concrete contingencies of her own personal history and the ethically redundant urban culture that produced it. Her somewhat contrived exhilaration as she drives is bound up with the eradication of memory. Whilst, 'at night', images of her husband, lover, and friends, the violently self-destructive film producer BZ and his wife Helene, 'flood her mind ... she never thought about that on the freeway' (pp. 16–17). The freeway produces a gaze that fixates on the spectacle of the present, and closes off the memory of the past. Thus, Mariah's mind is concentrated on the effort 'to keep her eyes on the mainstream, the great pilings, the Cyclone fencing, the deadly oleander, the luminous signs, the organism which absorbed all her reflexes, all her attention' (p. 15). Later on, the experience of the freeway becomes internalised, to the degree that merely imagining 'driving straight on into the hard white empty core of the world' (p. 161), lulls Mariah into dreamless sleep, liberating her from the burden of her personal history, from narrative itself.

The system of transportation that defines Los Angeles is not merely, then, an instrumental source of mobility, but a mode of being, a force that structures the urban subject's relation to time and space. Mariah's wholesale surrender to its logic works as a kind of displacement of bodily agency on to the car and the road. Driving on the freeway, that is, is less a way of reinventing the subject's embodied relation to the city, than of severing that relation altogether, in an attempt to find a time free of history, and a space liberated from geography. 'All her attention', her intellectual and affective capacity, is absorbed into this 'hard white empty core of the world', white and empty because apparently uncoloured and unfilled by the material struggles of everyday life. Didion, moreover, conveys the naturalized status of the world of the freeway for Mariah, by deploying a jarringly distorted natural metaphor to render the latter's experience of driving: 'she drove it as a riverman runs a river, every day more attuned to its currents, its deceptions ... ' (p. 14). In this conflation of nature and technology can be glimpsed a further allegorical figuration of the former's lost transparency, its melancholy inscription by the transient forces of history and culture.

As H. Jennifer Brady observes, however, Mariah 'is forced to recognize the failure of her attempt to find a refuge from thought and memory on the freeway'.[41] Her attempt to escape these contingencies by constructing the freeways as the site of a perpetual present gives way to the disarming realisation that they do not float above, and oblivious to, specific places, but rather connect them. The freeways, that is, both produce, and are produced by, their history and geography, and cannot function as a fully autonomous space abstracted from those forces. Mariah symbolically confronts this reality when the hallucinatory rhythm of the freeway is broken by her unintentional drive beyond it, to the Nevada town of Baker. This accident forces her to contemplate the possibility of participating once more in her personal life by telephoning her estranged husband Carter, who is shooting a film nearby. Once the freeways have caused this confrontation with the contingencies of her own history, they are effectively disenchanted for her. Thus, 'On the way back to the city the traffic was heavy and the hot wind blew sand through her windows and the radio got on her nerves and after that Mariah did not go back on the freeway except as a way of getting somewhere' (p. 33). The very space valued for its illusory status as a refuge from the everyday experience of the body suddenly transmutes, in Mariah's perception, into a site of material surfeit, effecting an unwelcome awareness both of the body and of the materiality of the environment (the traffic, the sand, and the radio).

For Benjamin, it is precisely this surfeit of meaning that distinguishes allegory from myth. In allegory, we recall, history inscribes the object with a kind of superabundance of determinations, rendering it illegible. Mariah embraces this illegibility, whilst simultaneously disavowing its historicity. In this respect, her involuntary recognition of the materiality of the freeway reads as

KING ALFRED'S COLLEGE
LIBRARY

a moment in which the 'frozenness' of the allegorical image is ruptured.

Mariah's existence, then, is predicated on the effort to elude the traumatising effects of her own history, most particularly the abortion that constitutes the central event of the novel. Imposed upon her by Carter, Mariah is able to come to terms with the abortion only by dissociating it from her own desires and motivations, and by reducing the experience to one moment in a flat, undifferentiated tableau of other moments. As she herself has it,

> No moment more or less important than any other moment, all the same: the pain as the doctor scraped signified nothing beyond itself, no more constituted the pattern of life than did the movie on television in the living room of this house in Encino. (p. 81)

The movie on television serves here as an emblem of the proliferation of signs in Mariah's present, obscuring any pattern of meaning or significance in its visual order, just as the abortion itself is drained of any affective charge in being integrated into the screen of her abstracted experience. Mariah wills this flattening of lived time and space, perceiving her predicament at one remove, as when the abortionist, during the drive to the 'house in Encino', talks nonchalantly of his intentions to buy a Camaro; the incongruous conversation:

> significantly altered her perception of reality: she saw now she was not a woman on her way to have an abortion. She was a woman parking a Corvette outside a tract house while a man in white pants talked to her about buying a Camaro. (p. 78)

The uncompromisingly detached manner of rendering the scene bears comparison with Didion's image of the suicidal woman on the sixteenth-floor ledge. In both instances, there is at work a kind of willed reification of the object, subtended by an impassivity before its opaque historicity. Mariah's shift of perception signifies a willed reversal of her perspectival relation to the world, in which she disavows her status as subject of her own experience and embraces the position of the object. Just as Carter refers to the abortionist with cold detachment as 'the only man in LA County who does clean work' (p. 54), Mariah describes herself as 'a radical surgeon of my own life. Never discuss. Cut. In that way I resemble the only man in Los Angeles County who does clean work' (p. 202). Bent on severing her capacity for 'discussion' from her orientation to the world, her life becomes a series of impenetrable gestures, whether sexual, professional or emotional. The imperative to 'cut' is grounded in an impulse to take on the status of object, to be relieved of the responsibility for her existence. Indeed, the cinematic term 'cut' constitutes an apt designation of her narrative strategy. The cut serves to interrupt the flow of narrative progress; it is the primary instrument of montage, the visual frame through which Mariah focalises her lifeworld. Montage, that is, is a form of counternarrative, privileging the production over the integration of images, an impulse reenacted in the repeated rendering of Mariah's visual horizon as an undifferentiated tableau of objects which refuses narrative resolution. Mariah negotiates subjective existence, then, by striving to melt into the undifferentiated object-world of signs that characterises her experience of Los Angeles, whether the freeways, the cinema and television, or the sexual and social life of Hollywood's parties. The effort to achieve this objectified state, however, is continuously frustrated by the persistence of memory, the involuntary awareness of her situated embodiment in a personal and social history. I have suggested that her drive home on the freeway from Baker functions very much in this way, as a moment of rupture in the apparently seamless hallucinatory surface of Los Angeles. Mariah's jolting memories of her mother, eaten by the coyotes of the Nevada desert, and of her aborted child, similarly penetrate the undifferentiated screen of presentness on which she projects her existence.

When she begins crying inconsolably, 'in the sun on the Western street', the narratorial voice remarks that 'she had deliberately not counted the months but must have been counting them unawares, because this was the day, the day the baby would have been born' (p. 140). Each of these moments, then, affirm Buci-Glucksmann's insight that the allegorical is a fundamentally disruptive force, generated by a disjunctive and overdetermined history. Mariah's perpetual refusal to recognise the historicity of the sign, her will to find in its opacity a melancholy liberation from thought and action, is repeatedly frustrated at these moments.

In the representation of this moment, then, can be identified the central tension in Didion's writings, especially those centred on Los Angeles. Whilst her images bear witness to the impossibility of narrative resolution, as well as of a transcendent eye, in doing so they tend to disavow their historicity wholesale. Nevertheless, countering this tendency to refuse history in both her journalism and fiction, is the fitful recognition this objectified landscape is produced by historical trauma. The past, then, to be sure, enters Didion's writings only as a marker of loss, as a rebuke to the present lifeworld of unstable opacity. Yet in these occasional traces of the past, whether social or personal, can be glimpsed the latent imperative to view the apparently impenetrable landscape of Los Angeles through the lens of history, even as that history frustrates any attempt to represent it transparently.

James Ellroy, Los Angeles and the spectacular crisis of masculinity

Didion's vision of Los Angeles as the terrain of an abstracted present in which the past surfaces only in the form of indeterminate memory traces, arguably finds its inversion in James Ellroy's crime fiction. Ellroy's four-volume chronicle of the postwar period in Los Angeles subjects the city's baroque criminal history and developmental geography to relentless interrogation. Urban history emerges from this confrontation as less indeterminate than startlingly overdetermined, mired in the interpenetration of corrupt political, economic and sexual forces, and generative of violently fractured subjectivities. Thus, whilst both writers identify a crisis of visual authority in the experience of Los Angeles, their means of dramatising and negotiating the history of that crisis are very different.

Mike Davis describes the LA Quartet as a 'delirious parody' of the noir genre, 'an almost unendurable wordstorm of perversity and gore', and censures Ellroy for 'extinguishing the genre's tensions' (p. 45). He goes on to contend that the 'pitch blackness' of Ellroy's Los Angeles leaves 'no light ... to cast shadows and evil becomes a forensic banality. The result feels very much like the actual moral texture of the Reagan-Bush era: a supersaturation of corruption that fails any longer to outrage or even interest' (p. 45). Davis's moralistic evaluation ironically elides a certain continuity of texture between Ellroy's and his own narrative of Los Angeles; in particular, the conception of the city as a locus of the erosion of critical agency in the face of implacably hostile material forces, and the consequent identification of violently displaced and distorted forms of resistance. However, in each writer (and in contrast to Didion), Los Angeles is projected less as severed from than as inextricably bound up with the dynamics of history and geography. The LA Quartet, spanning some twenty-three years in the life of the city, intricately maps its postwar boom, playing out Gothic dramas of criminal excess within the context of the reshaping of its built landscape by the convergent forces of land development and mass cultural spectacle. The labyrinthine plots of the novels reveal these phenomena to be underpinned by a confluence of explosive political and economic interests, a violent inversion of the dazzling spectacle Los Angeles projects outward, via the media. The destabilising experience of this logic of creative destruction is expressed foremost in the crisis-ridden masculinity of the Quartet's protagonists. If the Benjaminian *flaneur* is empowered by his capacity to exert a certain perceptual control over the city, by activating a visual mobility that eludes the instrumental imperatives of capitalism, the policemen who dominate Ellroy's novels represent *flaneurie* in a new and distorted form, an urban subjectivity that now operates not with critical autonomy, but in the service of a corrupt informal coalition of urban politicians, racketeers and developers. Just as Benjamin read in the discarded objects of late nineteenth-century Paris the fossilised 'ur-forms' of modernity, Ellroy's reinvention of the emergent landscape of postwar Los Angeles traces the origins of postmodern urbanity. In so doing, it offers an allegorical representation of Los Angeles' disintegrative postwar landscape. As he has explicitly asserted, Ellroy's shift of narrative perspective from the Chandlerian private eye to the waged cop constitutes a critique of the romanticised and historically inaccurate figuration of crime as existential conflict between alienated individual and urban modernity, and so marks the progressive cooptation of *flaneurie* by the State.[42] His protagonists' experience of a veritable conspiracy of material forces shaping the urban landscape is felt as a devaluation of status from active subject to victimised object. The masculine anxiety generated by this collapse is articulated by way of a displaced rage against an apparently feminised urban object-world. This object-world takes a bewildering array of forms, from the murdered prostitute at the centre of *The Black Dahlia*, to the manipulative promiscuity of communist organiser Claire De Haven in *The Big Nowhere*, and the prostitutes surgically transformed to double as movie stars in *LA Confidential*.[43] The male protagonists of these fictions consistently express their impotence before these emblems of the 'destructive principle' of the allegorical feminine in the form of violent misogyny and racism. The explosive map of the historical and geographical dynamics of postwar Los Angeles can thus be glimpsed in the representation of a traumatised (white) masculinity, for when Ellroy's cops investigate the murders of women, they are in effect tracing the disintegrative narratives of postwar urban space. Perhaps the most significant, and sinister, feature of Ellroy's urban object-world, however, is that it contains not only the officially sanctioned mass spectacle that pervades Los Angeles, but equally its 'bastard' progeny: shadowing the commodified images of Hollywood, Disneyland, the Dodgers Stadium and other emblems of the hegemony of spectacle are their violent inversions. The entranced subject of Benjamin's 'dreamworld' of mass culture, once that world is revealed as the product of specific historical and spatial processes, is 'awakened' less to conscious political engagement, than to the 'nightmare' double that looms beneath its surface. Indeed, in the most startling realisation of this awakening, the murder case at the centre of *LA Confidential* is finally tied to the grotesquely distorted animations that Raymond Dieterling, a barely concealed fictionalisation of Walt Disney and founder of the tellingly named 'Dream-a-Dream Land', creates for his illegitimate son. Dieterling's buried creative history thus serves as a discomfitingly literal enactment of Benjamin's famous dictum: 'There is no document of civilization which is not at the same time a document of barbarism.'[44] Indeed, this doubled logic of civilisation and barbarism is at the heart of Ellroy's fiction; the official narrative of Los Angeles' developmental progress, projected by its power elite, is perpetually haunted by counternarratives of a secret and disintegrative cultural history. Ellroy's novels, whilst ferociously demystifying the spectacular lifeworld of Los Angeles, do not appear to make that world any more available to the agency of the individual or collective urban eye; on the contrary, the material terrors of history and geography are if anything more destructive of the imperatives of ethics and politics (other than the corrupt variety) than the dazzling signs that conceal them.

Crucially, in the context of this discussion, the destabilising relation of the Quartet's protagonists to the landscape of postwar Los Angeles is played out foremost on the plane of vision. The novels are haunted by a recurring pattern of the mutilation of the eye. Masculine rage and criminal psychosis, frequently directed against women and homosexuals, are fixated on blinding, conflating the power of the Other with their visual capacity. A number of protagonists, notably Danny Upshaw in *The Big Nowhere*, attempt to maintain a hold on their perceptual control over the dizzying scenarios they confront, by deploying specifically visual strategies. Thus Upshaw, thrown into sexual confusion by his arousal before a homosexual orgy he is covertly surveilling, attempts to reassert a masculine vision by becoming 'Man Camera', taking up the forensic science technique of 'screening details from the perpetrator's viewpoint' (p. 94). By thus abstracting his vision from bodily experience, he is able to defer his crisis of sexual definition.

Visuality, then, is the conceptual and material ground of both the dynamic of the urban process, and of the anxieties it generates. It is this dynamic that I wish to explore in a detailed examination of *The Black Dahlia*, arguably the novel most explicitly concerned with the relations between visual agency and urban spectacle. It is perhaps the Quartet's culminating novel, however, *White Jazz*, which most intensely dramatises the peculiar violence of this struggle over vision.[45]

White Jazz is narrated by Dave Klein, a slum landlord, attorney and cop with extensive Mafia connections, involuntarily drawn into a power struggle at the highest levels of the LAPD, between Chief of Detectives Ed Exley and the wholly corrupt Captain Dudley Smith. Initiated in the novel that precedes *White Jazz*, *LA Confidential*, the conflict centres on the ruthless Exley's attempts to thwart Smith's criminal project to attain command of underground markets in the racially and economically 'contained' area of Southside Los Angeles. Smith's machinations are only one example of the Quartet's fascination with the character of urban space as a site of perpetual and violent contestation. To reiterate, these contestations repeatedly take visual form, as Klein comes to discover, during his investigation into the Gothically dysfunctional Kafesjian family, police-protected (and Smith-protected) cornerstone of the Southside narcotics racket. Recruited during the case as an unwitting pawn in Exley's very personal campaign against Smith, Klein becomes a target of Smith's merciless drive to terrorise his adversaries. Thus, when called to a clandestine meeting with Johnny Duhamel, a young 'Exley recruit', to see evidence against Smith in the Kafesjian case, Klein finds himself instead being beaten and drugged by, we later discover, Smith and his henchmen. The latter coerce the drug-addled and delirious Klein into hacking Duhamel to death, and film the act as evidential ammunition against Exley. Klein renders the subsequent experience of watching the film semi-consciously, thus:

> A white screen.
> Cut to:
> Johnny Duhamel naked.
> Cut to:
> Dave Klein swinging a sword: ...
> Cut to:
> Johnny begging – mute sound.
> Cut to:
> Dave Klein thrashing – stabbing, missing. (p. 205)

The breathless montage of images, denoted with an exaggerated economy, conveys a sense of a wholly disempowered vision, divested of the capacity to interpret, or exert control over, the object. Klein witnesses himself as a disembodied image on the screen. The camera, that is, and the film projected on screen, both effect and exhibit Klein's enforced displacement from his own sight, a displacement that constitutes the basis of his consequent, traumatised sense of impotence. Moreover, this literal assault on the eye, enforcing Klein's perceptual shift from subject to object of vision, is rooted in the violent struggle for control over urban space as a source of criminal profiteering.

Smith's exploitation of the anxieties bound up with visuality, however, is motivated by a drive for sexual, as much as economic, power. A part of his extensive project to dominate the criminal networks of Los Angeles is concentrated in the covert filming of sexual couplings, and in the making of absurd B-movies fixated on perverse forms of sexuality (notably incest) to distribute profitably amongst other voyeurs, as well as to power his own fantasies. Smith's voyeurism is a further manifestation of the imperative to power expressed at the level of vision. Furthermore, he is able to tap into the same impulses to visual domination in Klein, when the latter confronts him. 'Watching', he claims, is

> ... a dispensation for all the grand work of containment I'll be doing. I view it as a means to touch compelling filth without succumbing to it.
> FLASH: Lucille nude.
> You're a watcher, lad. You've touched your own dark capacities and now you enjoy the surcease of simple watching.
> FLASH: whore-pad windows. (p. 312)

As the passage demonstrates, Smith's calculating rhetoric works to conjure up voyeuristic images in Klein's mind, and so to throw into relief his destabilised vision. Klein experiences the 'flashes' of female objects caught unawares as blows to his perceptual authority, markers of a disintegrative masculine identity. Smith's more developed voyeuristic impulse, in contrast, is an expression of a ruthlessly objectifying vision, abstracting the covertly observed erotic image from its 'filthy' bodily materiality. The protagonists, then, are clearly conscious of the status of vision as a primary site of contestation over urban power.

It is this consciousness that informs Klein's elaborate revenge against Smith. Klein's plot involves the use of a key informant on Smith's interests in narcotics and pornography, psychotic ex-convict and photographer Wylie Bullock. Bullock's autobiographical confession to Klein, beginning with the shotgun murder of his parents in a tavern by a vagrant crazed and blinded by poisonous bootleg whisky, is a narrative of his insinuation into the heart of the criminal network controlled by Smith and the Kafesjians. He tells of discovering Smith's whitewash as chief investigator of his parents' murder, of witnessing a 'huddled' conference between Smith and J.C. Kafesjian and connecting the former to the bootlegged whisky, of his consequent, and uncoincidental, conviction for peddling pornography, his cultivation of a friendship with Kafesjians' suspected son Richie Herrick, and Herrick's confidences regarding his 'peeping' of his half-sister Lucille. Becoming a voyeur of Richie's incestuous voyeurism, Bullock is inserted into a complex web of visual power relations, presided over by Dudley Smith. His mounting derangement comes to take the form of an internal voice, 'Eyeball Man', telling him how to take revenge against Smith. Taking a job as cameraman on a low-budget vampire movie, financed by gangster Mickey Cohen and backed by Smith's policing authority, he begins, at the behest of 'Eyeball Man', the series of blindings and murders that form the basis of Klein's original investigations, of, first, the Kafesjians' dogs, and, subsequently, their associates, the Herrick family.

In this brief outline of the network of visual relations that informs
the distorted motivations of the principle players in this elaborate
drama of crime and incest can be glimpsed a partial map of the
dynamics of urban power. Smith and J.C. Kafesjian's bootlegged
alcohol is a source of exploitative profiteering that causes an enraged
blindness, able to articulate itself only through random and excessive
violence. Bootlegged alcohol and, later, narcotics, function for
Smith as means of keeping 'Negroes ... dope-sedated' (p. 321), whilst
ensuring that urban rage can be expressed only 'blindly', via random
psychosis that poses no threat to the established social and economic
order. In this respect, Ellroy gives fictional form to the distorted
forms of resistance bound up with, according to Stanley Aronowitz,
the 'crisis in historical materialism'.[46] For Aronowitz, labour's
displacement from 'the logical centre of historical change' (p. 126),
brings into being new and multiplicitous modes of dissent which,
bereft of a determinate position within the hegemony of economic
and political power, are frequently articulated in violent and
incoherent form.

Dudley Smith, as we have seen, later becomes engaged in the
production of a different, less literal kind of visual assault, namely
pornography, which is equally plugged into his intentions to
maintain control over the city's shifting landscape. His awareness
of the political content of vision enables him to preside over the
fraught web of incestuous voyeurism that structures the relations
between the Kafesjian and Herrick children (whose paternity, due
to mutual cuckolding, is uncertain). Smith's understanding of
how power relations are played out visually enables him to
manipulate those relations to his political and economic advantage.
It is only once Bullock is made aware of the crucially visual
inflection of Smith's strategies that he is able to counter them, to
devastating effect. Having wreaked revenge on the Kafesjians and
Herricks, he is prevented from extending his campaign of visual
mutilation to Smith himself only by his arrest. Klein, however, his
own rage fuelled by Smith's filming of his drug-induced murder
of Duhamel, calculatedly lets Bullock loose on his nemesis in a
moment of startlingly graphic violence. Bullock claws and bites
at Smith, screaming 'EYEBALL MAN!', until, as Klein flatly
presents it, he is 'Ripping at his eyes./ Look: One gushing red eye
socket' (p. 333).

White Jazz, then, represents visuality as a terrain fraught with
extraordinary tensions and drives, on which the struggles for social
and economic power, as well as the distorted forms of resistance
to that power, are staged. Bullock's (and Klein's) final act of
vengeance against Smith constitutes a displacement of collective
urban rage to the level of atomised and incoherent psychosis. In
the world of the Quartet, then, the oppositional impulse is locked

into a self-perpetuating crisis of visual violence and domination, and consequently mutates into a mere effect of the grizzly phantasmagoria of urban experience.

The crisis of urban subjectivity dramatised in *White Jazz* is projected initially in the Quartet's opening novel, *The Black Dahlia*. Here, it is tortuously bound up with the post-war phenomenon of Los Angeles' emergent predominance in mass spectacle and land development. An intricate fictionalisation of an actual case, the novel centres on the brutalisation and murder of a young prostitute and aspiring movie star (the titular 'Black Dahlia'). Revealing both the dark web of connections to the murder of a powerful Hollywood developer and his family, and the appropriation of the case as a public spectacle by the press, the novel establishes the complex and highly-charged relation between urban politics and spectacle. Indeed, this relation is thematised before the central murder is discovered, in the events that lead to the narrator, Dwight 'Bucky' Bleichert's assignation to the case.

Bleichert is a former heavyweight boxer turned cop, his apparently solid masculine identity called into question by a reputation for padding his undefeated fight record with victories over synthetically built-up middleweights, and for shopping Japanese friends to the FBI during the war. In the opening pages of the novel, he is offered the prospect of moving from his routinised work as a uniformed traffic cop to a place on the LAPD's Warrants Squad in exchange for participation in a match with a fellow former boxer already on Warrants, Sergeant Lee Blanchard. The contest is the proposition of Machiavellian District Attorney, Ellis Loew, who sees in it the potential to employ spectacle as a means of drawing back public enthusiasm for a police force whose battered reputation, after revelations of wartime corruption, has rather muddied the prospect of winning the forthcoming vote over Proposition B, to allocate greater financial resources to it. As Loew himself puts it, 'We need to build up morale within the Department, and we need to impress the voters with the quality of our men. Wholesome white boxers are a big draw ...' (p. 28). The ensuing local media frenzy once the contest is announced, projecting a prototype American showdown between Blanchard, 'Mr. Fire', 'the poet of brute strength', and Bleichert, 'Mr. Ice', 'the counter poet of speed and guile' (p. 26), effectively displays the interlocking mechanisms of urban political interests and media spectacle. The boxing match organised for popular entertainment serves as a means of augmenting economically the power of the police, in a disturbingly literal realisation of mass spectacle's function as a regulatory social force.

The context for this burgeoning relation between the politics and spectacle of the city is elaborated by Bleichert, shortly before the discovery of Elizabeth Short's corpse. In the hard-boiled descriptive vocabulary characteristic of Ellroy's acute noir pastiche, Bleichert remarks that,

> The district's main drag ... spelled 'postwar boom' like a neon sign. Every block from Jefferson to Leimert was lined with dilapidated, once grand houses being torn down, their facades being replaced by giant billboards advertising department stores, jumbo shopping centres, kiddie parks and movie theatres ... it hit me that by 1950 this part of L.A. would be unrecognizable. (p. 77)

Bleichert's figuration of the landscape of the postwar boom as a 'neon sign' aptly designates the peculiarly spectacular character of the new urban dynamic. The drama that proceeds will be intimately bound up with this process of creative destruction that will bring the new object-world of urban consumer culture (department stores, amusement parks and cinemas), predicated on the deployment of spectacle, into being. Indeed, the centrality of spectacle to this new urban space is prefigured in the use of 'giant billboards' to 'advertise' the alluring consumerist future, the emergent 'kaleidoscopic' city that defines, for Edward Soja, the decentred logic of postmodernity. The semiotics of the new urbanity come across as Benjaminian 'wish images' divested of their dialectical charge, their utopian energy absorbed wholesale by the marketing strategies of the entrepeneurial developers. The new spaces, furthermore, are crucially 'feminine', foregrounding the pleasures of domestic consumption, 'family' leisure and, in the case of the movie theatres, female spectatorship. Their destabilising effect on masculine identity is, then, bound up with their dazzling appearance as floating signs 'unmoored', to use Soja's term, from any material foundations.

It is significant that Bleichert registers these seismic shifts in urban form just prior to the unearthing, on 39th Street and Norton Avenue, of the corpse that will haunt the remainder of the novel. Elizabeth Short's murder is a bleak narrative of the insertion of a young woman into this kaleidoscopic new space, graphically enacting the violent inversion of the utopian individualism (with its fantasies of stardom and romance) intrinsic to Hollywood. Caught, as we gradually discover, in the network of destructive mechanisms of urban development and spectacle, and the startlingly destabilised forms of familial, gender and sexual identity that they generate, her murder is a terrible emblem of the underside of the new Los Angeles. Bleichert's unsparingly clinical description of the mutilated corpse potently communicates this sense of urban shock. Cut in half at the waist, he notes that,

A large triangle had been gouged out of the left thigh ... the flaps
of skin behind the gash were pulled back; there were no organs
inside ... the breasts were dotted with cigarette burns, the right
one hanging loose ... the girl's face ... was one huge purpled
bruise, the nose crushed deep into the facial cavity, the mouth
cut ear to ear into a smile that leered up at you, somehow
mocking the rest of the brutality inflicted. (p. 87)

The excesses of brutalisation documented here take on a particularly
disturbing resonance in the context of an allegorical reading of Los
Angeles. Elizabeth Short, as we find in the pages that follow, has
aspired to the realisation of the full catalogue of 'wish images'
projected by Hollywood. That is, she seeks to become that object
of consumer desire and mass veneration, the screen goddess, which
most embodies the new logic of urban spectacle. This 'feminine'
object-world has been a consistent repository of masculine anxiety
and rage in postmodern American fiction; in the above passage can
be glimpsed the accumulated force of that rage, concentrated in
the image of a single female body. It is perhaps the grotesque leer
of the mouth, a taunting distortion of the smiling female object,
that most graphically conveys this sense of viciously inverted
fantasy. Betty Short's corpse, that is, potently enacts the graphic
fragmentation of the feminine wrought by postmodernity's allegorical
crisis of seeing.

The Short murder's brutality is not, however, incommensurable
with its potential for political appropriation. On the contrary, it is
just its intimations of unconstrained and unaccountable evil that
render it so expedient an urban political spectacle. As Blanchard
puts it, attempting to persuade Bleichert of its value in career
terms, 'It's a showcase ... to show the voters that passing the bond
issue got them a bulldog police force' (p. 92). The consequent
politicised packaging of the case as a display of the dangerous
forces at large in the city, and of the imperative to contain them,
is predicated on its crude narrative construction via the media. This
elision of the case's complex inflections, in favour of a symbolic
narrative of good and evil for easy public consumption, is tellingly
figured in Bleichert's image of Ellis Loew before the radio
microphones. As the latter speaks to his listeners of the 'vivisection
of a lovely young woman', Bleichert notes the American Legion
poppy on his lapel, and remarks that it was probably bought from
'the wino legionnaire who slept in the hall of records parking lot –
a man he had once vigorously prosecuted for vagrancy' (p. 102).
The poppy serves as a potent allegorical image; a 'wish image' of
collective memory and meaning in its outward display, and a
counterimage, as Bleichert reveals, of a latent material history of
urban power and domination. Indeed, it reads as a historical and

geographical mutation of Benjamin's counterimages (the vagrant, for example) of the spectacular facades of Hausmann's Paris. The Black Dahlia is to become another 'flower' charged by this dialectic of collective spectacle (the 'glamorous siren headed for Hollywood stardom' (p. 147), constructed by the 'official' media narrative of her life and death), and urban power (the actual network of material forces – developers, policemen and pornographers – embroiled in her murder). Loew's function is to efface the doubleness of her image, to refuse any information that might counter its transparency.

Bleichert's investigation takes him through the range of Los Angeles subcultures and institutions that have impacted on Short's life and death, from the lesbian bars of Crenshaw Boulevard and seedy rented rooms of aspiring starlets, to the monied and elite spaces of the Sprague family and the Hughes empire. His inquiries yield an increasingly convoluted map of Short's place in these interlocking urban spaces, one that shatters her media image as an unwitting and innocent victim of a cruelly indifferent city. Questioning a fellow aspirant actress and former roommate, Sheryl Saddon, he learns of the significance of the black clothing that has earned Short her popular sobriquet. Saddon tells Bleichert of Betty Short's compulsive lying, which would extend to her explanations of her three-day absences, her 'marriages' to war heroes, and her donning of black outfits 'because her father died or because she was mourning the boys who died in the war' (p. 123; her father, we have already learned, is alive). The black clothing is also 'a gimmick to impress casting directors' (p. 123), and so serves in more than one way as a marker of elusiveness and guile.

The image of the Black Dahlia thus emerges with increasing force as a literally and figuratively dark 'shadow' of the luminous spectacle of Los Angeles' 'dreamworld'. Indeed, the gathering storm of revelations about Short's final days renders Ellis Loew's public projection of a 'lovely young girl' frustratingly difficult to sustain. Short emerges as an embodiment of Buci-Glucksmann's allegorical feminine, 'seraphic and hell-black by turns' (p. 78). The mass spectacle of the feminine, available to easy consumption in its officially sanctioned form, becomes dangerously destabilising of this hegemonic illusion as its inverted double. As a signifier of promiscuity and deceit, and a repository of masculine desire, anxiety and rage, 'black' is the violently material negative of Hollywood's immaterial spectacles.

The catalogue of atrocities wrought on Short's body by Ramona Sprague and the other members of her family is the culminating articulation of the uncontainable rage generated by the projection of crisis-ridden sexual and gender identities on to this inverted image. Part of the novel's profoundly unsettling effect, however, is derived from the way in which the crisis of gender that the Black Dahlia's image embodies is replicated in the policemen investigating her murder. Both Bleichert and Blanchard experience the accumulating evidence surrounding the murder as an assault on their sexual integrity. As they discover the many layers of sordid exploitation that mark Betty Short's last days, she becomes for each of them a tortuously elusive female object, bringing to the surface the anxieties at the heart of their relation to the urban spectacle. Moreover, this conflict between masculine subject and feminine object is once more played out directly on the plane of the visual, most notably during the scene in which the policemen assigned to the case watch a pornographic film in which Short appears. The film is shot in 'grainy black and white', on a pastiche ancient Egyptian film set (which, as I shall show, will emerge as central to the murder), and reveals her 'wearing only stockings and doing an inept hoochie-koochie dance' (p. 180). Bleichert goes on to describe how his 'groin clenched' (p. 180), whilst Blanchard, after witnessing simulated and enforced lesbian sex between Short and a younger girl, 'stood in front of the screen, blinking from the hot white light in his eyes. He wheeled round and ripped the obscenity down ...' (p. 181).

The 'hot white light' that obscures Blanchard's field of vision is an apposite figuration of the effect of the film itself. Blanchard's response to the film is an expression less of moral outrage than of his own implication in the misogynistic violence displayed on screen and in the corrupt formations that produce it. The novel goes on to reveal him as tied to organised crime and, more important, a suppressor of crucial evidence in the Short case. Blanchard, we climactically learn, knew the identity of her murderer, and of the complex circumstances surrounding her affair with Madeleine Sprague and eventual murder. Unbeknownst to Bleichert, a tantalising clue to these circumstances is visible in the film, namely the set. The set is the backdrop to a Keystone Cops movie, whose real-life creator, Mack Sennet, is a business partner of the fictionalised developer, Emmett Sprague. Sprague and Sennett are engaged in a joint venture to develop the Hollywood Hills and the set is housed in property owned by the former. The labyrinthine web of relations that ties Short's torture and murder to this development project is clarified when Bleichert sees Sprague's 'Assistant Director' credit at the end of the Keystone Cops movie. The significance of this relation between property speculation and the film industry is displayed in the implicitly doubled status of the set as an emblem of both dominant Hollywood culture and its violently twisted progeny. The pornographic film compels Blanchard to recognise how these apparent polarities inhere in one another; mainstream spectacle is exposed as parasitic on a hidden history of misogyny and economic exploitation. His secret knowledge of this history is expressed by his inarticulable rage before the film that bears witness to it, and by the temporary 'blindness' he experiences in the face of the light that projects it. Blanchard's characteristic swagger, a mark of controlled and confident masculine embodiment, is here reduced to a quivering absence of control, encapsulated by his loss of vision in standing up before the screen. The shadow world that haunts the abstracted images of mass spectacle, is experienced by Blanchard as a crisis of masculinity.

Madeleine Sprague's history is similarly bound up with Betty Short's, as an occasional lover, seduced in the lesbian bars of Crenshaw Boulevard, and as the provider of the Egyptian film set for the pornographic film. She also procures Short for George Tilden, her father's disfigured and disturbed business partner; it is this encounter with Tilden that leads to Betty's prolonged torture and murder. Madeleine also emerges as Blanchard's murderer, motivated by the imperative to silence the one individual who knows the Sprague family's role in the Short case. Finally, her striking resemblance to Short leads to her compulsive imitation of her around the seedy bars of 8th Street. Madeleine, in her connections to her father's corrupt development interests, in her own dark sexual pathology (including an ongoing affair with Emmett) and in her obsessive transformations into the Black Dahlia, comes to represent Short in distorted form, foregrounding the disruptive forces that would conspire in her murder. Madeleine, that is, becomes the Black Dahlia divested of the utopian individualism that had characterised Betty Short's naive hankering for stardom, and so reduced to an emblem of the destabilising new urbanity generated by the likes of Emmett Sprague.

Drawn into an affair with Madeleine, as a means, for her, of ensuring his silence in the face of revelations of her family's involvement, Bleichert's relation to her becomes increasingly haunted by the Black Dahlia's shadowy sexual presence. This experience of Madeleine as Betty is registered visually, when he describes how, in the midst of a sexual clinch, '... I made Madeleine Betty – made her eyes blue instead of hazel, made her body Betty's body from the stag film, made her silently mouth, "No, please"' (pp. 210–11).

The transmutations that Bleichert witnesses tauntingly elude his perceptual control. Betty, as an interruptive female object, almost literally invades his field of vision; an object that embodies simultaneously the abstracted fantasies of pornography and the misogynistic force (Betty mouthing 'No, please') that brings those fantasies into being. Madeleine's interchangeability with Betty, then, becomes a further expression of the deceptive logic of feminised urbanity that threatens the integrity of Bleichert's masculinity. If Madeleine functions as the active, conscious representative of particular material interests and processes (the Sprague family and their development projects), and Betty as the hapless victim of those processes, the two women nevertheless constitute for Bleichert an interlocking articulation of the city. This doubleness is as profoundly disorientating for Bleichert as for Blanchard, for the same reason that it displays both the dazzling 'wish imagery' of urban spectacle, and the destructive material processes that produce it. Once masculine sexual identity is confronted by the relentless dynamic of an urbanity that eludes its visual control (as figured by the interchangeable images of Madeleine and Betty), it is predictably traumatised. Bleichert's mounting obsession with the case and the young woman at its centre, and its destructive effects on his marriage, career and mental stability, all bear witness to this trauma.

The articulation of violent misogyny via Ellroy's recurrent trope of blinding, identified already in *White Jazz*, provides further evidence of the profoundly deranged masculinity that drives the events of the novel. The perpetrator of this assault on sight in *The Black Dahlia* is Fritz Vogel, a corrupt cop attached to the Short murder case. Vogel and his son Johnny (also a cop) themselves come under suspicion of the murder when Bleichert traces Johnny as the client of a prostitution job during the 'missing' days prior to Betty's death. Questioning Sally Stinson, Betty's mentor in the business, he learns of the incident that had Vogel transferred from Administrative Vice squad. Believing he had caught syphilis from a black prostitute, Vogel '"... shook down a house in Watts and made all the girls do him before he took the cure. He made them rub his thing in their eyes, and two of the girls went blind"' (p. 251). The structure of domination that characterises visual relations between masculine subject and feminine object is here almost unpalatably literalised. The syphilitic policeman embodies masculine authority at the limits of dislocation, whilst the black prostitutes function as a degraded repository of his rage. If, for Benjamin and Buci-Glucksmann, Baudelaire's prostitute constitutes the most potent counterimage of the dazzling dreamworld of the modern metropolis, the prostitute's blinding at the hands of a sadistic policeman can be read as a bleak narrative of the fate of that counterimage in the landscape of postwar Los Angeles. Here, the final degradation of the female object's agency takes the form of a viciously enforced eradication of sight and, implicitly, of the capacity to negotiate the predicament of displacement that the experience of prostitution brings about.

In the crisis-ridden masculinity that plagues the cop protagonists of *The Black Dahlia*, and the Quartet in general, then, can be read the monumental shift in the visual logic of Los Angeles wrought by the city's postwar boom. The grandiose images of early modern

Paris, from the arcades to the World's Fairs, dialectical symbols, for Benjamin, of both shattering economic power and utopian social hope, have become, in Ellroy's Los Angeles, kaleidoscopic neon abstractions enshrining perpetual consumer desire and naturalising the urban 'dreamworld' of modern commodity culture. If Benjamin describes the subjective experience of modern Paris as one of 'shock', the subjectivity produced by postwar Los Angeles might be termed a kind of 'hypershock', a hypertrophied anxiety before an object-world that seems to resist and destabilise the eye. This new, traumatised subjectivity is clearly tied to the increasingly pervasive figuration of the landscape of mass spectacle as feminine, as exemplified by Ellroy's protagonists, whose experience of urban change is concentrated in their relations with women. The bodily agency of the city's policemen, supposedly the most controlled and authoritative urban subjects, appears to have been possessed by the invasive forces of mass spectacle that the Black Dahlia and the Sprague family encapsulate.

The Sprague family presides over these violent mutations in the landscape of Los Angeles. Characterised by a kind of Gothic hyper-dysfunctionality that takes in adultery, incest and murder, the Spragues' intricate web of connections to the Short case emerges in a startling procession of revelations during the climactic pages of the novel. As Betty Short's torture and murder is discovered by Bleichert to have taken place in one of the shacks in the Hollywood Hills built by Emmett Sprague, and owned in conjunction with Mack Sennett, the links forged by the novel, between Emmett's corrupt development project, the emergent visual dominance of Hollywood spectacle and the Short murder, converge on a particularly charged flashpoint in the approach to the climax. Bleichert is called urgently by Harry Sears, a fellow investigator, to examine the recently stumbled-upon cinderblock hut in which Betty Short spent her last days. His walk through the dense scrubland of the hills is coloured by the image of, quite literally, the birth of Hollywood, that is, by the execution of Mack Sennett's plan to remove the last four letters of the 'Hollywoodland' sign that hovers over his tract, and so to project to the world perhaps the most enduring emblem of the long and dense history of Los Angeles spectacle.

Bleichert, then, is confronted by a double image of urban development. On the one hand, he sees the phantasmagoric mass spectacle of the sign, accompanied by a band striking up 'Hooray for Hollywood', and a crowd of gawking 'rubberneckers ... and political types' (p. 338), and on the other, its secret and blood-drenched underside. The hut is a grotesquely inverted phantasmagoria, with its side walls 'papered with pornographic photographs of crippled and disfigured women ... a mattress on the floor ... caked with layers and layers of blood ... close-up shots

of diseased organs oozing blood and pus' (p. 338). Crucially, both
the abstracted spectacle of the Hollywood sign and its unpalatably
visceral negative looming beneath, are tied to the same economic
force, namely Emmett Sprague's development interests. The
playing of 'There's No Business Like Show Business' that provides
the musical score to the disappearance of the fourth and final letter
takes on a bitterly doubled charge when counterpointed by the
images of butchery lurking beneath the sign. This confrontation
with the perverse visual dynamics of Hollywood is experienced by
Bleichert as the extreme limit of urban shock, in which the most
potent global image of the mass cultural urban 'dreamworld' is
brought into startling conjunction with its counterimage of bodily
mutilation. These parallel images thus encapsulate the postwar
period's doubled developmental logic, a logic generative of both
the official narrative projected by urban spectacle and the counternarrative articulated by the intensely destabilised gender identity
violently figured in the corpse of Elizabeth Short.

The pages that remain are taken up with Bleichert's interrogations
of Madeleine and Emmett and, finally, Ramona Sprague, by means
of establishing the bizarre events, resentments and desires that
result in the identification of the latter as Short's murderer. These
confrontations clarify explicitly the dysfunctional familial relations
underlying the murder of Elizabeth Short, as well as the private and
public phenomena that help to produce them. The first of these
highly fraught interviews begins after Bleichert walks in on Madeleine
and Emmett fondling one another whilst engaged in a discussion
about the latter's mounting legal problems. These centre on the
approaching grand jury probe into his health and safety violations
in building houses with poor materials and shoddy workmanship.
Bleichert has established that Short has been murdered in one of
these houses, apparently by Emmett's friend George Tilden. When
he confronts Emmett with the accusation against Tilden, the
former is persuaded to give an account of his relationship with the
latter. Tilden, his former army comrade and business partner, he
reveals, is the natural father of Madeleine, the result of an affair
with Ramona after Emmett had refused to provide her with a
child. After discovering Tilden to be Madeleine's father, he 'played
tic-tac-toe on his face' (p. 345) with a knife, leaving him permanently
disfigured, and went on to show remorse by finding him work tending
his property and hauling garbage for the city. He goes on to tell of
George's fascination for internal organs, and of his own obligation
to George for his role in saving his life during the war. Madeleine
goes on to confess how this burden of obligation led to her procuring
Betty Short for Tilden, after the latter has been aroused by watching
Betty in the pornographic film made, with Madeleine's permission,
in one of Emmett's vacant houses (on Mack Sennett's Egyptian

film set). Both Madeleine and George insist that they had no suspicion of George's murderous tendencies. They also excuse their own apparently incestuous relationship on the basis of Madeleine's true paternity.

In these confessions to Bleichert can be excavated the interlocking crises of gender, sexuality and the family inscribed into the processes of urban restructuring in which Emmett so actively participates. His corrupt manoeuvres in property speculation, executed in conjunction with the power elite of the film industry, give rise to the skewed relations and impulses that culminate in the Black Dahlia murder. George and Emmett begin their (Scottish) immigrant lives as friends, a relationship that turns bitter when Emmett is obliged to George after being hidden by him under a pile of German corpses during an incident in combat (during World War I), and consequently escaping death. George's secret knowledge of Emmett's cowardice acts as a taunting drain on the latter's masculine identity, compounded when he is cuckolded by the same man who saved his life. His masculinity is further destabilised when George and Ramona direct and film Madeleine, her sister Martha, and their friends, in a series of macabre pageants symbolically reenacting Emmett's various acts of corruption, including the collapse of his shacks in the earthquake of 1933, as well as his desperate crawling beneath German corpses. Emmett's occupation as a contractor and emerging heavyweight in the Los Angeles property market of the 1920s, then, quickly becomes a source of marital estrangement, resulting in Ramona's affair with George. Emmett's consequent relation to George, precariously combining uncontainable rage with guilty obligation, expresses a radically destabilised masculine subjectivity. This subjectivity is registered very visibly in George's disfigured face, as well as in Emmett's anxious assumption of the obligation to find George work on city maintenance projects. George's existence, that is, serves as a taunting marker of the new, profoundly unsettled masculinity brought into being by Emmett's role in the shifting urban landscape. His would-be incestuous, if unconsummated, relation to Madeleine, and increasing neglect of Ramona, further mark the penetration of this disrupted masculine identity into the arena of the family, culminating in the calamitous events of January 1947.

The Black Dahlia murder constitutes the final convergence of the crises of sexual and familial identity experienced by Madeleine, George and Ramona, on the body of Elizabeth Short. These crises, to reiterate, are produced by, and played out on, the dislocated terrain of Emmett's corrupt property holdings, and are registered in explicitly visual forms. Thus, Madeleine's narcissistic obsession with her resemblance to Short leads to their affair, and to her eventual provision of her father and Mack Sennett's film set and property for the making of a pornographic film. Her manipulative exploitation of the Black Dahlia persona to entrap Bleichert after the murder demonstrates her consciousness of its capacity to unsettle masculine sexual and epistemological authority. George's covert voyeuristic pleasure in the making of the film, meanwhile, results in his blackmailing of Emmett, demanding sex with Short in exchange for his silence over 'the family's sordid past and present' (p. 369). Emmett's reluctant consent to the terms is overheard by Ramona, whose explosive resentment is finally realised when Betty Short arrives at the Sprague house on January 12 for her liaison with George. George's spurning of Ramona's advances is now bitterly compounded by his lust for a girl who 'looked so much like Madeleine that it felt that the cruelest of jokes was being played on her' (p. 369). Betty's resemblance to her and George's own child, that is, acts as a taunting visual embodiment of her own displacement by the processes of urban change in which Emmett has invested his masculine identity. If Madeleine is the direct product of that displacement, Betty is its haunting shadow and replication (George is fixated on her to the exclusion of Ramona), and as such draws out the incendiary rage accumulated through the years of her husband's corrupt speculations. It is no coincidence, furthermore, that the liaison that eclipses her own sexual presence takes place in 'one of his [Emmett's] abandoneds on North Beechwood' (p. 369). It is in this dilapidated residue of Emmett's early ventures into Los Angeles real estate that Ramona determines to reverse her experience as displaced object by violently transposing that status on to Betty Short.

The torturous mutilations to which Ramona subjects Betty, after breaking in on the couple and knocking her unconscious with a baseball bat (as well as persuading George to consent to her torture by promising him her extracted internal organs), become symbolic inscriptions of this rage. When Short's corpse is driven by George and Ramona to 39th and Norton '– a lot that Georgie used to tend for the city' (p. 370), the collapse of the Benjaminian 'wish image' that Betty represented in life, into the 'ruin' of consumer culture that her corpse has become, is complete. The fatally mutilated prostitute and aspiring movie star, lying on the city street tended by an accessory to her murder, and presumably developed by the murderer's husband, tears apart, like the prostitutes of Baudelaire's poetry, the harmonising pretensions of the new urbanity embodied in Mack Sennett's 'Hollywood' sign. The corpse palpably underscores the resistance of postwar urban history's counterimages to narrative resolution. Bleichert's (counter)narrative demonstrates rather its own failure to make sense of the disintegrative history which results in the Short murder.

The Black Dahlia, then, and indeed, the LA Quartet as a whole, reveals the degraded counterimages which shadow the 'official' images of urban spectacle. Despite the relentless identification of the material forces of politics and economics at work in the construction of Los Angeles' dazzling facade, however, there is little sense that history and geography can illuminate a path of resistance to urban domination. The implacable dynamics of urban change paralyse any gesture towards political or ethical opposition. Embodiment is reduced by the unremitting processes of urban change to an enraged masculine subjectivity, more often directed towards the brutalisation of women, who function as repositories of male hysteria, than towards identifiable forces of political and economic power. The interpenetrative dynamics of history and geography, though potently dramatised, are divested of any utopian charge. Ellroy's fiction thus interrogates the crisis of perception produced by the displacement of the detective as narrative master-subject.

Didion and Ellroy offer very different responses to the crises in visual relations that Los Angeles generates. Both foreground a spectacular urbanity whose ceaselessly transformative development has reversed the perceptual relations of urban subject and object, engendering a crisis of visual authority. Didion negotiates this crisis by way of a melancholic resignation to the impotence of the gaze in the face of the city. Ellroy's protagonists, in contrast, driven by a hypertrophied will to penetrate the city's criminal history, are forced to confront the destabilising surfeit of meanings that lie buried beneath its spectacular surface. If Didion's tendency is to abstract the urban subject's relation to time and history, Ellroy's is rather to situate that subject in a history that is implacably overdetermined, rendered illegible by the sheer weight of the material forces which have shaped it. Both writers, however, seem reluctant to see the reversibility of visual relations engendered by the city as a condition for the activation of politics and ethics. Postmodern Los Angeles thus emerges as what Buci-Glucksmann terms a 'Catastrophist Space', a site at which the agency of the eye is irreversibly paralysed. In figuring Los Angeles as a site at which the privileged vantage-point of the master-subject is untenable, however, each writer unwittingly opens up a very Benjaminian question: might not the catastrophe of the urban eye be a condition for the activation of new forms of critical vision?

Conclusion

The critical energy buried within the figuration of postmodernity's 'catastrophic' culture of spectacle has been a central concern
of this book. With this concern in mind, I have aimed to be alert
throughout to the incongruities, as well as homologies, between
theoretical and fictional negotiations of postmodern spectacle. In
particular, where my theoretical model identifies, in postmodernity's displacement of the narrating eye, the condition for a mobile
and situated cultural politics, my readings in fiction suggest the lived
experience of that displacement to be one of anxiety, melancholy
and rage. There is little sense, in any of the six very different writers
discussed, of a positive relation to the postmodern lifeworld. It is
above all in conceptualising these incongruities that I have been
informed by, and indebted to, the critical vision of Walter Benjamin,
for it is in Benjamin that catastrophe and redemption emerge as
the two sides of consumer spectacle's coin. His essay on Baudelaire,
for example, far from eliding the rage and despair with which the
poet envisions Hausmann's Paris, finds in this response precisely
that perceptual acuity which could penetrate the space and time
of 'the victors'.[1]

I have taken up Benjamin's interpretative strategies in my attempts
to mobilise the allegorical impulse of postmodern American fiction
for a critical politics of vision. Each writer foregrounds the precarious
position of the narrating eye in the face of America's proliferating
lifeworld of spectacle. As a critic, however, I have been concerned
not to read these thematics of perceptual trauma as mere degraded
symptoms of spectacle's systemic power. Rather, I have looked to
the cultural and political horizons that this trauma might open up.
In particular, the object's power to withstand the subjective gaze,
so persistently figured by the writing discussed, presages a new
reversibility of visual relations, one that positions the eye in a
dialogic and mobile relation to its lifeworld. In this way, the
phantasmagoria of consumer culture reveals its buried utopian
energy and allegory's melancholic gaze becomes simultaneously a
critical one. This transformative energy is released most potently
on the plane of gender; the crisis of perceptual control I have
attempted to trace enacts the failure of the masculine gaze to
contain and fix its feminine object. Allegory's interruptive force,

as Christine Buci-Glucksmann has shown, finds its exemplary embodiment in the deceptive, ambiguous figure of Woman.[2]

Thus, Norman Mailer's fetish of the body as a locus of existential authenticity yields increasingly, over the course of his career, to the destabilising ambiguity of mass culture, or, in his own terms, to the 'womanisation' of America.[3] Cinematographic writing, in turn, dramatises a crisis of the perceptual opposition of subject and object, in which the unreadable force of the 'feminine' eludes and explodes the masculine narrator's optic control. Finally, postmodern Los Angeles' feminised mass cultural landscape produces an intensely disintegrative vision, registered by Didion in the form of narrative arrest and by Ellroy in the traumatised eyes of his protagonists.

These 'catastrophic' interruptions of visual authority speak to the imperative to construct new ways of seeing, which refuse both the abstracted vantage-point of the master-subject and the victimised perspective of the object. Postmodern American writing, in dramatising the erosion of visual authority engendered by mass spectacle, opens us to the path of vision's potential reinvention. My critical aim has been to help illuminate that path.

Notes

N.B.: Throughout the notes, where two dates are given, the first denotes the date of original publication, the second the date of the edition used.

Introduction

1. The phrase, of course, is the title of Guy Debord's seminal polemic, *Society of the Spectacle* (1967; Detroit, MI: Black and Red Press, 1993).
2. Of other work in the field, Samuel Coale, *In Hawthorne's Shadow* (Lexington, KY: University of Kentucky Press, 1988) has perhaps come closest to the deployment of a visual model, but its literary-historical formalism puts it at some distance from the concerns foregrounded here. Two other texts have addressed the visualities of American fiction: Rachel Bowlby's study of literary naturalism and the growth of commodity culture, *Just Looking* (London: Methuen, 1985) has a chapter on Dreiser; Carolyn Porter's study of nineteenth-century and modernist American fiction, *Seeing and Being* (Middletown, CT: Wesleyan University Press, 1981) is a Lukacsian inquiry into the problem of reification in Emerson, James, Adams and Faulkner. Whilst both these texts have been suggestive, they are both historically and methodologically divergent from the present study.
3. Jean Baudrillard, *America* (1986; trans. Chris Turner, London: Verso, 1992).
4. Jean Baudrillard, *Le Guerre de Golfe n'y a pas a lieu* (Paris: Gallimard, 1991).
5. For further elaboration of this argument, see Chapter 1 below, as well as David M. Levin (ed.), *Modernity and the Hegemony of Vision* (Berkeley, CA: University of California Press, 1993) and Martin Jay, *Downcast Eyes* (Berkeley, CA; Oxford: University of California Press, 1993).
6. Richard Godden, *Fictions of Capital* (Cambridge: Cambridge University Press, 1990).
7. On the relation between mass culture and the 'feminine', see Andreas Huyssen, *After the Great Divide* (Basingstoke: Macmillan, 1986), and Christine Buci-Glucksmann, *Baroque Reason: The Aesthetics of Modernity* (1984, trans. Patrick Camiller, London: Sage, 1994).
8. Craig Owens, 'The allegorical impulse: toward a theory of postmodernism' and 'The allegorical impulse, part 2', in S. Bryson *et al.* (eds), *Beyond Recognition* (Berkeley, CA: University of California Press, 1992).

9. Benjamin's concept of 'porosity' is expounded in 'Naples' (1925), in *One-Way Street and Other Writings* (1978; trans. Edmund Jephcott and Kingsley Shorter, London: Verso, 1992).

10. Martin Jay, *Downcast Eyes* (1993).

Chapter 1

1. A similar position on Baudrillard is worked out in Hal Foster, *Recodings* (Seattle, WA: Bay Press, 1985).

2. Jean Baudrillard, *Simulations* (1976; trans. Paul Foss, Paul Patton and Philip Beitchman, New York, NY: Semiotext(e), 1983), p. l0.

3. Douglas Kellner, *Jean Baudrillard: From Marxism to Postmodernism and Beyond* (Oxford: Polity Press, 1989), p. 155.

4. Jean Baudrillard, *Symbolic Exchange and Death* (1976; trans. Iain Hamilton Grant, London: Sage, 1993), p. 18.

5. For an interesting account of this genealogy, see Jean-Philippe Mathy, *Extreme-Occident: French Intellectuals and America* (Chicago, IL: University of Chicago Press, 1993).

6. Walter Benjamin, 'Theses on the philosophy of history' (1950) in *Illuminations* (1955; trans. Harry Zohn, London: Fontana, 1992); see also in *Illuminations* 'The storyteller' (1936) and 'The image of Proust' (1929).

7. Christine Buci-Glucksmann, *Baroque Reason: The Aesthetics of Modernity* (1984; trans. Patrick Camiller, London: Sage, 1994); Craig Owens, 'The allegorical impulse: toward a theory of postmodernism' and 'The allegorical impulse, part 2' in L. Tillman *et al.* (eds), *Beyond Recognition* (Berkeley, CA: University of California Press, 1992).

8. Richard Godden, *Fictions of Capital* (Cambridge: Cambridge University Press, 1990).

9. Peter Nicholls, 'Violence, recognition, and some versions of modernism', in *Parataxis* no. 4, summer, 1993, p. 25.

10. Guy Debord, *Society of the Spectacle* (1967; Detroit, MI: Black and Red Press, 1983), para 4.

11. Dale Carter, *The Final Frontier* (London: Verso, 1988).

12. David Harvey, *The Condition of Postmodernity* (Oxford: Blackwell, 1992).

13. Hal Foster, *Recodings* (1985).

14. Anthony Woodiwiss, *Postmodernity USA* (London: Sage, 1993).

15. Walter Benjamin, 'The storyteller' (1936) in *Illuminations* (1955; 1992).

16. See especially Maurice Merleau-Ponty, *The Phenomenology of Perception* (1945; trans. Colin Smith, London: Routledge, 1992).

17. Friedrich Nietzsche, *Thus Spoke Zarathustra* (1885; trans. R. J. Hollingdale, Harmondsworth: Penguin, 1991).

18. Gary Shapiro, 'In the shadows of philosophy: Nietzsche and the question of vision' in D.M. Levin (ed.), *Modernity and the Hegemony of Vision* (Berkeley, CA: University of California Press, 1993).

19. Martin Heidegger, 'The age of the world picture' (1938) in W. Lovitt (ed.), *The Question Concerning Technology and Other Essays* (New York, NY: Harper and Row, 1977).

20. Maurice Merleau-Ponty, *Phenomenology of Perception*.

21. Maurice Merleau-Ponty, 'Concerning Marxism' (1945) and 'Marxism and philosophy' (1946), in *Sense and Non-Sense* (trans. Hubert L. Dreyfus and P.A. Dreyfus, Evanston, IL: Northwestern University Press, 1991), p. 120.

22. Walter Benjamin, 'Theses on the philosophy of history' (1950) in *Illuminations*.

23. Walter Benjamin, 'Surrealism' (1929), in *One-Way Street and Other Writings* (1978, trans. Edmund Jephcott and Kingsley Shorter, London: Verso, 1992).

24. Martin Jay, 'The disenchantment of the eye: surrealism and the crisis of ocularcentrism', in L. Taylor (ed.), *Visualizing Theory* (London: Routledge, 1994, reprinted from Jay's own *Downcast Eyes* (1993)), p. 185.

25. Michael Taussig, 'Physiognomic aspects of visual worlds', in L. Taylor (ed.) *Visualizing Theory*, p. 169.

26. Stanley Aronowitz, *The Crisis in Historical Materialism* (New York, NY: J.F. Bergin, 1983).

27. Homi Bhabha, *The Location of Culture* (London: Routledge, 1994).

28. Susan Buck-Morss, *The Dialectics of Seeing: Walter Benjamin and the Arcades Project* (Cambridge, MA: MIT Press, 1993).

29. Walter Benjamin, *The Origins of German Tragic Drama* (1962; trans. John Osborne, London: Verso, 1992).

30. I am thinking here especially of Paul de Man's *Allegories of Reading* (New Haven: Yale University Press, 1979) as well as his essay *The Rhetoric of Temporality in Blindness and Insight* (1971; Minneapolis: University of Minnesota Press, 1983). Deborah L. Madsen's recently published study, *Allegory in America: From Puritanism to Postmodernism* (Basingstoke: Macmillan, 1996) draws much on de Man for its reading of postmodern American fiction, as well as, more generally, a tradition of American rhetorical studies exemplified by the likes of Sacvan Bercovich and Larzer Ziff. There is much in Madsen's work that converges with the present study – for example, the argument that the modern allegorical image reveals and exploits a gap between the realms of appearance and reality, and that postmodern allegorical language is established within and through a discontinuous temporality. The founding premises of our respective projects are rather different, however: Madsen's intention is to locate postmodern allegory within a much broader genealogy of rhetoric rooted in 'ancient Hellenistic and Roman cultures' (p. 5). As will now be clear, the model of allegory developed here is less formally specific. Rather than reading texts as interventions in the trajectory of a literary form, I want to posit allegory, following Benjamin, as the articulation of a historically specific crisis of seeing.

31. The large number of studies of 'self-reflexiveness' in postmodern fiction include Linda Hutcheon, *Narcissistic Narrative* (London: Methuen, 1986); Patricia Waugh, *Metafiction* (London: Methuen, 1984); and Brian McHale's more comprehensive *Postmodernist Fiction* (London: Routledge, 1986).

32. Robert Coover, 'The babysitter' in *Pricksongs and Descants* (1969; London: Picador, 1971).

33. Christine Buci-Glucksmann, *Baroque Reason*; Peter Nicholls, 'Divergences: modernism, postmodernism, Jameson and Lyotard', in *Critical Quarterly*, vol. 33, no. 3, Autumn 1991, 1–18.
34. On this question, see also Andreas Huyssen, *After the Great Divide* (Basingstoke: Macmillan, 1986). Huyssen discusses modernism's conflation of the feminine with the new world of mass cultural spectacle.
35. Peter Nicholls, 'Divergences'.
36. Fredric Jameson, 'Postmodernism, or, the cultural logic of late capitalism', in his book of that title (London: Verso, 1991).

Chapter 2

1. Thomas Flynn, *Sartre and Marxist Existentialism* (Chicago, IL: University of Chicago Press, 1984), p. 3.
2. Joseph Wenke, *Mailer's America* (Hanover, CT: University Press of New England, 1987). It may be worth mentioning that I have found most existing Mailer criticism ahistorical and impressionistic, with a marked tendency to use his ongoing autocritique as an unproblematic critical lens. Of the better work on Mailer, I have found suggestive, along with Wenke's book, Richard Poirier, *Mailer* (London: Fontana, 1973); Laura Adams, *Existential Battles: The Growth of Norman Mailer* (Athens, OH: Ohio University Press, 1976); and Richard Lehan's chapter on Mailer in *A Dangerous Crossing* (Carbondale, IL: University of Southern Illinois Press, 1973). There is a dearth of material, good or bad, on Mailer's recent work.
3. Richard Godden, *Fictions of Capital: Essays in the American Novel from James to Mailer* (Cambridge: Cambridge University Press, 1990).
4. Norman Mailer, *Harlot's Ghost* (New York: Ballantine, 1991).
5. Dale Carter, *The Final Frontier* (London: Verso, 1988).
6. Norman Mailer, *The Naked and the Dead* (1949; London: Flamingo, 1993).
7. Christine Buci-Glucksmann, *Baroque Reason: The Aesthetics of Modernity* (1984; trans. Patrick Camiller, London: Sage, 1994).
8. Norman Mailer, 'Petty notes on some sex in America', in *Cannibals and Christians* (1967; London: Granada, 1979), pp. 136–7.
9. Norman Mailer, *Barbary Shore* (1951; New York, NY: Carol and Graft, 1988); Mailer makes the claim in Peter Manso, *Mailer: His Life and Times* (New York, NY: Viking, 1985).
10. Walter Benjamin, *The Origins of German Tragic Drama* (1963; trans. John Osborne, London: Verso, 1992), p. 175.
11. Robert J. Begiebing, *Acts of Regeneration: Allegory and Archetype in the Fiction of Norman Mailer* (Columbia, MO: University of Missouri Press, 1980).
12. Maurice Merleau-Ponty, *The Phenomenology of Perception* (1945; trans. Colin Smith, London: Routledge, 1992).
13. Norman Mailer, *The Deer Park* (1957; London: Flamingo, 1994).
14. Mailer's typically bombastic projection of the unwritten work is to be found in 'Last advertisement for myself before the way out', in his *Advertisements for Myself* (1961; London: Granada, 1985), p. 391.

15. Samuel Coale, *In Hawthorne's Shadow: American Romance from Melville to Mailer* (Lexington, KY: University of Kentucky Press, 1988).

16. On postmodernism's shift away from this kind of narrative perspective, see Peter Nicholls, 'Divergences: modernism, postmodernism, Jameson and Lyotard', in *Critical Quarterly* vol. 33, no. 3, Autumn 1991, 1–18.

17. Norman Mailer, *Advertisements for Myself*.

18. Norman Mailer, 'From surplus value to the mass media', in *Advertisements for Myself*.

19. See especially Theodor Adorno and Max Horkheimer, 'The culture industry: enlightenment as mass deception', in *Dialectic of Enlightenment* (1944; trans. John Cumming, London: Verso, 1989); the pivotal text in French Marxism's postwar 'cultural turn' was Henri Lefebvre's *Critique of Everyday Life* (1946; trans. John Moore, London: Verso, 1992).

20. Norman Mailer, 'A note on comparative pornography', in *Advertisements for Myself*.

21. See Susan Buck-Morss, *The Dialectics of Seeing: Walter Benjamin and the Arcades Project* (Cambridge, MA: MIT Press, 1993).

22. Norman Mailer, 'Advertisements for myself on the way out', in *Advertisements for Myself*.

23. Douglas Kellner, *Jean Baudrillard: From Marxism to Postmodernism and Beyond* (Oxford: Polity Press, 1989), p. 155.

24. Craig Owens, 'Toward a theory of postmodernism: the allegorical impulse', in S. Bryson *et al.* (eds), *Beyond Recognition* (Berkeley, CA: University of California Press, 1992).

25. Norman Mailer, *An American Dream* (1966; London: Mayflower 1970); *Ancient Evenings* (New York: Warner Books, 1983).

26. Norman Mailer, 'The metaphysics of the belly', in *The Presidential Papers* (1964; London: Panther, 1976), p. 301.

27. Norman Mailer, 'On totalitarianism', in *The Presidential Papers*. The paper is a selection from Mailer's *Esquire* column of 1963, 'The big bite'. References are to the August column.

28. The term (*Unverborgenheit*) recurs throughout Heidegger. See for example, 'The question concerning technology' in W. Lovitt (ed.), *The Question Concerning Technology and Other Essays* (1955; New York, NY: Harper and Row, 1977), p. 11.

29. Norman Mailer, 'An impolite interview', from 'The sixth presidential paper: a Kennedy miscellany', in *The Presidential Papers*, p. 141, emphasis Mailer's.

30. Norman Mailer, 'In the red light: a history of the Republican convention in 1964', in *Cannibals and Christians*, p. 22.

31. Norman Mailer, 'The political economy of time', in *Cannibals and Christians*, p. 237.

32. Norman Mailer, 'Petty notes on some sex in America', in *Cannibals and Christians*, p. 139.

33. Andreas Huyssen, *After the Great Divide: Modernism, Mass Culture, Postmodernism* (Basingstoke: Macmillan, 1986).

34. Norman Mailer, 'The argument reinvigorated', in *Cannibals and Christians*.

35. Richard Poirier, *Mailer*, p. 107.

36. Guy Debord, *Society of the Spectacle* (1967; Detroit, MI: Black and Red Press, 1983).
37. Norman Mailer, 'The playwright as critic', in *Existential Errands* (New York, NY: Signet, 1973), p. 76.
38. Norman Mailer, 'The White Negro', in *Advertisements for Myself*, p. 277.
39. Norman Mailer, 'The time of her Time', in *Advertisements for Myself*.
40. Walter Benjamin, 'Theses on the philosophy of history' (1950), in *Illuminations* (1955; trans. Harry Zohn, London: Fontana, 1992).
41. Norman Mailer, 'Hip, hell and the navigator', in *Advertisements for Myself*, p. 308.
42. Norman Mailer, 'An eye on Picasso', in *Advertisements for Myself*, p. 377. Mailer has developed this view of Picasso at much greater length in his recently published biography, *A Portrait of Picasso as a Young Man* (1997).
43. Norman Mailer, 'Ten thousand words a minute', from 'Eleventh presidential paper: death', in *The Presidential Papers*.
44. Friedrich Nietzsche, *Thus Spoke Zarathustra* (1885: trans. R. J. Hollingdale, Harmondsworth: Penguin, 1991).
45. Martin Heidegger, 'The question concerning technology', in W. Lovitt (ed.), *The Question Concerning Technology and Other Essays*.
46. Martin Heidegger, 'The word of Nietzsche: God Is Dead', in W. Lovitt (ed.), *The Question Concerning Technology and Other Essays*.
47. Maurice Merleau-Ponty, *The Phenomenology of Perception*.
48. Norman Mailer, *The Prisoner of Sex* (London: Sphere, 1971), p. 173.
49. Norman Mailer, 'A course in film-making', in *Existential Errands; Of A Fire on the Moon* (London: Pan, 1970); *Why Are We In Vietnam?* (1967: London: Panther, 1970).
50. Christopher Walker, 'Terminal Fictions: Death in the Post-war American Novel' (University of Sussex; unpublished DPhil thesis, 1991).
51. Anthony Woodiwiss, *Postmodernity USA* (London: Sage, 1993), p. 86.
52. David Harvey, *The Condition of Postmodernity* (Oxford: Blackwell 1992). See especially Part 2.
53. Norman Mailer, 'Our argument picturesquely continued', in *Cannibals and Christians*.
54. Norman Mailer, *The Executioner's Song* (1979; London: Arena, 1989).
55. Victor Marchetti and John D. Marks, *The CIA and the Cult of Intelligence* (New York, NY: Alfred A. Knopf, 1974).
56. Jean Baudrillard, *Simulations* (1976: trans. Paul Foss, Paul Panon and Philip Beitchman, New York, NY: Semiotext(e), 1983).
57. Homi Bhabha, *The Location of Culture* (London: Routledge, 1994).

Chapter 3

1. Walter Benjamin, *The Origins of German Tragic Drama* (1962; trans. John Osborne, London: Verso 1992), p. 199.
2. Craig Owens, 'The allegorical impulse, part 2: toward a theory of postmodernism', in S. Bryson *et al.* (eds), *Beyond Recognition* (Berkeley, CA: University of California Press, 1992), p. 80.

3. Martin Jay, *Downcast Eyes: The Denigration of Vision in Twentieth Century French Thought* (Berkeley, CA: University of California Press, 1993); Andre Bazin, 'The myth of total cinema', from 'What is cinema?' (1946), in G. Mast, M. Cohen, L. Braudy (eds), *Film Theory and Criticism: Introductory Readings* (New York, NY: Oxford University Press 1992).

4. Andre Bazin, 'De Sica: metteur en scene', from 'What is cinema?', in G. Mast *et al.* (eds), *Film Theory and Criticism.*

5. Andre Bazin, 'The myth of total cinema', in G. Mast *et al.* (eds), *Film Theory and Criticism.*

6. Jean-Louis Braudy, 'Ideological effects of the basic cinematographic apparatus' (1974), in G. Mast *et al.* (eds), *Film Theory and Criticism.*

7. The Lacanian version of Baudry's critique equates the transcendent perspective of ideology with the phallic order's effacement of visual discontinuity, and hence of sexual difference. For further elaboration, see Daniel Dayan, 'The tutor code of classical cinema', and Colin McCabe, 'Theory of film: principles of realism and pleasure', in G. Mast *et al.* (eds), *Film Theory and Criticism.*

8. See especially Paul Virilio, *War and Cinema: The Logistics of Perception* (1984; London: Verso, 1992).

9. Paul Virilio, *Lost Dimension* (1984: trans. Daniel Moshenberg, New York, NY: Semiotext(e), 1991), p. 13.

10. Constance Penley, 'Feminism, film theory and the bachelor machines', in *The Future of an Illusion: Feminism, Film Theory and Psychoanalysis* (London: Routledge, 1989).

11. Walter Benjamin, 'The work of art in the age of mechanical reproduction' (1936), in *Illuminations* (1955: trans. Harry Zohn, London: Fontana, 1992).

12. Michael Taussig, 'Physiognomic aspects of visual worlds', in L. Taylor (ed.), *Visualizing Theory* (London: Routledge, 1994).

13. Maurice Merleau-Ponty, 'The film and the new psychology', in *Sense and Non-Sense* (1947; trans. Hubert L. Dreyfus and P.A. Dreyfus, Evanston, IL: Nortwestern University Press, 1991).

14. Vivian Sobchack, *The Address of the Eye* (Princeton, NJ: University of Princeton Press, 1992).

15. Gilles Deleuze, *Cinema-1: The Movement-Image* (London: Athlone, 1986).

16. Derek Taylor, 'Phantasmatic genealogy', in T.W. Busch and S. Gallagher (eds), *Merleau-Ponty, Hermeneutics and Postmodernism* (Albany, NY: SUNY Press, 1992).

17. Stephen Kellman, 'The cinematic novel: tracking a concept', in *Modern Fiction Studies* vol. 33, no. 3, Autumn 1987, 470–6.

18. Gavriel Moses, *The Nickel Was for the Movies: Film in the Novel from Pirandello to Puig* (Berkeley, CA: University of California Press, 1995). I came across Moses' exhaustive study of what he terms the 'film novel' only at the very last stages of this book's preparation. Consequently, I have been unable to integrate the full range of his arguments concerning the formal and thematic characteristics of this sub-genre into the present chapter. Nevertheless, the principal strategy of his book, to read in film novels dramatisations of some of the central issues in

film theory, albeit from a more formalist and genre-based perspective, dovetails with that of this chapter.

19. Alan Spiegel, *Fiction and the Camera Eye* (Charlottesville, VA: University of Virginia Press, 1976). Other studies of the penetration of literary by cinematic ways of seeing include E. Murray, *The Cinematic Imagination* (New York, NY: New York University Press, 1972); J. Harrington (ed.), *Film and / as Literature* (Englewood Cliffs, NJ: Prentice Hall, 1977); K. Cohen, *Writing in a Film Age* (Boulder, CO: University of Colorado Press, 1991).

20. What these divergent forms share, however, is an ongoing preoccupation with 'what became a major theme in film novels after the forties: the centrality and ambiguity of the spectator's role' (Moses, *The Nickel*, p. 192).

21. Jerzy Kosinski, *The Painted Bird* (1966; London: Arrow, 1982). Biographical material can be found in a range of Kosinski criticism, including Paul R. Lilly's book, listed below.

22. Samuel Coale, 'The cinematic self of Jerzy Kosinski', in *Modern Fiction Studies* vol. 20, no. 3, Autumn 1974, 364–70; Kosinski makes the point in his long essay on *Steps*, *The Art of the Self* (1968), p. 15.

23. Jerzy Kosinski, *Steps* (1968; New York, NY: Vintage, 1988); *Cockpit* (1972; London: Arcade, 1993).

24. Dale Carter, *The Final Frontier* (London: Verso, 1988).

25. Paul R. Lilly, *Words in Search of Victims: The Achievement of Jerzy Kosinski* (Kent, OH: Ohio's State University Press, 1988).

26. I am indebted here to David Harvey's account of 'concrete abstraction' in *The Urban Experience* (Oxford: Blackwell, 1989), pp. 166–70.

27. Jerzy Kosinski, *Pinball* (London: Michael Joseph, 1982).

28. Jean-Paul Sartre, *Being and Nothingness* (1942; trans. Hazel Barnes, London: Methuen, 1981).

29. Christine Buci-Glucksmann, *Baroque Reason: The Aesthetics of Modernism* (1984; trans. Patrick Camiller, London: Sage, 1994).

30. Jerzy Kosinski, *Being There* (1972: London: Black Swan, 1992).

31. Herbert B. Rothschild Jr., 'Jerzy Kosinski's *Being There*: Coriolanus in postmodern dress', in *Contemporary Literature* vol. 29, no. 1, p. 57.

32. David Harvey, *The Condition of Postmodernity* (Oxford: Blackwell, 1992), p. 328; Stanley Aronowitz, *The Crisis in Historical Materialism* (New York, NY: J.F. Bergin, 1981), p. 126.

33. Robert Coover, 'The phantom of the movie palace', in *A Night at the Movies, or, You Must Remember This* (London: Picador, 1989).

34. Robert Coover, 'Panel game', in *Pricksongs and Descants* (1969: London: Picador, 1971).

35. Paul Maltby, *Dissident Postmodernists: Barthelme, Coover, Pynchon* (Philadelphia, PA: University of Pennsylvania Press, 1991). Maltby's chapter on Coover claims him for an explicitly political strain in postmodern writing, usefully extending the formalist thematics of self-reflexivity and fictional 'play' foregrounded in most Coover criticism; see for example, Louis Gordon, *Robert Coover: The Universal Fiction-making Process* (Carbondale, IL: Southern Illinois University Press 1983); J.L. Cope, *Robert Coover's Fictions* (Baltimore, MD: Johns Hopkins University Press, 1986); and Thomas G. Kennedy,

Robert Coover: A Study of the Short Fiction (New York, NY: Twayne Press, 1992).

36. Paul Virilio, *War and Cinema*.

37. Robert Coover, 'Morris in chains', in *Pricksongs and Descants*.

38. Robert Coover, 'The wayfarer', in *Pricksongs and Descants*.

39. Friedrich Nietzsche, *Thus Spoke Zarathustra* (1885; trans. R.J. Hollingdale, Harmondsworth: Penguin, 1991), p. 92.

40. Peter Nicholls, 'Violence, recognition, and some versions of modernism', in *Parataxis* no. 4, Summer 1993, 19–35.

41. Robert Coover, *The Public Burning* (New York, NY: Viking, 1977).

42. Fredric Jameson, 'Postmodernism, or, the cultural logic of late capitalism', in his book of that title (London: Verso, 1991), p. 34.

43. Robert Coover, Preface to the 'Seven Exemplary Fictions', in *Pricksongs and Descants*, pp. 60–2.

44. Stephen Dixon, *Movies* (San Francisco, CA: North Point Press, 1983).

45. Jerome Klinkowitz, 'Stephen Dixon: experimental realism', in *North American Review* vol. 266, no. 1, November 1981, 54–6. This very short piece appears to be the only available critical work on Dixon.

46. Stephen Dixon, 'Meeting Aline', in *Time to Go* (Baltimore, MD: Johns Hopkins University Press, 1984).

47. Stephen Dixon, 'The moviemaker', in *Movies*.

48. Andreas Huyssen, *After the Great Divide: Modernism, Mass Culture, Postmodernism* (Basingstoke: Macmillan, 1986), p. 47.

49. Stephen Dixon, 'My dear', in *Movies*.

50. Stephen Dixon, 'Joke', in *Movies*.

51. Peter Nicholls, 'Divergences: modernism, postmodernism, Jameson and Lyotard', in *Critical Quarterly* vol. 33, no. 3, Autumn 1991, 1–18.

Chapter 4

1. Gavriel Moses, *The Nickel Was for the Movies: Film in the Novel from Pirandello to Puig* (Berkeley, CA: University of California Press, 1995), p. xviii.

2. See Paul Virilio, *War and Cinema: The Logistics of Perception* (1984; London: Verso 1992); *Lost Dimension* (1984; trans. Daniel Moshenberg, New York, NY: Semiotext(e), 1991); and *The Aesthetics of Disappearance* (1980: trans. Philip Beitchman, New York, NY: Semiotext(e), 1991).

3. Paul Virilio, *Lost Dimension*.

4. Edward Soja, *Postmodern Geographies* (London: Verso, 1989), pp. 13–16.

5. Maurice Merleau-Ponty, *The Phenomenology of Perception* (1945; trans. Colin Smith, London: Routledge, 1992).

6. Walter Benjamin, 'On some motifs in Baudelaire' (1939), in *Illuminations* (1955; trans. Harry Zohn, London: Fontana, 1992).

7. Christine Buci-Glucksmann, *Baroque Reason: The Aesthetics of Modernity* (1984; trans. Patrick Camiller, London: Sage, 1994).

8. Walter Benjamin, 'Naples' in *One-Way Street and Other Writings* (1925; trans. Edmund Jephcott and Kingsley Shorter, London: Verso, 1992).

9. Walter Benjamin, 'Hashish in Marseilles' (1932), in *One-Way Street*.
10. Susan Buck-Morss, *The Dialectics of Seeing: Walter Benjamin and the Arcades Project* (Cambridge, MA: MIT Press 1993).
11. Edward Soja, 'It all comes together in Los Angeles', in *Postmodern Geographies*.
12. David Harvey, *The Urban Experience* (Oxford: Blackwell, 1989).
13. Guy Debord, *Society of the Spectacle* (1967; Detroit, MI: Black and Red Press, 1983), para 4.
14. Mike Davis, *City of Quartz: Excavating the Future in Los Angeles* (London: Vintage, 1990).
15. Paul Virilio, *Lost Dimension*, p. 23.
16. Jean Baudrillard, *America* (1986: trans. Chris Turner, London: Verso, 1992).
17. Rayner Banham, *Los Angeles: The Architecture of Four Ecologies* (Harmondsworth: Penguin, 1971).
18. Fredric Jameson, 'Postmodernism, or, the cultural logic of late capitalism', in his book of that title (London: Verso, 1991).
19. Mike Davis, 'Urban renaissance and the spirit of postmodernism', in *New Left Review* no. 151, May/June 1985, 107–13.
20. Fredric Jameson, 'Spatial equivalents in the world system', in *Postmodernism*, p. 125.
21. Alan Spiegel, *Fiction and the Camera Eye* (Charlottesville, VA: University of Virginia Press, 1976).
22. David Fine, 'Introduction', in D. Fine (ed.), *Los Angeles in Fiction: A Collection of Original Essays* (Albuquerque, NM: University of New Mexico Press, 1984), p.3.
23. Charles L. Crow, 'Home and transcendence in Los Angeles fiction', in D. Fine (ed.), *Los Angeles in Fiction*, p. 191.
24. Hal Foster, *Recodings* (Seattle, NA: Bay Press, 1985), p. 168.
25. Joan Didion, 'LA notebook', in *Slouching Towards Bethlehem* (1969; Harmondsworth: Penguin, 1974), p. 114; 'On morality', in *Slouching Towards Bethlehem*, p. 132.
26. Mark Z. Muggli, 'The poetics of Joan Didion's journalism', in *American Literature* vol. 59, no. 3, p. 405.
27. Joan Didion, 'The white album', in *The White Album* (Harmondsworth: Penguin, 1979), p. 44.
28. Samuel Coale, 'Didion's disorder: an American romancer's art', in *Critique*, vol. 21, no. 3, 161.
29. David Harvey, *The Condition of Postmodernity* (Oxford: Blackwell, 1992), p. 328.
30. Jerzy Kosinski, *Steps* (1968; New York, NY: Vintage, 1988).
31. Fredric Jameson, *Postmodernism*, pp. 8–9.
32. Craig Owens, 'The allegorical impulse: towards a theory of postmodernism', in S. Bryson *et al.* (eds), *Beyond Recognition* (Berkeley, CA: University of California Press, 1992), p. 57.
33. Joan Didion, 'The women's movement', in *The White Album*, p. 117.
34. Joan Didion, 'On the morning after the sixties', in *The White Album*, p. 208.
35. Joan Didion, 'LA notebook', p. 179.

36. Joan Didion, 'Pacific distances', in *After Henry* (New York, NY: Vintage, 1992. Published in Britain as *Sentimental Journeys*, Harmondsworth: Penguin), p. 112.

37. Joan Didion, 'LA days' in *After Henry*, p. 150.

38. Joan Didion, 'Times mirror Square' in *After Henry*, p. 230.

39. Joan Didion, *Play It As It Lays* (1967; New York, NY: Signet, 1970).

40. Cynthia Griffin Wolf, 'Play It As It Lays: Didion and the diver heroine', in *Contemporary Literature*, vol. 24, no. 1, Winter 1983, p. 488.

41. H. Jennifer Brady, 'Points west, then and now: the fiction of Joan Didion', in *Contemporary Literature*, vol. 20, no. 4, Summer 1979, p. 464.

42. Ellroy has polemicised against Chandler's romanticism in a number of places, most notably in a Channel 4 documentary by Nicola Barker, 'White Jazz', broadcast in May 1995.

43. James Ellroy, *The Black Dahlia* (1984); *The Big Nowhere* (1988); *LA Confidential* (1990). All published London: Arrow.

44. Walter Benjamin, 'Theses on the philosophy of history' (1950), in *Illuminations*, p. 248.

45. James Ellroy, *White Jazz* (London: Arrow, 1992).

46. Stanley Aronowitz, *The Crisis in Historical Materialism* (New York, NY: J.F. Bergin, 1983).

Conclusion

1. Walter Benjamin, 'On some motifs in Baudelaire' (1939), in *Illuminations* (1955; trans. Harry Zohn, London: Fontana, 1992); 'Theses on the philosophy of history' (1950), in *Illuminations*, p. 246.

2. Christine Buci-Glucksmann, *Baroque Reason: The Aesthetics of Modernity* (1984; trans. Patrick Camiller, London: Sage, 1994).

3. Norman Mailer, 'Petty notes on some sex in America', in *Cannibals and Christians* (1967; London: Granada, 1979), pp. 136–7.

Select bibliography

N.B.: Where two dates are given, the first denotes the date of original publication, the second the date of the edition used.

Primary sources

Coover, Robert, *Pricksongs and Descants* (1969; London: Picador, 1971).
—— *The Public Burning* (New York: Viking, 1977).
—— *A Night at the Movies, or, You Must Remember This* (London: Picador, 1989).
Didion, Joan, *Play It As It Lays* (1967; New York: Signet,1970).
—— *Slouching Towards Bethlehem* (1968; Harmondsworth: Penguin, 1974).
—— *The White Album* (Harmondsworth: Penguin, 1979).
—— *After Henry* (New York: Vintage, 1992; published in Britain by Penguin (Harmondsworth) under the title of *Sentimental Journeys*).
Dixon, Stephen, *14 Stories* (Baltimore, MD: Johns Hopkins University Press, 1980).
—— *Movies* (San Francisco: North Point Press, 1983).
—— *Time to Go* (Baltimore, MD: Johns Hopkins University Press, 1984).
—— *Friends: More Will and Macna Stories* (Santa Maria, CA: Asylum Arts, 1990).
Ellroy, James, *The Black Dahlia* (London: Arrow, 1984).
—— *The Big Nowhere* (London: Arrow, 1988).
—— *LA Confidential* (London: Arrow, 1990).
—— *White Jazz* (London: Arrow, 1992).
Kosinski, Jerzy, *The Painted Bird* (1996; London: Arrow, 1982).
—— *Pinball* (London: Michael Joseph, 1983).
—— *Steps* (1968; New York, NY: Vintage, 1988).
—— *Being There* (1972; London: Black Swan, 1992).
—— *Cockpit* (1972; London: Arcade, 1992).
Mailer, Norman, *The Naked and the Dead* (1949; London: Flamingo, 1993).
—— *Barbary Shore* (1951; New York, NY: Carol and Graft, 1988).
—— *The Deer Park* (1957; London: Flamingo, 1994).
—— *Advertisements for Myself* (1961; London: Granada, 1985).
—— *The Presidential Papers* (1964; London: Panther, 1976).
—— *An American Dream* (1966; London: Mayflower, 1970).
—— *Cannibals and Christians* (1967; London: Granada, 1979).
—— *Why Are We In Vietnam?* (1967; London: Panther, 1970).
—— *The Armies of the Night* (1968; New York, NY: Signet, 1990).
—— *Of a Fire on the Moon* (London: Pan, 1970).

—— *The Prisoner of Sex* (London: Sphere, 1971).

—— *Existential Errands* (New York, NY: Signet, 1973).

—— *The Executioner's Song* (1979; London: Arena, 1989).

—— *Ancient Evenings* (New York, NY: Warner Books, 1983).

—— *Harlot's Ghost* (New York, NY: Ballantine, 1991).

Secondary sources

Literary criticism: general

Bowlby, Rachel, *Just Looking: Consumer Cuture in Dreiser, Gissing and Zola* (London: Methuen, 1985).

Coale, Samuel, *In Hawthorne's Shadow: American Romance from Melville to Mailer* (Lexington, KY: University of Kentucky Press, 1988).

Fine, David, 'Introduction', in D. Fine (ed.), *Los Angeles in Fiction: A Collection of Oriqinal Essays* (Albuquerque, NM: University of New Mexico Press, 1984).

Godden, Richard, *Fictions of Capital: Essays in the American Novel from James to Mailer* (Cambridge: Cambridge University Press, 1990).

Kellman, Stephen, 'The cinematic novel: tracking a concept', *Modern Fiction Studies* vol. 33, no. 4, Autumn 1987, 470–6.

Lehan, Richard, *A Dangerous Crossing* (Carbondale, IL: University of Southern Illinois Press, 1973).

McHale, Brian, *Postmodernist Fiction* (London: Routledge, 1986).

Madsen, Deborah L., *Allegory in America: From Puritanism to Postmodernism* (Basingstoke: Macmillan, 1996).

Maltby, Paul, *Dissident Postmodernists: Barthelme, Coover, Pynchon* (Philadelphia: University of Pennsylvania Press, 1991).

Moses, Gavriel, *The Nickel Was for the Movies: Film in the Novel from Pirandello to Puig* (Berkeley, CA: University of California Press, 1995).

Nicholls, Peter, 'Violence, recognition, and some versions of modernism', *Parataxis* no. 4, Summer 1993, 19–35.

—— 'Divergences: modernism, postmodernism, Jameson and Lyotard', *Critical Quarterly* vol. 33, no. 3, Autumn 1991, 1–18.

Porter, Carolyn, *Seeing and Being: The Plight of the Participant Observer in Emerson, James, Adams and Faulkner* (Middletown, CT: Wesleyan University Press, 1981).

Spiegel, Alan, *Fiction and the Camera Eye* (Charlottesville, VA: University of Virginia Press, 1976).

Walker, Christopher, 'Terminal Fictions: Death in the Post-war American Novel' (Universtity of Sussex: Unpublished DPhil dissertation, 1991).

Literary criticism: individual authors

Adams, Laura, *Existential Battles: The Growth of Norman Mailer* (Athens, OH: Ohio University Press, 1976).

Begiebing, Robert J., *Acts of Regeneration: Allegory and Archetype in the Fiction of Norman Mailer* (Columbia, MO: University of Missouri Press, 1980).

Coale, Samuel, 'The cinematic self of Jerzy Kosinski', *Modern Fiction Studies* vol. 20, no. 3, Autumn 1974, 364–70.

—— 'Didion's disorder: an American romancer's art', *Critique* vol. 21, no. 3, 161–70.

Kennedy, Thomas G., *Robert Coover: A Study of the Short Fiction* (New York: Twayne Press, 1992).

Klinkowitz, Jerome, 'Stephen Dixon: experimental realism', *North American Review* vol. 266, no. 1, November 1981, 54–6.

Lilly, Paul R., *Words in Search of Victims: The Achievement of Jerzy Kosinski* (Kent, OH: Kent State University Press, 1988).

Manso, Peter, *Mailer: His Life and Times* (New York, NY: Viking, 1985).

Poirier, Richard, *Mailer* (London: Fontana, 1973).

Wenke, Joseph, *Mailer's America* (Hanover, CT: University Press of New England, 1987).

Cultural theory/history

Adorno, Theodor and Horkheimer, Max, *Dialectic of Enlightenment* (1944; trans. John Cumming, London: Verso, 1989).

Aronowitz, Stanley, *The Crisis in Historical Materialism* (New York, NY: J.F. Bergin, 1983).

Baudrillard, Jean, *Symbolic Exchange and Death* (1976; trans. Iain Hamilton Grant, London: Sage, 1993).

—— *Simulations* (1976; trans. Paul Foss, Paul Panon and Philip Beitchman, New York, NY: Semiotext(e), 1983).

—— *In the Shadow of the Silent Majorities* (trans. Paul Foss, John Johnson and Paul Patton, New York, NY: Semiotext(e), 1983).

—— *The Ecstasy of Communication* (trans. Bernard and Caroline Schutz, New York, NY: Semiotext(e), 1988).

—— *Le Guerre de Golfe n'y a pas a lien* (Paris: Gallimard, 1991).

—— *America* (trans. Chris Turner, London: Verso, 1992).

Benjamin, Walter, *The Origins of German Tragic Drama* (1963; trans. John Osborne, London: Verso, 1992).

—— *Charles Baudelaire: A lyric poet in the era of high capitalism* (1973; trans. Harry Zohn, London: Verso, 1992).

—— *Illuminations* (trans. Harry Zohn, London: Fontana, 1992).

—— *One-Way Street and Other Writings* (1978; trans. Edmund Jephcott and Kingsley Shorter, London: Verso 1992).

Bhabha, Homi, *The Location of Culture* (London: Routledge, 1994).

Buci-Glucksmann, Christine, *Baroque Reason: The Aesthetics of Modernity* (1984; trans. Patrick Camiller, London: Sage, 1994).

Buck-Morss, Susan, *The Dialectics of Seeing: Walter Benjamin and the Arcades Project* (Cambridge, MA: MIT Press, 1993).

Carter, Dale, *The Final Frontier* (London: Verso, 1988).

Debord, Guy, *Society of the Spectacle* (1967; Detroit, MI: Black and Red Press, 1993).

Foster, Hal, *Recodings* (Seattle, WA: Bay Press, 1985).

—— (ed.) *Vision and Visuality* (New York: Dia, 1993).

Harvey, David, *The Condition of Postmodernity* (Oxford: Blackwell, 1992).

Huyssen, Andreas, *After the Great Divide: Modernism, Mass Culture, Postmodernism* (Basingstoke: Macmillan, 1986).

Jameson, Fredric, *Postmodernism, or, The Cultural Logic of Late Capitalism* (London: Verso, 1991).

Jay, Martin, *Downcast Eyes: The Denigration of Vision in Twentieth Century French Thought* (Berkeley, CA; Oxford: University of California Press, 1993).

Jencks, Chris, 'The centrality of the eye in Western culture: an introduction', in C. Jencks (ed.), *Visual Culture* (London: Routledge, 1995).

Kellner, Douglas, *Jean Baudrillard: From Marxism to Postmodernism and Beyond* (Oxford: Polity Press, 1989).

Lefebvre, Henri, *Critique of Everday Life* (1946; trans. John Moore; London: Verso, 1992).

Lowe, Donald M., *History of Bourgeois Perception* (Brighton: Harvester-Wheatsheaf, 1982).

Marchetti, Victor and Marks, John D., *The CIA and the Cult of Intelligence* (New York: Alfred A. Knopf, 1974).

Mathy, Jean-Philippe, *Extreme-Occident: French Intellectuals and America* (Chicago, IL: University of Chicago Press, 1993).

Melville, S. and Readings, B. (eds), *Vision and Textuality* (Basingstoke: Macmillan, 1995).

Owens, Craig, 'The allegorical impulse: toward a theory of postmodernism' and 'The allegorical imulse, part 2' in S. Bryson, B. Kruger, L. Tillman and J. Weinstock (eds), *Beyond Recognition* (Berkeley, CA: University of California Press, 1992).

Taussig, Michael, 'Physiognomic aspects of visual worlds', in L. Taylor (ed.), *Visualizing Theory* (London: Routledge, 1994).

Virilio, Paul, *Speed and Politics: An Essay on Dromology* (1977; trans. Mark Polizzotti, New York, NY: Semiotext(e), 1986).

—— *The Aesthetics of Disappearance* (1990; trans. Philip Beitchman, New York, NY: Semiotext(e), 1991).

—— *Lost Dimension* (1984; trans. Daniel Moshenberg, New York: Semiotext(e), 1991).

Woodiwiss, Anthony, *Postmodernity USA* (London: Sage, 1993).

Philosophy

Flynn, Thomas, *Sartre and Marxist Existentialism* (Chicago, IL: University of Chicago Press, 1984).

Heidegger, Martin, *The Ouestion Concerning Technology and Other Essays* (trans. and ed. William Lovitt, New York: Harper and Row, 1977).

Levin, David M., 'Decline and fall: ocularcentrism in Heidegger's reading of the history of metaphysics', in D.M. Levin (ed.), *Modernity and the Hegemony of Vision* (Berkeley, CA: University of California Press, 1993).

Merleau-Ponty, Maurice, *The Phenomenology of Perception* (1945; trans. Colin Smith, London: Routledge 1992).

—— *Sense and Non-Sense* (1947; trans. Hubert L. Dreyfus and Patricia Allen Dreyfus, Evanston, IL: Northwestern University Press, 1991).

Nietzsche, Friedrich, *Thus Spoke Zarathustra* (1885; trans. R.J. Hollingdale, Harmondsworth: Penguin, 1991).

—— *Beyond Good and Evil* (1886; trans. R.J. Hollingdale, Harmondsworth: Penguin, 1990).

Sartre, Jean-Paul, *Being and Nothingness* (1942; trans. Hazel Barnes, London: Methuen, 1981).

Vattimo, Gianni, *The End of Modernity: Nihilism and Hermeneutics in Postmodern Culture* (1985; trans. Jon R. Snyder, Baltimore, MD: Johns Hopkins University Press, 1991).

Zimmerman, Michael, *Heidegger's Confrontation with Modernity: Technology, Politics and Art* (Bloomington, IN: University of Indiana Press, 1990).

Film theory

Bazin, Andre, 'The myth of total cinema', from 'What is cinema?' (1946), in G. Mast, M. Cohen and L. Braudy (eds), *Film Theory and Criticism: Introductory Readings* (New York, NY: Oxford University Press, 1992, 4th edition).

—— 'DeSica: Metteur en Scene', from 'What is Cinema?', in G. Mast, *et al.* (eds), *Film Theory and Criticism*.

Braudy, Jean-Louis, 'Ideological effects of the basic cinematographic apparatus' (1974), in G. Mast *et al.* (eds), *Film Theory and Criticism*.

Deleuze, Gilles, *Cinema-1: The Movement Image* (London: Athlone, 1986).

Mulvey, Laura, 'Visual pleasure and narrative cinema' (1975), in G. Mast *et al.* (eds), *Film Theory and Criticism*.

Penley, Constance, *The Future of An Illusion: Feminism, Film Theory and Psychoanalysis* (London: Routledge, 1989).

Sobchack, Vivian, *The Address of the Eye: A Phenomenology of Film Experience* (Princeton, NJ: University of Princeton Press, 1992).

Virilio, Paul, *War and Cinema: The Logistics of Perception* (1984; London: Verso, 1992).

Urban theory/Los Angeles

Banham, Rayner, *Los Angeles: The Architecture of Four Ecologies* (Harmondsworth: Penguin, 1971).

Davis, Mike, *City of Quartz: Excavating the Future in Los Angeles* (London: Vintage, 1990).

—— 'Urban renaissance and the spirit of postmodernism', *New Left Review* no. 151, May/June 1985, 107–13.

Harvey, David, *The Urban Experience* (Oxford: Blackwell, 1989).

Soja, Edward, *Postmodern Geographies* (London: Verso, 1989).

Sorkin, Michael (ed.), *Variations on a Theme Park: The American City and the End of Public Space* (New York: Hill and Wang, 1992).

Virilio, Paul, *Lost Dimension* (1984; trans. Daniel Moshenberg, New York, NY: Semiotext(e), 1991).

Index

All names in quotation marks are fictional (or fictionalised historical) characters.

KING ALFRED'S COLLEGE
LIBRARY